GLOBAL MATTERS

GLOBAL MATTERS

The Transnational Turn in Literary Studies

PAUL JAY

CORNELL UNIVERSITY PRESS
ITHACA AND LONDON

First published 2010 by Cornell University Press
First printing, Cornell Paperbacks, 2010

Printed in the United States of America

Library of Congress Cataloging-in-Publication Data

Jay, Paul, 1946–
   Global matters : the transnational turn in literary studies / Paul Jay.
      p. cm.
   Includes bibliographical references and index.
   ISBN 978-0-8014-4900-0 (cloth : alk. paper) — ISBN 978-0-8014-7607-5 (pbk. : alk. paper)
   1. Commonwealth fiction (English)—History and criticism.   2. Literature, Comparative—Commonwealth
(English) and English.   3. Literature, Comparative—English and Commonwealth (English).   4. Literature,
Comparative—Commonwealth (English) and American.   5. Literature, Comparative—American and
Commonwealth (English).   6. Transnationalism in literature.   7. Globalization in literature.   8. Multi-
culturalism in literature.   9. Literature and globalization.   I. Title.
   PR9084J39   2010
   809—dc22   2010005687

Cloth printing   10   9   8   7   6   5   4   3   2   1
Paperback printing   10   9   8   7   6   5   4   3   2   1

For my parents, Lester and Midge Jay

Contents

ACKNOWLEDGMENTS

Global Matters: The Transnational Turn in Literary Studies had its genesis in a paper on border studies and globalization I gave at the Modern Language Association convention in San Francisco in 1998 that crystallized in an essay on globalization and the future of literary studies that appeared in *PMLA* in 2001 and then evolved during the next few years in lectures at Pennsylvania State University, Lewis University, Texas Tech University, and in conference papers delivered in Rome, Honolulu, Washington DC, New Orleans, Milwaukee, and elsewhere. I want to thank the many people who attended those lectures for their keen attention, probing questions, and constructive feedback. My book would not have taken intelligent shape without those lively discussions.

Of course books like this are not just the product of solitary research and writing. More often than not, they evolve in the classroom, out of the give-and-take we have with our students. I have been blessed to teach at an institution, Loyola University Chicago, that not only values scholarship but understands and facilitates the crucial link between original research and successful undergraduate and graduate teaching. The material in this book has grown out of free-wheeling discussions I have had with my students in courses about the impact of globalization on literature and its study at a variety of levels. I owe a debt of gratitude to those students, to my university, and to the English department, where I have been given the opportunity to teach a range of experimental courses connected to my research and to engage my students in wide-ranging discussions of virtually every topic and text covered in this book.

My chairpersons during this period, Suzanne Gossett, Timothy Austin, Frank Fennell, and Joyce Wexler, have been incredibly supportive and I want to thank them. A university research leave in the spring of 2006 proved indispensible to finishing an early draft of this book, and I thank the university very much for its support. I also want to thank the Fulbright Program for a grant that allowed me to travel to India for five weeks with a group of scholars in the summer of 2008, a trip that dramatically affected my understanding of the impact of globalization in developing countries. Particular thanks go to Madhuri Deshmukh and Katherine Schuster for writing the grant and organizing the trip and to Ranjith Henry, our fabulous guide in India. He turned out to be an extraordinarily knowledgeable companion during my weeks there, and I learned much in my discussions with him. Finally, one's intellectual life grows out of one's engagement with friends and colleagues, in conversation, argument, and laughter. I want to thank, in particular, Harveen Sachdeva Mann for being such a wonderful friend and helping me over the years to gain a deeper, if tentative and evolving, understanding of India, its history, culture, people, and literature. I also want to thank Badia Ahad, Jay Boersma, Suzanne Bost, Pamela Caughie, David Chinitz, Deborah Holdstein, Steve Jones, Tom Kaminski, David Kaplan, Anil Lal, Mary Mackay, Nasrin Qader, and Edward Wheatley for their friendship and support. I have also benefited from my conversations and correspondence with two extraordinary writers, Aravind Adiga and Junot Díaz, from whom I have learned much. Special thanks go to Ross Miller, my partner in half-wittery and sneak-outs, whose knowledge and brilliance have kept me in competitive shape for over twenty-five years.

During the time I have been at work on this project I have benefited from the support, encouragement, and intelligence of my family, who made this book in its present form possible. My wonderful, indefatigable, and vibrant mother, Midge Jay, passed away just months before this book was finished. I miss her terribly and hope this book stands as a tribute to her marvelous spirit and intellectual energy. We all owe our mothers our lives, but she was something special.

I cannot imagine life without my two wonderful brothers, Criss and Greg. Their love and support has been of incalculable value, but I have benefited enormously, as well, from our conversations about literature, art, culture, and politics, and much of what I have learned from them has found its way into this book. Many readers will be familiar with Gregory Jay's work on American literature and multiculturalism. The quality of his books and essays speak for themselves.

His great intelligence and critical and theoretical savvy has been a secret weapon of mine for many, many years, and thanking him enough is just not possible. Criss Jay is an extraordinarily gifted poet and musician whose eloquence, intellect, and music are well known to his students, friends, fellow writers, and readers. I have been blessed to spend countless hours in conversations with him, especially about the literature and culture of the Southwest, conversations that have contributed enormously to the quality of this book. I thank him with all my heart for his love and his indispensible intellectual and moral support.

My wife and companion for over thirty years, Lynn Woodbury, has been unfailing in her love and support during the years I have been working on this book, years in which she has been chairing her own department of English at Oakton Community College in Des Plaines, Illinois. I cannot imagine life without her as my partner, both as a companion and co-parent, and as an intellectual friend whose wise advice and sound ideas have been invaluable. It is impossible to express fully my love and gratitude to her. Our son, Darren, has grown from a teenager into a young man while I wrote this book, and I am so proud to be his father. His intelligence, wit, and exquisite sense of taste are a marvel. His pitch-perfect riffs on all things related to popular culture have entertained and educated me, and it is simply a joy to have him in my life.

Finally, I want to thank my editor at Cornell University Press, Peter J. Potter, who saw a book in the jumble of pages I initially sent him and did a brilliant job teasing it out and helping to give it shape. This book would not be what it is without his wise editorial suggestions (and, of course, whatever failings it might have are my own). He's been a dream editor. I also want to express my gratitude to the two very astute readers for Cornell, Susan Stanford Friedman and Sanjay Krishnan, who were so encouraging but also full of smart suggestions for improving the manuscript.

Scattered parts of this book previously appeared in the journals *PMLA, Arizona Quarterly, Ariel, American Literary History,* and the book *Globalization and the Humanities: Field Imaginaries, Virtual Worlds, and Emergent Sensibilities,* edited by David Leiwei Li, Hong Kong University Press. I am grateful to each for permission to reprint.

Global Matters

Introduction

The Transnational Turn in Literary Studies

Since the rise of critical theory in the 1970s, nothing has reshaped literary and cultural studies more than its embrace of transnationalism. It has productively complicated the nationalist paradigm long dominant in these fields, transformed the nature of the locations we study, and focused our attention on forms of cultural production that take place in the liminal spaces between real and imagined borders. This transformation has exploded under the forces of globalization, but it has its roots in political movements outside of the academy and theoretical developments within it that run back to the early 1960s. The civil rights movement and then later the women's movement, the Chicana/o movement, and the gay and lesbian rights movement transformed the demographics of the student body and then the professoriate in U.S. higher education. These demographic changes brought a revolution in both the texts and the issues treated by scholars in literary and cultural studies. Work on women writers and African American, Latina/o, Native American, Asian American, gay, lesbian, and queer literatures transformed the curriculum of literature departments and the research agenda of its faculty in ways that dramatically reconfigured the historical and geographical boundaries of traditional practices. During the same period postcolonial studies emerged to challenge the primacy of discrete national literatures and what seemed like their insular concerns, providing a framework for studying literature and culture in a transnational context that moved beyond and explicitly questioned older Eurocentric models of "comparative" analysis. However, the transnational turn in literary studies began in earnest when the study of minority, multicultural, and postcolonial literatures began to intersect with work done under the auspices of the emerging study of globalization.

This turn, of course, has been a controversial one. My aim in this book is to explore the nature and history of these controversies. As some scholars define globalization as a contemporary phenomenon linked to the development of electronic media, the rise of transnational corporations, global financial institutions, and proliferating forms of entertainment that easily leap national boundaries, others define it as a historical phenomenon running back to at least the sixteenth century and incorporating the histories of colonization, decolonization, and postcolonialism. Many insist that globalization is largely an economic and political phenomenon and that it therefore ought to be studied from a materialist point of view. Others maintain that globalization is a more broadly cultural phenomenon, and they draw on cultural theory in ways that are roundly criticized by those in the materialist camp.

There are also vigorous debates about the economic consequences of globalization and the impact it has on individual agency. Some see economic globalization as a rising tide that eventually *will* lift all boats, while others point to class inequities and the extent to which some countries, such as India, feel the benefits of globalization mainly in urban areas. Many scholars insist that globalization, characterized as it is by the exchange of cultural commodities central to the fashioning of identity and the exercise of social power, facilitates new forms of agency, while others lament what they see as the oppressively homogenizing effects of cultural globalization. Whereas scholars once ignored the role of gender in studying both the impact and benefits of globalization, over the last ten years gender has become a crucial object of analysis in the study of globalization. Finally, attention to the global flow of cash, cultural commodities, and media necessarily calls our attention to transnational contexts and locations of exchange, and some critics believe it does so in a way that can blind us to the nature of local circumstances, practices, and needs.

My goal in this book is to review and intervene in each of these debates. First of all, I challenge the idea that the transnational turn in literary and cultural studies can simply be linked to recent developments related to what we have come to call "globalization." In fact, this turn has roots that run back through theoretical developments in the humanities and social and political movements outside of the academy that began in the 1960s. In addition, I argue that it is a mistake to approach globalization itself as a contemporary phenomenon and that it makes much more sense to take a historical view in which globalization is dated as beginning in at least the sixteenth century and covering a time span that includes the long histories of imperialism, colonization, decolonization, and postcolonialism. This is both a historically sound approach to globalization *and* it has the practical benefit of historicizing literary and cultural studies, rescuing it from those who see globalization as a strictly contemporary or postmodern phenomenon.

Furthermore, in my view the debate over whether globalization is an economic or cultural phenomenon is based on a false distinction. We cannot neatly separate economic from cultural commodities; when commodities travel, culture travels, and when culture travels, commodities travel. Materialist critics are therefore wrong when they claim that a culturalist model is inappropriate for studying what is essentially an economic phenomenon. And, yet, cultural critics are also mistaken when they ignore the economic and material aspects of globalization. As for homogenization and agency, there are no such things as pure, autonomous cultures that are not "contaminated," as Kwame Appiah puts it, by productive contact with other cultures.[1] Indeed, "homogenization" has emerged as something of a false villain in debates about globalization, in that similarity or uniformity is as much undone by contact with other cultures as it is enforced by it. The same can be said about agency, which is often linked to debates about homogenization. We tend to link agency to cultural autonomy and to measure cultural autonomy in terms of a society's ability to protect its cultural identity from being watered down or erased by alien cultural forms; but every culture is always shaped by other cultures, and agency has more to do with the intelligent and imaginative negotiation of cross-cultural contact than with avoiding such contact. Agency from this point of view is a function of that negotiation, not its victim. And, clearly, agency is variously enabled and circumscribed by gender. The study of globalization both inside and outside of literary studies will not work without attention to this gender difference. As I point out in the chapters ahead, this was a problem in early studies of globalization that is being remedied by an increasing engagement between globalization studies and feminist studies.

Finally, I argue that the center-periphery model for the study of globalization (one that sees power, commodities, and influence flowing from urban centers in the West to a peripheral developing world) needs to be complicated. In fact, globalization is characterized by complex back-and-forth flows of people and cultural forms in which the appropriation and transformation of things—music, film, food, fashion—raise questions about the rigidity of the center-periphery model. While the institutional infrastructures of economic globalization still tend to be defined by this center-periphery model, emerging forms of agency at the cultural level are beginning to loosen its hold. And what we have increasingly come to recognize about the locations we study is that they are not fixed, static, or unchanging. We create the locations we study, and this recognition ought to encourage us to continue to remap the geographies of literary and cultural forms.

One claim that is often made against the changes ushered in by the transnational turn in literary studies is that it has led to a debilitating fragmentation. Principles of coherence that have guided the field for decades have given way to a focus on pluralities, differences, hybrid identities, and complicated transnational geographies that are seemingly incoherent and unmanageable. I do not agree, because I believe that literary studies as a field has always *thrived* on fragmentation and challenges to coherence. The field continually builds on the strength of new critical approaches and paradigm shifts, which may seem at first as though they are fragmenting the discipline when in fact they are renewing it. This is what has been happening as literary and cultural studies have taken a transnational turn; and in my view this turn is both a positive and an exciting one, promising new forms and expressions of coherence.

It is certainly true that the globalizing of literary studies challenges some traditional and often valuable practices in ways that have become controversial. It is no surprise that globalization studies, especially to the extent that they are associated with departments of English, are often seen as a threat to the already transnationalized fields of comparative literature or postcolonial studies. The relationship, for example, between globalization studies in English departments and postcolonial studies has been vexed. It is easy to misconstrue the argument that globalization has a long history that includes the epochs of imperialism, colonialism, decolonization, and postcolonialism as an attempt to discount or marginalize the importance of these historical processes, to replace focused attention on the specific histories of imperialism and colonialism with a more generalized but vague study of global flows of commodities and cultural forms. This is, I believe, a real danger, but I also think it is often based on misunderstanding—and in any case, it is an effect that can, and should, be avoided. If globalization offers a critical framework that moves the disciplines of literary and cultural studies toward a new transnational coherence, it will only do so if its relationship to postcolonial studies can be thought through in a responsible way.

With regard to a recurrent concern that scholars and critics in the field of English are trying to take over transnational approaches to the study of literature that are better left to comparatists, I want to be clear at the outset that although my book is primarily about the transnational turn in literary studies in English I am not arguing that English departments should have some kind of privileged position in the study of cultural and literary forms of globalization. Nor am I arguing that "global literature" (however we choose to define that term) is primarily being written in English. The relationship of literary production to globalization is complex and multifaceted, irreducible by definition to literature produced in a particular language or constellation of nations. (Indeed, such a practice must acknowledge that much of the literature we study predates the formation of modern nation-states altogether.) To study this relationship requires the careful analysis across historical periods of a transnational range of writers in a variety of languages from a variety of perspectives.[2] Indeed, in the humanities we have historically had a number of different paradigms for studying literature in a transnational framework, principal among them being commonwealth studies, comparative literature, and postcolonial studies. While the first often focused much too narrowly on literature written in English in a colonialist context, the other two have covered literature written on every continent and in myriad languages from a point of view increasingly critical of colonialism and the kind of Eurocentrism informing early approaches to the comparative study of literature. Since the late 1990s, the discourses of multiculturalism, border studies, diaspora studies, and cosmopolitanism have been invoked in various ways to help underwrite a transnational approach to literary studies.

From this perspective, the discipline of English is in many ways a latecomer to the field of transnational literary studies. It was not until the developments I have sketched out that scholars and critics working in English departments began to think seriously about reorganizing areas of study in global rather than national contexts defined by conventional historical periods.[3] My interest here is in tracking these developments. I want to explore the various social, economic, cultural, and political imperatives that have led to the creation of earlier transnational paradigms for the study of culture and literature in the humanities and to consider how they model approaches that can help inform work on globalization in English. Again, the aim here is not to assert the primacy of English in the study of globalization's effects on culture and literature but to recognize that, like a number of other disciplines, English literature and those who study it have been profoundly affected by the processes of globalization.

Given this fact, I want to help develop a theoretical and methodological framework for studying these effects.[4] In so doing I aim to question the default narrative for historicizing English,[5] one in which the history of English and American literature is studied through the lens of conventional national histories, guided by the sometimes unconscious assumption that the history of these literatures began with the history of *nations* and with relatively little attention paid to the transnational forces at work in their production. I do not mean to discount the importance of national approaches to the study of English, but I do want to advocate other approaches based on a global reframing of the origins, production, and concerns of what we have called "English" literature, to look closely at how the production of English literature itself has increasingly become transnational, and how it has become engaged with a set of issues related to globalization.

In the chapters that follow I review and, I hope, clarify many of the key issues in globalization studies that I have been discussing thus far. In addition, I examine a number of contemporary literary texts produced in the context of globalization in order to develop some models for the reading and analysis of fiction that are both a product of and engaged with the forces of globalization. The book is structured to emphasize this double focus. Whereas the chapters in part 1 deal with theoretical, critical, and institutional issues related to the transnational turn in literary studies, those in part 2 analyze a representative range of contemporary literary texts produced by a group of transnational writers whose fiction both represents the impact of globalization on the production of English and engages a range of issues related to the economic, social, cultural, and political forces globalization is unleashing.

The chapters in part 1 develop a thorough analysis of globalization and its relationship to historical forces that have contributed to the transnationalizing of literary studies in general and English literature in particular. In chapter 1 I argue that social movements outside the university that became linked to the rise of minority, multicultural, and postcolonial studies laid the groundwork for the transnationalizing of literary studies, and I survey the impact of globalization since at least the early 1990s on this trend and on the academy more generally. I explore, in particular, how developments in the field of literary criticism and theory spurred by the profession's combined interests in the differences that locations, ethnicities, genders, race, and sexualities make in the production of identities and in the nature of experience have accelerated the discipline's transnational turn. These changes have been controversial, and in this chapter I discuss some of the key controversies, analyze the positions of some important critics on both sides of the issues (including Bill Readings, Edward Said, Ania Loomba, Masao Miyoshi, Susan Stanford Friedman, Arjun Appadurai, and Kwame Appiah), and provide something of a road map for negotiating their concerns.

In chapter 2 I step back from these debates in order to sift through a competing set of answers to the question, what is globalization? I explore the evolution in the West of globalization as an academic field of study, beginning as it did among economists, political scientists, and sociologists before migrating later to literary and cultural studies. One of the key questions here has to do with how we historicize globalization. I review competing positions taken by critics such as Roland Robertson and Malcolm Waters, who argue that globalization has a long history, and others such as Anthony Giddens and David Harvey, who insist it is a contemporary phenomenon. I argue that the long historical perspective taken by Robertson and Giddens is more accurate and offers a better framework for the study of globalization in both the humanities and social sciences. I connect these general debates about the historical character of globalization to the more specific and pressing question of how colonialism, decolonization, and the experience of postcoloniality are related to globalization. The whole question of how we ought to reconcile these historical epochs, and what the relationship ought to be between postcolonial and globalization studies, is a vexing one, and critics have taken a range of positions on the problem, from Simon During's insistence that globalization theory can be a tool for redescribing the entire history of colonization, decolonization, and postcoloniality to Masao Miyoshi's insistence that globalization as both a socioeconomic process and a field of study can only have a corrupting influence on work in the humanities and social sciences. I agree here that Miyoshi's position ought to give us pause. He is certainly right that we must scrutinize the university's complicity with the forces of global capital if we want to insure that our work contributes to, and does not inadvertently work against, social justice; and he is right that more attention must be paid to the debilitating effects of globalization on the economies and environments of postcolonial countries. We also need to guard against facile approaches to the study of cultural globalization that tend to simply celebrate diversity and hybridity without thinking critically enough about its effects. That said, I also argue that During is fundamentally correct in seeing globalization as a long historical process and that we have to include as central to that history the whole arc of imperialism, colonization, decolonization, and postcoloniality. In doing so we need to be careful to foreground these histories as absolutely central to the evolution of globalization, avoiding a position that seems to privilege some amorphous (and teleological) concept of "global change" over one that treats colonialism and its aftermath as the driving force of globalization.

In chapter 3 I turn my attention to debates over whether globalization ought to be studied as an economic or a cultural phenomenon. While there are critics, such as Miyoshi and H. D. Harootunian, who insist that globalization ought to be treated as a wholly economic process using a thoroughly materialist methodology purged of culturalism, others, such as Appadurai, Appiah, and James Clifford insist on the fundamentally reciprocal relationship between economic and cultural forms of globalization and argue for a more syncretic model of analysis that tends to privilege culturalist models. Here I argue that while we need to make distinctions between cultural and economic processes and conditions, and that we need to be careful to distinguish between the semiotic, representational, and imaginary on the one hand and the lived reality of material and economic relations on the other, economic and cultural systems have become so intertwined that it makes little sense to advocate for a strictly materialist or a strictly culturalist model for studying the effects of globalization. From this perspective, both sides share some blame in creating an overly schematic or one-sided approach to the study of globalization. If contemporary theory influenced by deconstruction has taught us anything, it is that the binary division between the economic and the cultural is a false one, that we need to interrogate how each term is constructed in contrast to the other and how the binary tends to mask a much more complicated set of processes than either term by itself can reference.

In chapter 4, the final chapter in part 1, I explore how the transnational turn in literary studies has resulted in a wholesale remapping of the *locations* we study. This remapping has grown out of a focus on migration and cross-cultural experience, generally, and a particular interest in tracing complicated histories of displacement. In the United States this has led scholars in African, Asian, Native American, and Latina/o literary and cultural studies to turn what used to be a narrow U.S. focus into a hemispheric and even global one (the United States, Canada, Mexico, the Caribbean, Latin America, Africa, and the "Pacific Rim"), so that the locations that now come under the rubric of "American studies" have become transnational. Likewise, the study of "British" literature has moved productively away from a narrow focus on the British Isles, Western Europe, and the United States to include the histories and geographies of former British colonies (South Asian, African, New World) and the back-and-forth movement of people between them. These changes have had the salutary effect of helping us recognize that we create the spaces we study. I argue that as scholars and critics complicate the traditional attention we pay to nation-state locations by focusing our attention on transnational spaces and regions, we need to develop a clear sense of the constructedness of these regions. Rob Wilson presents a compelling model for this kind of work with his concept of critical regionalism, and I use it as my point of departure for an extended analysis of how work in the field of border studies in the Americas can provide a model for how to remap the geographical spaces of literary and cultural studies. In this context I find Paul Gilroy's conceptualizing of "the black Atlantic" particularly useful, and so I present an extended discussion of how his work on the Atlantic slave trade and its relationship to modernity can be usefully linked to the work of Mexican and Latin American theorists such as Edmundo O'Gorman, Nestor Canclini, and Edouard Glissant to produce a hemispheric approach to the literatures and cultures of the Americas.

The chapters in part 2 are designed to examine how a range of contemporary transnational writers working in English are using their fiction to explore the issues treated by the critics discussed in part 1. Taken together, these chapters present some models for how we can begin to deal critically—and in the classroom—with new literary works that embody the transnational turn in English. The texts I discuss in these chapters deal in various ways with the historical, social, and political forces at work shaping personal and cultural identity in transnationalized spaces from the Caribbean to London to South Asia under the combined historical effects of colonization, decolonization, postcoloniality, and globalization. These kinds of texts are transforming the scope of the national literatures to which they belong *and* pushing beyond national boundaries to imagine the global character of modern experience, contemporary culture, and the identities they produce. They document the transnationalizing of English literature, but more important, they engage the complex range of critical and theoretical issues discussed in part 1. That is, they reflect the globalization of English as a mode of literary production, but they also reflect *on* the historical, political, social, cultural, and personal issues of concern to critics.

In chapter 5 I begin by looking at three contemporary novels by South Asian writers—Arundhati Roy's *The God of Small Things* (1997), Vikram Chandra's *Red Earth and Pouring Rain* (1995), and Mohsin Hamid's *Moth Smoke* (2000). These three novels model in different ways the kind of dialectical relationship between colonialism, decolonization, postcolonialism, and globalization I insist in part 1 ought to inform the study of transnational literatures and cultures. Roy's novel contains a running critique of the effects of globalization in India, but it does not link those effects historically to colonialism in the kind of systematic way we find in Chandra's novel, which draws a clear line between the two histories. Hamid, on the other hand, tries to draw a clear distinction between the postcolonial condition and globalization, insisting that he belongs to a generation of "post–postcolonial" writers. Analyzing these novels together I draw attention to the challenge of treating categories such as the local and the global, the personal and the historical, and the cultural and the economic as if they represented fixed distinctions. Roy's novel in particular, with its contrast between the gods of big and small things, also suggests the difficulty of creating a totalizing historical view that does not, at the same time, take account of the local, the particular, and the personal. In this chapter I show how, taken together, these three novels dramatize why we cannot discuss postcolonial literature in isolation from the phenomenon of globalization and, conversely, that it is impossible to study globalization without dealing with complex local histories of colonialism and postcolonialism.

Roy, Chandra, and Hamid each write to some degree about characters who move back and forth between the East and the West, foregrounding forms of disruption, displacement, migration, and mobility caused by colonization, decolonization, and globalization. In chapter 6 I analyze a novel whose narrative structure is carefully calibrated to explore this kind of fluidity of movement across borders, Kiran Desai's *The Inheritance of Loss* (2006). Desai's novel contains two interrelated narratives. One is set in New York City and explores the contemporary effects of globalization on a group of diasporic migrant workers in a city that could be almost anywhere, while the alternating chapters, set in Kalimpong in West Bengal, analyze the persistent effects of colonialism on local ethnic conflicts with deep historical roots in the far north of what is now India. Desai's novel is particularly compelling, I argue, for the way in which it foregrounds how nationalism and globalization coexist even as globalization seems to be accelerating in different ways in multiple locations. In *The Inheritance of Loss* nationalism is not withering away under the effects of globalization but asserting itself in the face of the changes ushered in by globalization, and in ways that are connected to changes set in motion generations ago by colonialism. The links she draws between the experiences of migrant workers in New York City and nationalist revolutionaries in Kalimpong works to complicate our understanding of the relationship between nationalism and globalization and the extent to which they feed off each other, and they stress the uneven effects of economic globalization in places such as Kalimpong and New York. Desai's novel, moreover, focuses on the challenges faced by global migrant workers in metropolitan centers like New York in a way that questions the relatively upbeat vision of globalization's liberatory possibilities of a critic such as Appadurai. It draws a clear link between forms of cultural colonization under colonialism and globalization, while insisting in its treatment of nationalism in northeastern India that an obsession with cultural purity and anti-Westernization can be as debilitating as colonialism itself. (The novel is as critical of nationalism as it is of globalization.)

In chapter 7 I analyze how Zakes Mda's postapartheid South African novel published in 2000, *The Heart of Redness,* stages an elaborate and multileveled debate about tradition and modernization in the overlapping eras of colonialism and contemporary globalization. The novel explores both the cultural politics of identity in a newly liberated urban Johannesburg and struggles related to modernization in the villages of rural South Africa. Here the kind of mobility Desai explores is embodied in Mda's protagonist, Camagu, who has returned to a newly liberated South Africa after thirty years in the West. Camagu's journey from the United States to Johannesburg, and then to a historically important village near the sea, sets the stage for his exploration of how tensions around economic development and cultural preservation in the late twentieth century are linked historically to colonialism. I connect Mda's treatment of these issues with those of the critics discussed in part 1 (particularly Appadurai and Appiah) and explore how Mda's focus on the relationship between the political and the romantic, between eros and ecology, link the personal and the political in ways we can observe in a number of the novels I treat in this book.

The novel I discuss in chapter 8, Zadie Smith's *White Teeth* (2000), also deals with forms of displacement, migration, and mobility characteristic of colonization, postcolonization, and globalization, but it locates the intersecting effects of such movement in contemporary London and particularly explores multiculturalism and fundamentalism as two competing responses to the kind of diversity these forms of mobility produce. I analyze Smith's approach to the construction of personal and cultural identity in a mixed group of South Asian, Caribbean, and Anglo Londoners. In Smith's novel the colonial machinery has gone into reverse. The mobility of the colonizer has become the mobility of the colonized, as they retrace the journeys of those who conquered their ancestors. With the descendents of those dislocated by colonial conquest having relocated to the very center of colonial power, it is Englishness, not indigenousness, that is at stake. *White Teeth* traces the construction of postcolonial subjectivities among its South Asian and Caribbean characters in the colonizing metropolis, but it also is about how the complex forces it explores are remaking Englishness. I argue that Smith's novel transcends the categories of "British" or "postcolonial" fiction. She draws from these two traditions, but her novel has its roots in the hybrid mix of Asian and Caribbean cultural forms that have emerged in London and elsewhere since the late 1980s. Of particular importance is her critical engagement with multiculturalism as a strategy for dealing with difference in a contemporary and increasingly hybridized city like London, and how she contrasts this strategy with forms of fundamentalism emergent in the last decade of the twentieth century.

The book's final chapter is devoted to Junot Díaz's 2007 Pulitzer Prize–winning novel, *The Brief Wondrous Life of Oscar Wao*. Although Díaz is routinely treated as an American or a Latino writer, I insist on linking his novel to the transnational turn in English in order to underscore how it deals with a range of issues explored by Desai, Smith, and the other novelists I discuss. All of these novels are about mobility and displacement and thus shift the reader between multiple locations, engaging a new model of migration characterized by the back-and-forth movement of people across borders, at once insisting on the importance of location *and* deterritorializing the spaces in which their characters operate. In Díaz's novel we move back and forth between the eastern United States and the Dominican Republic, and between the years of Rafael Trujillo's dictatorship in the Dominican Republic (especially between the years 1942 and 1961) and the contemporary life of Díaz's young characters growing up in Patterson, New Jersey, in the 1980s and 1990s. I show how both the generational structure of the novel and the ways in which it shuttles between locations mirrors literary and narrative devices used in both *The Inheritance of Loss* and *White Teeth*. This enables me to demonstrate how Díaz's work is remarkably in sync with Desai's and Smith's when it comes to writing about personal and cultural identity, about how histories of displacement and the exercise of colonizing power cut across generations, and about the multiple effects of travel and displacement on people living in diasporic communities. I pay particular attention, finally, to Díaz's treatment of the relationship between masculinity, sexuality, storytelling, and power, a subject that has received relatively little attention in the other novels I discuss in part 2 or in the work of the critics I analyze in part 1. Attending to these relationships leads me to argue that the self-reflexive nature of *The Brief Wondrous Life of Oscar Wao* distinguishes it from the other novels. Díaz frames the novel as both a historical critique of colonialism and dictatorship in the Americas, systems linked to masculinity and storytelling, and as a kind of counterspell that uses the very narrative power it critiques to undo that power. Díaz's distinction between simple and troubled narratives becomes a metaphor for the kinds of texts I privilege here, critical and fictional narratives that complicate simple national narratives and narrow myths about purity and belonging. More than any other novel I treat here, Diaz's develops a sustained meditation on literary form, and on the role and power of storytelling to deal with historical and social injustice.

Taken together, the two parts of this book are designed to present a composite picture of the transnational turn in English both inside and outside the academy. This turn is driven by demographic changes produced by decolonization and globalization that have, in my lifetime, transformed cultural production and the nature of academic work both in the United States and abroad in ways that were unthinkable in the first two decades following World War II when I was growing up. Mobility is the key process here. The central transformation since the late 1960s is the general upward mobility of minority populations within the United States, who, as early as the late 1950s and early 1960s, began to demand access to educational opportunities that took them into colleges and universities and eventually to the front of the classroom. There they began to teach formerly ignored authors and subjects, producing in turn students who have changed the very nature of academic work in the humanities and social sciences. Mobility outside the university has had an equally dramatic impact, both in the United States and abroad. In the United States and in major metropolitan cities in Europe communities, shops, restaurants, churches, and schools are now made up of a challenging demographic mix of cultures from all over the world. In places outside the West, in South Asia, East Asia, and Africa, the forces of globalization are disrupting old patterns of economic production and traditional cultural practices in ways that have become profoundly controversial. The critics I discuss in part 1 are working hard to understand and analyze these changes, to identify the opportunities they have created and the problems they confront us with, while the creative writers whose work I turn to in part 2 chronicle the experiences of people around the world whose lives are being shaped by the accelerating forces of globalization, forces that offer unprecedented opportunity to some and deepening poverty and desperation to others.

Part I

GLOBALIZATION AND THE STUDY OF LITERATURE

1

Difference, Multiculturalism, and the Globalizing of Literary Studies

Roughly every ten years the Modern Language Association publishes a book entitled *Introduction to Scholarship in Modern Languages and Literatures.* The series began in 1952 in order to clarify the "aims and methods currently adopted in the fields of modern language scholarship in America" (vii). These books, aimed at an audience of advanced students and academics, provide a snapshot of professional scholarship at the time of their publication, including a comprehensive overview of current theories, methodologies, key issues, and fields of study. The newest edition was published in 2007 under the general editorship of David G. Nicholls, director of book publications for the MLA. According to Nicholls, the new volume "seeks to provide an orientation for future scholars and to take stock of trends in the field over the past decade and a half" (vii). It does not take long to see what those trends are. Here is how Doris Sommer begins the opening essay, entitled "Language, Culture, and Society":

To listen to the world now is to wake up from a romantic enchantment whose spell cast human subjects into vessels of one language, made language seem almost identical to nation, and made nation practically indistinguishable from state.... But today, *home* means not a here but a there, somewhere else, a loss for

migrant parents and a lack for the children.... By now, strangeness is the norm
in big cities worldwide, where urban life is recovering the heterogeneous and dynamic qualities that once defined the medieval metropolis. (3)

What has broken the spell of the romantic enchantment of one home, one
language, one nation, one stable place? "Globalization, . [the] push of peoples
from poor countries to richer ones and the pull of market logic beyond national
economies into regional and even broader arrangements" (3).[1] Beyond its effects
on markets and economies, the push and pull of globalization, Sommer rightly
points out, has also produced a "reshuffling [of] the cultural map of languages
and literatures" (3). "Hardly any spaces are left to the tidy coincidence that some
of us imagined between national culture and sovereign state," for countries and
national cultures are interlocked by a web of markets and migrant workers, and
they "depend on news and books written in one place, published in another,
and marketed to a world of readers" (4). This means, according to Sommer,
that "reading, writing, and speaking—verbal creativity in general—often cross
national boundaries and thereby transgress the lines of proper (or proprietary)
language" (4).[2]

The theme Sommer sketches out here is registered in the book's essays covering new developments in traditional fields including linguistics, poetics, textual
scholarship, historical scholarship, interpretation, comparative literature, and
translation studies, as well as in those dealing with newly established or emergent fields such as "cultural studies," "feminisms, genders, sexualities," "race and
ethnicity," and "migrations, diasporas, and borders."[3] Taken together, these essays dramatize how, in an age of accelerating globalization, the profession of
literary studies has shifted away from scholarly practices and critical paradigms
rooted in the nation, the universality of experience, and a shared "humanity"
that supposedly links all people and has increasingly turned its attention to the
study of difference and diversity within newly transnationalized fields of study.
What Sommer calls our "romantic enchantment" with the nation as a "home"
for single literatures and languages (English, American, Spanish, Italian, Japanese, etc.) has been displaced by a new, more contemporary engagement with
transnational spaces, hybrid identities, and subjectivities grounded in differences
related to race, class, gender, and sexual orientation, and the study of how culture and its practices are shaped and reshaped in border zones and liminal spaces
that transgress the clear lines between states and the more fuzzy ones between
nations.

Sommer is certainly right that the transnational turn in literary and cultural
studies can be traced in part to the accelerating forces of both economic and cultural globalization. Indeed, much of my book is taken up with an analysis and

assessment of the role globalization has played in fostering the kinds of changes Sommer discusses. However, I do not believe the transnationalizing of literary studies can be explained simply as a response to globalization, especially if we define globalization as a relatively contemporary phenomenon related to new technologies of travel and communication and the complex intersection of national economies and cultures. The transnationalizing of literary studies has to be understood as the effect of a more complicated set of intersecting forces dating back to the late 1960s, forces operating both within and outside the academy. They include the breakdown of a late nineteenth-century Arnoldian model of literary study grounded in an aestheticized, ahistorical, liberal-humanist set of assumptions about the nature and value of literature and culture; the development outside the academy of social and political movements, including the anti–Vietnam War movement, the civil rights movement, the women's movement, and the gay rights movement, and the rise of theoretical and critical practices within the academy dominated by a sustained and critical attention to difference (deconstruction; feminist and gender studies; work on race, class, and sexual orientation; and minority, multicultural, and postcolonial literatures). If we are going to understand how and why national paradigms for the study of literature have broken down in the age of globalization, it is important that we grasp the dramatic role this shift in our attention from sameness to difference has played in facilitating this transformation.

The Arnoldian model of literary studies, part of a more general response in the Victorian period among ruling class cultural arbiters to liberal reform and shifting class structures, was rooted in sameness. Students and professors were to study "the best that has been said and thought" from a position of disinterest, and "the best" was defined by criteria that were both ahistorical and universal. Following Matthew Arnold, the "best" literature is the literature that has managed to transcend the local, historical circumstances of its production and come to embody universal truths about reality and what it means to be human. The "best" literature links "men" because it engages that which is universal for all men. The best criticism is disinterested in the sense that it suspends our different interests and biases in the act of understanding the work as "in itself it really is." Literary texts have singular, essential natures; those with the "best" natures transcend differences and link us to something fundamentally human we all share, and so the canon we study comprises literary texts unified by what they have in common. The critique of this way of thinking about literature and its study is too well known to rehearse, but the main point has always been that Arnold's was a radically dehistoricizing, idealizing, and aestheticizing approach that provided cover for a masculine, interested, politicized conception of literary study masking its particular interests by calling them universal.[4]

What Sommer calls our "romantic enchantment" with sameness and singularity rooted in discrete national literatures evolved under this Arnoldian rubric, a rubric that operated pretty much intact until the 1960s. What happened then is also a familiar story but worth a brief review in the context of the argument I am making. It is a story, at bottom, about the shift from a critical rubric based on sameness to one based on difference. This shift developed both inside and outside the academy, though the forces intersected in dramatic fashion. Within the academy, the interest in difference developed narrowly under the influence, first, of structuralist theory and, later, and more broadly, the deconstructionism of Jacques Derrida and the work of Michel Foucault. Structuralism as a theory of signification taught us that meaning was produced not through sameness (some kind of inherent connection between words and things) but through difference, the play of binary oppositions in arbitrary systems of signification (where nature and culture or purity and hybridity do not have inherent meanings but rather derive their meanings from being set in a binary relationship). Meaning is not inherent but systematic, the product of a play of differences. Derridean deconstructionism developed as both an elaboration and a critique of structuralism. Deconstruction deepened our focus on the central role of difference in the production of meaning by insisting that the structuralist explanation of how meaning is produced was too neat, that in pointing out that a sign was made up of a signifier (a word or image) and a signified (the concept to which the word or image refers) structuralists developed a system that was deceptively self-contained. Language, Derrida argued, has a lot more play in it than the structuralists allowed for. What they called the signified was just another signifier that deferred meaning, hence the concept of *différance,* the idea that words always end up introducing difference and deferring meaning at the same time.

This approach to analyzing the production of meaning and its circulation was revolutionary, but for many critics it seemed focused too narrowly on textual matters and linguistic play. The work of Michel Foucault emerged as a kind of antidote to this focus on textual play, with critics like Hans Bertens arguing that where Derrida was narrowly interested in the role of difference in the operations of "textual power," Foucault was interested in "social power" (157). While this is a helpful distinction in general terms, it misses the extent to which Derrida was quite interested in social as well as textual power (Derrida subjects distinctions like that between textual and social power to deconstructive analysis), but Bertens also plays down the extent to which Foucault operated within a deconstructive framework deployed in the interests of historical, social, political, and institutional analyses. Foucault's classic treatment of sexuality, for example, models a certain way of doing theory that, as Jonathan Culler has argued, is nearly paradigmatic in terms of what theory *does*.[5] For Foucault, "sexuality" is a discursive term. We cannot understand very much about sexuality by try-ing to understand its "nature," without studying how it has been constructed historically, discursively, and ideologically in specific cultures at specific times. The difference between heterosexuality and homosexuality is not a difference of inherent natural qualities but a difference instituted and regulated by dis-courses about sexuality that are historically embedded. We now regularly make the same argument about literature and race and gender that Foucault made about sexuality. None of these things exists in and of themselves. Literature, race, gender, and sexuality are defined and regulated by discursive regimes based on difference that operate ideologically and through institutions to both enable and restrict certain forms of agency. The very nature of "truth" in any instance is not immanent but based on difference, and regimes that regulate and police the truth (formal and informal) all operate by enforcing behaviors and identities as-sociated with socially and historically articulated values based on the interests of those who wield the power to enforce them.

Foucault employs a deconstructive theoretical framework that shifts our at-tention from so-called inherent qualities and sameness to the productive role of difference in a critical landscape more engaged with social, cultural, and politi-cal forms than was early deconstruction. This is why his work has become so central to more political and historical forms of criticism developing in his wake. However, these forms of criticism (feminist, new historicist, African American, postcolonial, gay, lesbian, and queer, etc.) would not have been possible without the wider political movements I mentioned earlier. All of these movements con-tributed to the accelerating study of difference in literary and cultural studies and in the humanities generally, but, perhaps more important, they transformed the demographic makeup of the student population and then the professoriate in ways that have become nearly revolutionary. Indeed, it is the intersection of these demographic changes with theoretical innovations in our understanding of the key role difference makes in the production and regulation of meaning that set the stage for the transnationalizing of literary studies. In this regard the social and political movements I mentioned earlier turned out to be crucial. The civil rights movement opened up colleges and universities to an African American population who had been systematically excluded from higher education, as the Chicana/o movement did for Latino/a students and professors. The Immigration and Nationality Act of 1965 lifted restrictive immigration policies against Asian, Latin American, Mexican, and other non-Anglo populations and helped fuel a demographic transformation of the United States.[6] The women's movement began in the late 1960s to bring significant numbers of women into professional schools and graduate programs, and the gay rights movement brought a whole range of formerly ignored issues and authors (and students and professors) into the classroom. By the late1970s the student body had changed, but so too had the professoriate. With an increasing number of minority, women, and openly gay faculty members came a transformation in the texts taught and the issues foregrounded. This did not happen as part of someone's political agenda. It was the predictable effect of dramatic demographic changes produced by social justice movements that began in the street and ended in the courts. The academy today now reflects the population of the United States—and its disparate interests and experiences—much more than it did in, say, the mid-1960s.

With these changes, the study of different literatures (African American, Latina/o, Native American, and Asian American, etc.), and the representation of difference *in* literature began to systematically complicate scholarship in modern languages and literatures and to transform what it meant to get a "literary" education. The guiding principle of literary studies—that the literature we ought to study gets its significance from its engagement with universal human experiences that transcend historical circumstances—got turned nearly on its head. The imperative to *historicize* the texts we study, to pay attention to the material circumstances of both their production and consumption, and to recognize the *differences* historical and material circumstances make in what we think of as literature and how we engage with it as students and scholars, became central to the enterprise of literary studies. Formerly marginal texts by women and "minority" writers began to get sustained attention; the literary canon, in the first stages of these changes, became productively complicated by the inclusion of these texts and, at a later stage, began to disappear altogether as the principle for organizing the texts we study. At the same time, narrow attention to the formal, aesthetic, and linguistic characteristics of literary texts became complicated by increasing attention to the ways in which they reflect, and reflect on, experiences and identities determined by the social and ideological forces of gender, class, race, sexual orientation, and migration across national borders.

While at the height of the so-called culture wars critics of this transformation complained that literary studies specifically and the humanities in general had become hijacked by the Left and politicized (as if traditional forms of literary study were not always political themselves), something much more complicated and valuable was happening. The dominant paradigm for identifying what counted as "literature" was changing, and the range of issues engaged by literary scholars was shifting dramatically away from a narrow aesthetic basis to a broadly social and even anthropological one. The literature we studied, wrote about, and taught became more representative and thus more complicated. The older, unitary, aestheticized, ahistorical, and universalizing paradigm for literary studies that developed in the late nineteenth and early twentieth centuries collapsed under the imperative to understand literature as a multicultural object of knowledge full of social and cultural information and expressive of a whole range of different experiences and identities. By the mid-1970s the unitary model, which had framed literary studies in English in wholly national terms as "British" and "American," had become complicated in extraordinarily rich ways. The case in American studies, for example, was dramatic. In a short period of time the narrow canon of American writers that was used to establish and then control the study of "American" literature in the early twentieth century exploded, and with it went the unitary model for study, which saw literature as embodying an "American" identity regulated by the pressures of assimilation and sameness. A wave of African American, Chicana/o, Native American, and Asian American scholars joined with others to produce whole new fields of study that challenged first the hegemony of Anglo-American literature in the U.S. canon and then the national model of American studies itself. This should not be seen in negative terms as the *fragmentation* of coherence in literary studies but as a broad and socially valuable corrective to flawed ways of making choices about what ought to be studied in higher education. In its earlier guise, "American" literary studies was "American" in only the narrowest sense of the term, comprising literature produced largely by white males, first in New England and then later in the Midwest, the South, and the West. In fact, as critics began to point out in the late 1970s and early 1980s, the term "America" had been hijacked by "American" studies in the interests of defining a very limited geographical and historical framework for the work it did. As numerous critics began to point out, the Americas comprise all of North, Central, and South America, and a truly "American" studies ought to focus in complex ways on literary production across the borders of these disparate but linked locations.[7] By the mid-1980s "American" literary studies, under the productive pressure of Chicana/o, African American, Asian, and Native American critics had begun to transform itself into a study of the literatures of the Americas, a practice in which U.S. literatures became engaged with those produced along the U.S., Canadian, Mexican, and Caribbean borders, specifically, in the Americas, generally, and among writers belonging to the African (and now South Asian) diaspora. This change was so dramatic that by 2004, Shelly Fisher Fishkin, president of the American Studies Association, devoted her long presidential address to cataloguing what she called the transnational turn in American studies.[8] The story here is clear. As long as the study of "American" literature stuck to the analysis of Anglo-American texts and traditions it remained a scholarly enterprise focused narrowly on a British-U.S. axis of exchange in which the experience of mostly white male authors defined the norm. But once the study of literature became engaged with texts by writers both male and female of African, Native, Asian, Mexican, and Latin American descent, the roots *and* the routes of American literature, and the histories of those who both produced and populated its texts, became a transnational affair.⁹

Many of these changes paralleled the rise of postcolonial studies, a development made possible in part by the general opening up of literary studies to the analysis of formerly marginal texts by minority writers I have been discussing. That is, the evolving study of Native American, African, Asian, and Latino/a texts in the United States and elsewhere in the 1970s and 1980s helped set the stage for postcolonial studies. I address this at length in later chapters about this field, its status as a transnational practice, and its relationship to globalization, but a few key points are worth making here.

As a practice that simultaneously analyzed texts produced outside of Western Europe in former colonies *and* subjected the history of British literature to an analysis of its engagement with imperialism and colonialism (Edward Said's *Culture and Imperialism* is a key example), postcolonial studies had the effect of undermining the Eurocentricity of literary studies in the West *and* subjecting a European literary tradition to historical and material critiques that dramatically transformed traditional critical discourse. Here again, the shift was away from sameness (under the older traditional paradigms of comparative literature, that is, the question of what *united* literatures from disparate locations) to difference— racial, class, and cultural. Like the analyses of minority and multicultural texts ushered in by the rise of African, Native, Asian, and Hispanic American studies, postcolonial studies organized itself around the study of difference, focused attention on alternative histories and experiences, and, perhaps most important, required engagement with texts and issues that cut across national boundaries.

Postcolonial studies has to a significant degree been the offspring of the very diasporic formations it studies (though of course it does not limit itself by any means to such study). Here again shifting demographics are as important as shifting critical practices. The postcolonial *period,* central to the history of globalization, has been characterized by displacement, migration, and mobility that helped transform both the student bodies and the professoriate of Western academic institutions. Postcolonial literature enters the curriculum and spurs new scholarly work in the West in part as the result of this mobility. With migration to U.S. and western European academic institutions of scholars and critics having roots in postcolonial countries, and with growing diasporic communities (Africa, South Asian, Asian, etc.) feeding the student body of these institutions, came a whole new generation of students and professors dedicated to expanding the geographical scope of literary studies and, with it, the identities, experiences, and histories it encompasses.

The replacement of a unitary, ahistorical, and universalizing model for literary studies with one focused on difference and influenced by the rise of minority, multicultural, and postcolonial studies happened well before anyone in the academy started talking much about globalization. Globalization, in the sense Doris Sommer invokes it, becomes central to the transnationalizing of literary studies because it *merges* with the kinds of changes I have been discussing. Economic and cultural globalization have both worked to dramatically accelerate the kind of demographic changes that are central to changes in critical and scholarly practices in literary studies. All of these changes have converged in ways that have led to the transnationalizing of literary studies. The opening of U.S. and other Western academic institutions to minority and postcolonial students, the movement of some of those students into the professoriate, and the ways in which their work has challenged and to a significant degree overturned older critical practices has transformed what used to be a largely nationalist enterprise into an increasingly transnational practice, whether measured in terms of the transnational turn in American or modernist studies,[10] the impact of postcolonial studies on British literary studies, or the more general sense in which the curriculum in English, Romance languages, and comparative literary studies departments has complicated national models by the attention we now pay to the porousness of borders and to cross-cultural, transnational, and even postnational experiences.

Globalization has thus played an important part in the transnationalizing of literary studies, but it is not the singular cause of this dramatic change. Rather, the forces of economic and cultural globalization outside of the academy, and the development of theories and practices for its study *inside* the academy, have dramatically accelerated a longer history of change. While popular public discussion of globalization can be dated from the publication in June 2000 of Thomas L. Friedman's *The Lexus and the Olive Tree,* globalization had already become a popular topic among academics in a number of fields, where, since the early 1990s, scholars in economics, political science, sociology, film and communications, and cultural and literary studies had been writing about its effects.[11] By the time Friedman published his book, the study of globalization had already migrated from departments of economy and political science through sociology departments and cultural studies programs into the field of literary studies. What started out as a relatively narrow field dedicated to tracking the rise of an increasingly global network of economic relations dominated by transnational corporations had steadily evolved into a globalized field of cultural studies, as scholars and critics in a range of disciplines in the humanities and social sciences came to recognize that commodities, currencies, and cultures are inseparable, that the globalization of economies brings with it the globalization of cultures, and that, indeed, it is nearly impossible to figure out where economic globalization stops and cultural globalization begins.

Academic studies of globalization have increasingly turned to the question of its general impact on the university, and more specifically to the question of how globalization is changing the nature and scope of work within the disciplines. One of the first books to do this was *The University in Ruins* (1998) by Bill Readings. In it Readings develops a trenchant analysis of the impact globalization had on the North American university in the last decades of the twentieth century, focusing on how the demise of the nation-state affected the humanities in general and literary studies in particular. He reminds us that the rise of the modern university is intimately connected to the evolution of the modern nation-state, that the needs of nationalism and the operations of the university were deeply connected from the outset. In Readings's view, the modern university, which evolved under Wilhelm von Humboldt at the University of Berlin beginning in 1810 and was later adopted in the United States (7), always had a "national cultural mission" (3), in part because the modern idea of "culture" and the modern idea of the nation developed in close relation to one another (12), so much so that the "university . . . has historically been the primary institution of national culture in the modern nation-state" (12).

In the view of Readings, however, globalization began very quickly to put an end to all this. With the contemporary shift from national economies to a global one, with the proliferation of electronic media able to transmit information instantaneously across national boundaries, and with the power of transnational corporations rivaling that of the nation-state, the university is undergoing a profound reorientation. "The University," Readings writes, "is becoming a different kind of institution, one that is no longer linked to the destiny of the nation-state by virtue of its role as a producer, protector, and inculcator of an idea of national culture" (3). Because "the process of economic globalization brings with it the relative decline of the nation-state" the university is undergoing a fundamental reorientation away from serving the needs of the nation-state toward serving the needs of transnational capital (3).

This change is having a particularly striking impact on the humanities in general and on the study of English in particular. The modern university grew out of the values of the Enlightenment and was committed to the cultivation of character, an aesthetic education, and the development in its students of the capacity for philosophical critique. The central role of philosophy in this enterprise, and the later importance of a literary education as formulated by Matthew Arnold, who saw literature as central to his programmatic effort to use culture in England as a bulwark against a rising working class, underscore the important role English played in the modern university. "The current crisis of the University in the West" in the age of globalization, Readings insists, "proceeds from a fundamental shift in its social role and internal systems, one which means that the centrality of the traditional humanistic disciplines to the life of the University is no longer assured" (3), and that the role of English in particular is becoming radically transformed. In the United States, English has traditionally been part of a curricular world organized along the lines of a political map, the borders of which have neatly duplicated those of modern nation-states. If the conventional structures of literary study (English, French, Spanish, Italian, German, etc.) have been transparently nationalist, they mirror the aesthetic ideology of literary studies, one that can be traced to the linkage among nation, race, and literature forged in nineteenth-century Europe by writers like Hippolyte-Adolphe Taine and Matthew Arnold. In the United States Ralph Waldo Emerson and Walt Whitman articulated the need for a national literature decades before it became incorporated in the curricula of American universities. As Peter Carafiol and others have demonstrated, the structure of American literary studies in universities in the United States has always been informed by a broadly nationalist ideal.[12] While this ideal was based on forging an aesthetic and ideological consensus about culture and identity grounded in a limited set of texts unified around certain themes and values, we have seen how contemporary criticism became increasingly preoccupied with difference in ways that undermine the neat, superficial cultural homogeneity informing the study of national literatures.

This interest in difference, connected as it is to the study of minority, multicultural, postcolonial, and transnational literatures, was dramatically accelerated by the forces of globalization. It was also paralleled by a significant increase in the production of literature written in English outside the United States and Great Britain. As the locations from which English literature is produced have multiplied, the rationale for a nation-state model governing its study has appeared increasingly anachronistic. There is an obvious synchronicity between the transnational production of English and the transnationalizing of its study. The remarkable explosion of English literature produced outside Britain and the United States in the last decades of the twentieth century made it clear that "English" was becoming defined less by a nation than by a language. The globalization of English from this point of view is not a theoretical formulation or a political agenda developed by radicals in the humanities to displace the canon. It is a simple fact of contemporary history. English literature in the age of globalization is increasingly transnational, whether written by cosmopolitan writers like Salman Rushdie, Derek Walcott, Zadie Smith, Arundhati Roy, Junot Díaz, or Nadine Gordimer or by a host of lesser-known writers working in their home countries or in diasporic communities around the world, from Europe and Africa to the Caribbean and North America. For this reason, English literature is becoming increasingly more difficult to understand without recognizing its

relationship to a complicated web of transnational histories linked to the historical processes of globalization.

These changes, coming as they have in the wake of significant transformations in literary studies already ushered in by poststructuralist, feminist, and
postcolonial theories (among others), have been profoundly controversial. Critics
on the right have lamented the so-called dominance of theory and have complained about the politicization of literary studies. But even some progressive
critics such as the late Edward Said and Masao Miyoshi have lamented the combined effects of theory and globalization on the humanities, complaining that
it has led to intellectual fragmentation and created a proliferation of what appear to be largely uncoordinated efforts to create new subdisciplines and reorganize traditional curricula and programs. Clearly, the unprecedented explosion
of theorizing about literary language, interpretation, textuality, authorship, and
reading since the late 1960s has played an important role in overturning conventional approaches to literary study in the classroom, in criticism, and in the curriculum. But nothing has quite had the kind of transformative effect on literary
studies that globalization has had. This effect has all but undone the traditional
Eurocentrism of literary studies in the West. As Edward Said put it in "Globalizing Literary Study" (2001), "economic and political globalization... since the
end of the cold war... has been the enveloping context in which literary studies
are undertaken":

> The gradual emergence in the humanities of confused and fragmented paradigms
> of research, such as those available through the new fields of postcolonial, ethnic,
> and other particularistic or identity-based study, reflects the eclipse of the old au-
> thoritative, Eurocentric models and the new ascendancy of a globalized, postmod-
> ern consciousness from which, as Benita Parry and others have argued, the gravity
> of history has been excised. (66)

Said was obviously less than sanguine about these developments. Like Readings, he took the "deterioration of the position of the humanities" in the university to be a direct result of the "catastrophic effects of the global situation" (66).
The end of Eurocentrism, in his view, has simply left us with a hodge-podge of
critical approaches rooted in identity politics and shorn of a historical consciousness. In our rush to celebrate a "purely academic version of multiculturalism with
which many people in the real world of ethnic division, conflict and chauvinism
would find it difficult to identify," we miss paying attention to "sites of resistance
to the terrible negative effects of globalization" (66). The worst of these effects
for Said, beyond even the poverty and political divisions that attend globalization, is the "dominance of the United States as the only superpower left" (66).[13]

This dominance carries over into the realm of academic politics. Those of us who have worried about the extent to which global studies represents the recolonization of "Other" literatures by Western academics are concerned that the field of transnational literary studies is coming to be dominated by a single superpower. From this point of view, globalization represents a return of Western colonization, as postnational literary studies hitches itself to the globalization bandwagon and begins to subjugate the literature of the Other to its own paradigms. In this scenario, Eurocentrism is repackaged as globalization, and multiculturalism gives way to an inevitably leveling kind of cosmopolitanism. Moreover, to the extent that "English" as both a language and literature is privileged in discussions about globalization, it seems that the rich complexity of literature and cultural production under globalization is in danger of being subordinated to the powerful forces of this dominant discipline.[14]

Miyoshi has echoed Said's concerns. Indeed, he warns in "'Globalization' and the University" (1998) against the dangers of academic work in the humanities and social sciences becoming complicit with globalization.[15] He insists that the autonomy of faculty in the research university in general and the humanities in particular has been compromised by the kind of "academic capitalism" (39) that fuels globalization, and that changes we superficially celebrate as progressive—a focus, for example, on "particularity" and "diversity" (40)—in fact support the needs of global capitalism. In Miyoshi's view, the ideal of "multiplicity and difference" ends up endorsing economic globalization (40). Where others see a value in focusing on diversity and difference Miyoshi sees a debilitating strategy of division and fragmentation. "If the strategy of division and fragmentation is not contained and moderated with the idea of a totality," he writes, "it may very well lose its initial purpose and end up paradoxically in universal marginalization" (42). Miyoshi sketches out his position in a masterful, condensed overview of the impact of poststructuralist theory on concepts of universality and difference.[16] His main complaint about poststructuralist theory is that its antifoundationalist critique of universals left little room for the kind of totalizing perspective normally associated with Marxism. This development, in his view, began with the rejection of essence by Jean-Paul Sartre and other existentialists, and then became extended in the structuralism of Claude Lévi-Strauss (fueled, as Miyoshi sees it, by an "abandonment of totality as well as universalism" [41]). Miyoshi sees the value of Lévi-Strauss's work on cultural difference in its break with a "long-established tradition of Eurocentricity" in Western theory, but he isolates a number of problems with it. First, it tends to focus on cultures as diverse and therefore lacking common characteristics and traits, which he insists leads to a kind of "cognitive relativism" (41). Second, influenced by Saussurean linguistics, the "world" and "history" become understood reductively in textual and narratological terms, while "truth is assumed to be unrepresentable" (42). It follows, then, that "every culture or age has its own unique terms and discourses, which are thus judged incommensurable across the cultural and historical borders" (42). Finally, subjectivity and agency under the system of Lévi-Strauss are impossibly fragmented and ineffective in terms of mounting resistance to dominant forces. In Miyoshi's view, Lévi-Strauss leaves us with a world in which individual subjectivity is determined by discrete fragmented cultures, individual agency is "disallowed," and "political engagement is impossible" (42). Finally, "because of this erasure of political agency, the diversity of cultures paradoxically surrenders to the hegemonic center once again—very much as in the so-called global 'borderless' economy" (42).

Once this basic approach to culture and subjectivity took hold, according to Miyoshi's narrative, universality and totality became demonized "in favor of difference, particularity, incommensurability, and structure" (42). "Totalizing concepts" such as "humanity, civilization, history, and justice," along with "subtotalities" such as "region" and "nation," were rejected, and all "foundational ideas and concepts" came to be understood as thoroughly "historical and cultural constructs" (42). Miyoshi mounts a breathtaking condemnation of the effects of poststructuralist theory on thinking about domination and liberation, and the agency required for both, a condemnation based on his conviction that "an individual, a group, or a program requires a totality in which to position itself" if it is to mount an effective critique of anything (42). Such an effective critique, in his view, has been thoroughly compromised in the United States by the discourse of multiculturalism and a stress on identity politics, both of which, he asserts, have fractured and fragmented various oppressed populations in ways that have actually undermined political agency. Both multiculturalism and identity politics have what Miyoshi calls the "imprimatur" of the "philosophy of difference" (which runs from Sartre and Lévi-Strauss through Derrida, Foucault, feminism, and African American theory) and they have in his view contributed to a debilitating "multiplicity of perspectives, specializations and qualifications" that are "intensified by the rage for differentiation," particularly in humanities departments (46). Miyoshi sees all this as much worse than the New Criticism: "Worse than the fetishism of irony, paradox, and complexity a half century ago, the cant of hybridity, nuance, and diversity now pervades the humanities" so that they are "thoroughly disabled to take up the task of opposition, resistance, and confrontation" (48).[17]

Said and Miyoshi raise a number of challenging questions about the relationship between globalization and academic work in the humanities and social sciences. But are things really as bad as they claim? Is globalization itself simply the newest and most efficient agent of capitalist exploitation yet developed by the West, a process that relentlessly homogenizes and Westernizes the cultures it entangles in its net? Is the attention we pay in the academy to literatures and cultures formerly excluded by Eurocentrism corrupted by its association with a Western commitment to difference, diversity, multiculturalism, and cosmo-politanism that has already been cunningly co-opted within the university by English departments and outside of it by capitalism? And must we, along with Said and Miyoshi, think of globalization and postcolonial studies, multicultural-ism, gender studies, the study of "ethnic" literatures and other approaches that grow out of identity politics and a general attention to difference as hopelessly compromised and fragmenting?

I don't think so. The dangers these two critics warn of are real, but I want to offer a more hopeful narrative than those presented by Said and Miyoshi. In the first place, there is nothing new about "fragmentation" in literary studies. Fragmentation actually has a long history in literary studies and is integral to its development. Whether we consider the steady fragmentation in English of the "canon" from British texts to British and American texts to "global English," or from texts authored by white men to texts authored by women and minority writers, or whether we consider the historical proliferation of critical approaches ranging from philology, historicism, New Criticism, structuralism, deconstruc-tion, feminism, *New* Historicism, postcolonialism, ecocriticism, and the like, we see a discipline that has been constantly fragmenting and then reforming itself. In literary studies, as in most other academic disciplines, "coherence" and "frag-mentation" are interdependent. Coherence comes as a benefit of fragmentation. It isn't an alternative to it.

We need to be careful not to set up a historical view of literary studies in which a monolithic and coherent Eurocentrism remained dominant until postmodern fragmentation set in, a fragmentation specifically linked to the debilitating ef-fects of globalization and complicit with forms of multiculturalism hijacked by companies like Benetton in ads that are transparently commercial. This historical narrative is much too simplistic. Although literary studies in the West has been, as Said pointed out, dominated by Eurocentrism, disciplinary coherence within this framework broke down and reorganized itself with remarkable regularity during the whole of the twentieth century.[18] The current shift in literary studies, which Said and a host of contemporary critics across the ideological spectrum characterize as a new kind of fragmentation, simply represents another instance in which one form of coherence gives way to another as the discipline continues to evolve. Earlier instances of this so-called fragmentation often occurred along narrow lines related primarily to methodology (philological, rhetorical, formal-ist, historical, structuralist, poststructuralist, etc.), whereas recent forms of frag-mentation are related more to political and social movements (poststructuralist

Marxism, feminism, gay and lesbian studies, postcolonial studies, African American and border studies, and now, globalization studies). However, the apparent shift—from a postcolonial to a global perspective—is quite consistent with the way the discipline of literary studies has developed over the whole course of the twentieth century.

Like Said's, Miyoshi's concerns about globalization and the humanities are often compelling, but ultimately his argument is misguided and reductive. As I noted, his absolute distinction between particularity and totality is so rigid as to be counterproductive. He is certainly right that a preoccupation with difference has been the hallmark of critical and cultural theory since the late 1960s, but it is only from the perspective of someone who wants to maintain an outmoded collectivist imperative for social change that this preoccupation would appear politically conservative. To real political conservatives multiculturalism and identity politics (especially feminist, queer, and minority) appear central to the agenda of radical leftists both inside and outside the academy. Surely both of these positions fail to acknowledge the extent to which multiculturalism and identity politics have contributed, however awkwardly, to the improvement of social justice in the United States and elsewhere.[19] While Miyoshi wants to dismiss the important lessons poststructuralism has taught us about the reductive impulses and political dangers of totalizing systems and master narratives, it seems to me imperative we resist his dismissal of the local and the particular and his nostalgia for a manufactured essentialism no matter how progressive its political aims might be. The idea that particularity and totality are absolutely opposed to one another ought to be tempered by the recognition that they exist in dialectical relationship with each other. It may be that attention to particular differences makes it more difficult to see the total picture, but the kind of totality or universality Miyoshi endorses more often than not reduces, obscures, ignores, or rejects the legitimacy of local and particular differences when they threaten the constructed coherence of a totalizing master narrative. It may be better to run the risk of making a fetish of local differences than erasing them in the interests of a larger, totalized good.[20]

Miyoshi's wholesale condemnation of critics interested in multiculturalism and globalization is much too sweeping and flies in the face of other critics, who lament the politicization of work in the humanities and social sciences by professors they associate with the political left. For this reason it seems like an odd time to complain, as Miyoshi has done, that the humanities are in "retreat" from "intellectual and political resistance" (40). We live in a time when the humanities have been hammered by conservative and moderate critics alike for becoming mired in a pedagogy dominated by a left-leaning intellectual and political resistance that has supposedly compromised the autonomy and objectivity of academic inquiry (see, for example, David Horowitz's "Academic Bill of Rights"). Miyoshi's position begs the question of how the academy can be both captive to the Left's agenda of intellectual and political resistance and at the same time complicit with the ideology and needs of global capitalism.

Miyoshi offers helpful caution with regard to the relationship between academic scholarship and globalization. However, he gets himself in the somewhat paradoxical position of criticizing the use of globalization as a framework for rethinking work in the humanities and in area studies while at the same time calling for a global "all areas" point of view that eschews particularity and difference in the interests of producing new metanarratives. He insists that "the academics' work in this marketized world is to learn and watch problems in as many sites as they can keep track of, not in any specific areas, nations, races, ages, genders, or cultures, but in all areas, nations, races, ages, genders, and cultures. In other words, far from abandoning the master narratives, the critics and scholars in the humanities must restore the public rigor of the metanarratives" (49). From this point of view our work should ignore the enormous body of cautionary literature about master narratives, play down distinctions between specific areas and regions, and avoid anything but an overtly critical and persistently hostile scholarly posture toward globalization. Except for his antipathy toward global capitalism, it is never clear why a "totalized" system along the lines Miyoshi calls for could not be built around a historicized analysis and critique of the forces and effects of globalization. After all, one does not have to endorse globalization to study how its effects are having a totalizing effect on virtually every sphere of human endeavor. It is awkward to see Miyoshi on the one hand calling for a systematic macro approach to cultural analysis and on the other rejecting the study of globalization as one of its key components. It seems to me that both Said and Miyoshi are wrong to worry that the changes in literary and cultural studies I have been discussing in this chapter represent fragmentation or a loss of coherence. Rather, they represent the development of a new coherence (which will always be marked by some contradictions and be tentative by nature) in which histories of mobility, migration, and displacement get connected with a study of how cultures and identities and the politics that shape them develop across formerly fixed and overly narrow national geographies. Miyoshi's judgment that work on local and particular identities is debilitating because it disallows a collective perspective misses how fictions of the collective have served forces that have dominated and oppressed people who are marked *by* the collective as different. We are living in a period in which the historical value of attention to particular identities constituted by differences related to gender, ethnicity, race, and sexual orientation ought to seem clear.

While I have been arguing that there are problems with the positions taken by critics like Said and Miyoshi, they both raise a number of pressing questions worth exploring. What, in fact, is globalization, and when did it begin? How do the histories of colonialism and postcolonialism fit into the history of globalization? What kind of relationship obtains between the economic and cultural forces of globalization? In what sense do the discourses of multiculturalism and cosmopolitanism represent viable responses to managing difference in an age of increasing globalization? Or do they, as Miyoshi feared, simply feed the interests of an increasingly dominant system of global capital? What impact will the increasing attention to what we call global culture have on our study of literature in general and English literature in particular? And, finally, are the forms of personal and cultural hybridity produced by globalization destabilizing and to be lamented, or are they inevitable and potentially liberating? To begin to answer these questions it will help to first sort through some competing definitions of globalization, briefly exploring how the field of globalization studies developed before it migrated to cultural and literary studies, and asking ourselves how we ought to conceptualize globalization as we think about its relationship to literary and cultural production and its impact on the university.

What Is Globalization?

How we define globalization depends on how we *historicize* globalization. Many critics argue that globalization is a contemporary historical phenomenon defined by a dramatic kind of rupture from the past in which the flow of economic and cultural forces have swamped the borders of nation-states, that the development of electronic media forms in particular have changed entirely the nature of social, cultural, economic, and political relations. From this point of view globalization is a dramatically new phenomenon. Other critics, however, argue that globalization actually has a long history, that globalization in our own time should be seen as a significant acceleration of forces that have been in play since at least the sixteenth century and that are not simply Western in their origin. I endorse this view and believe we need to find a historically and theoretically sound way to reconcile the histories of trade, exploration, conquest, colonization, decolonization, and postcolonialism with the long history of globalization.

I want to examine in particular recent debates about postcolonialism and globalization because they foreground what is at stake in how we historicize globalization. While some critics fear that globalization studies threaten to replace a politically incisive form of critique (postcolonial studies) with a generalized and largely celebratory one, I believe this is a short-sighted and inaccurate assessment and that globalization and postcolonialism actually have a dialectical relationship with each other. The histories of the two are inseparable, and the transnational turn in literary and cultural studies will benefit greatly from our ability to articulate both the historical and the methodological relationship between them.

We also need to be careful about how we theorize the relationship between economic and cultural forms of globalization. In reviewing the spirited debate among critics about whether globalization is an economic or a cultural phenomenon, and the related argument about whether the study of globalization ought to be materialist or cultural, I take the position that a narrow exclusivist position on either side is wrong, that the very categories of "materialist" and "cultural" set up a false distinction. The process we call globalization is characterized by the *conflation* of cultural and economic forms. When commodities travel, culture travels, and cultural forms are nothing if not commodities. The study of globalization, therefore, requires an approach that is neither narrowly culturalist nor materialist but rather operates with an understanding of the interdependence and interrelationship of the two. This is an argument I will sketch out below but take up in more detail in chapter 3.

Historicizing Globalization

How we define globalization indeed depends on how it is historicized. If we think of globalization as comprising a set of economic, cultural, and political developments facilitated by the explosion of dramatically new electronic and digital technologies of communication and commercial activity, it will appear to be a contemporary, Western, postmodern, and postnational phenomenon. However, if we think of globalization more broadly as characterized by a complex set of intercultural encounters facilitated by successive historical shifts in forms of travel, communication, exploration, conquest, and trade that periodically accelerate in ways keyed to technological, economic, and political change, then globalization in our own time will appear to be the extension of relationships with a long and complex history both within and outside the West. While many journalists and critics think about globalization in the first way, I believe it is important to think of globalization in longer historical terms, not so much because it is more *accurate* than seeing globalization as a contemporary phenomenon (both positions have their merits), but because it affords us a more nuanced historical perspective regarding the development of globalization in our own time. To think of globalization as strictly a contemporary phenomenon requires that we define it in terms of a set of radically new developments related to technologies of travel and communication that in fact have a long history running back at least to the sixteenth century, if not earlier. The short view of globalization foregrounds the emergence of electronic, largely digital, forms of communication as a kind of rupture, and it sees new forms of physical mobility and the emergence of a global economy as singular and dramatically new forces that have fundamentally remade the world we live in. This way of defining globalization is valuable for the attention it pays to the role new media, communication systems, forms of travel, and economic relations and their governance have played in the contemporary transformation of personal experience and social relations. But it underplays how these changes are related to older, more incremental ones that have a long history and that call our attention to how brief the era of the nation-state has been and to patterns of continuity between the past and our own time.

A good example of the argument that globalization represents a historical rupture facilitated by dramatically new developments in media forms, financial relations, and ideologies is the now classic one Arjun Appadurai made in *Modernity at Large* (1996). For Appadurai, globalization is characterized by "disjunction" and "difference" (27). He postulates a "Global Now" (2) and argues that we have in the "past few decades" experienced "a general rupture in the tenor of intersocietal relations," a "dramatic and unprecedented break between tradition and modernity," indeed, a break "with all sorts of pasts" (3). This rupture takes "media and migration as its two major" causes, both of which have a profound effect on what he calls "*the work of the imagination* as a constitutive feature of modern subjectivity" (3). Appadurai's version of globalization is defined by the eruption of electronic media and the "new resources and new disciplines for the construction of imagined selves and imagined worlds" this media affords (3). It is about speed, immediacy, and convergence, the collapse of what David Harvey popularized as the time-space ratio, the "immediate" communication of textual and video information in a way that collapses the effect of distance, the circulation of bytes of information and "the immediacy of their absorption into public discourse" (3). This kind of immediacy is, for Appadurai, characterized by a set of "global flows" he characterizes using the metaphor of landscapes: ethnoscapes, mediascapes, technoscapes, financescapes, and ideoscapes (33). For Appadurai the landscapes of ethnicity, the media, technology, finance, and ideology have all ruptured into a complex set of global flows that have set loose contexts for the imaginative reformation of subjectivity across the borders of nation-states. While I believe this vision of globalization as a generally liberatory set of processes has some merit, I will be arguing in chapter 3 that it fails to account for how the unevenness of economic development under globalization limits opportunities for the kind of reformation of subjectivity Appadurai describes. What

I want to stress here is the theory of historical rupture that characterizes his definition of globalization. While Appadurai gives a nod to the historicity of some of
these changes, he insists that we understand globalization as an absolute break
with the past. "People, machinery, money, images and ideas now follow increasingly nonisomorphic paths...the sheer speed, scale, and volume of each of these
flows are now so great that the disjunctures have become central to the politics
of global culture" (37).

Appadurai's approach to globalization emphasizes rupture, speed, convergence, and disjunction at the expense of historicizing the forces that have led to
this rupture in the first place, and it stands in contrast to other approaches that
see globalization as a long historical process. It is important to recognize the
stakes for literary and cultural studies in these contrasting approaches. If globalization is seen as a fundamentally postmodern phenomenon then it would seem
limited as an explanatory paradigm to contemporary (and emerging) literatures
and cultures. But if globalization is a long historical process that dramatically accelerated in the last half of the twentieth century, then the globalization of literary studies cannot restrict itself to this contemporary acceleration.[1] In particular,
literature's relation to the processes of globalization as they manifest themselves
in a variety of historical periods—indeed, literature's facilitation of economic
and cultural globalization—is becoming a potentially important field of study
that can get short-circuited if we historicize globalization as a strictly postmodern
eruption.

While Appadurai aligns globalization with late modernity, Roland Robertson, a proponent of the idea that globalization has a long history, argues that
the process actually predates modernity and has been evolving since at least the
fifteenth century. He divides the history of globalization into five phases: "ger-
minal" (1400–1750), "incipient" (1750–1875), "take-off" (1875–1925), "struggle
for hegemony" (1925–69), and finally "uncertainty," which runs from 1969 to the
present (25–31). The key moments for Robertson in this long evolution toward
globalization include the collapse of Christendom; the development of maps and
maritime travel; the rise of the nation-state, global exploration, colonialism, the
creation of citizenship, passports, diplomacy and the entire paraphernalia of international relations; the rise of international communication and mass migration; the founding of organizations such as the League of Nations and the United
Nations; the outbreak of world wars; and the exploration of space and a developing sense that communities based on race, ethnicity, gender, sexual preference,
and so on, cut across national and state boundaries.

Robertson's approach to dating globalization is at odds with that of Appadurai and other postmodern theorists such as Anthony Giddens and David

Harvey. Giddens links globalization much more specifically to modernity—in particular, to the solidification of the nation-state under capitalism and to what Malcolm Waters calls the nation-state's "administrative competence" (achieved especially through surveillance and "industrialized military order" [48]). Highly industrialized, rationalized, and commodified nation-states in the twentieth century facilitated, in Giddens's view, the "'lifting out' of social relations from local contexts of interaction and their restructuring across time and space" (21). Like Immanuel Wallerstein, Giddens sees globalization in fundamentally economic terms, characterized by the dominance of transnational corporations, which turn the world into "a single market for commodities, labour and capital" (Waters 51). For Giddens globalization represents the "intensification of worldwide social relations that link distant localities in such a way that local happenings are shaped by events occurring many miles away and vice versa" (64). Whereas Robertson's approach suggests that literary and cultural forms produced in various periods may be connected to globalization, Giddens (like Appadurai) suggests a narrower relation between modernity and globalization, one in which literary and cultural studies and globalization primarily intersect in what we usually think of as the modern and postmodern periods. Harvey goes further than Giddens, insisting that globalization marks a fundamental break with modernity. For Giddens globalization is an extension of modernity, but for Harvey it is inextricably linked to postmodernity. Harvey's approach to globalization is keyed to the ways in which mechanization and technology increasingly diminish the constraints space puts on time. With the invention and growing sophistication of shipping, railways, motor, and air transport, the time it takes to move across space has continually shrunk, accelerating the collapse of boundaries and borders and facilitating economic and cultural globalization.

These developments have accelerated with the proliferation of electronic forms of communication, which allows for nearly instantaneous contact and for commercial transactions that cover the globe while virtually ignoring nation-state boundaries. These technologies (particularly the Internet) collapse the discontinuity between time and space in radically new ways. When I argue for a historical view of globalization that sees contemporary globalization as an *acceleration* of forces that have been at work for a few centuries, I am thinking in particular of the speed of change facilitated by the *convergence* of these new technologies. Appadurai gets at this phenomenon in his focus on how technologies related to and facilitating the various "scapes" he enumerates have intersected with one another and ramped up the pace of myriad global flows in our own time, producing what the media critic Henry Jenkins has called "convergence culture" in his book of the same name. If globalization in our own time can be said to represent a rupture from earlier forms, it is due to the phenomenon of convergence, "a word that," according to Jenkins,

> describes technological, industrial, cultural, and social changes in the ways media circulates within our culture. Some common ideas referenced by the term include the flow of content across multiple media platforms, the cooperation between multiple media industries, the search for new structures of media financing that fall at the interstices between old an new media, and the migratory behavior of media audiences who would go almost anywhere in search of the kind of entertainment experiences they want. Perhaps most broadly, media convergence refers to a situation in which multiple media systems coexist and where media content flows fluidly across them. Convergence is understood here as an ongoing process or series of intersections between different media systems, not a fixed relationship. (282)

Jenkins here articulates the kind of convergence that is at the center of Appadurai's mediascape, but the phenomenon of convergence has a much wider applicability in terms of understanding the accelerating forms of economic globalization in our own time, since the technologies Jenkins enumerates have become central in facilitating the global flow of cash, commodities, and knowledge. Indeed, Jenkins's notion of convergence culture mirrors Joseph Stiglitz's explanation of how economic globalization has dramatically accelerated in our own time as a linked set of institutional practices. Jenkins's exploration of how cultural forms are globally commodified in convergence culture is but one example of the general trend in all forms of economic globalization in an age of convergence.[2] The history of globalization, to a significant degree, is the history of accelerating convergences.

With the differences among Robertson, Giddens, and Harvey in mind, we can see that the question of what globalization is turns out to be inextricably linked to how it is historicized. Robertson's view of globalization is fundamentally different from those put forward by Appadurai, Giddens, and Harvey, and, as I have been suggesting, each one offers us a different context for thinking about how to globalize literary and cultural study. Following Robertson, the globalizing of literary and cultural studies would engage literatures and cultures from nearly every period, while, if—with Appadurai, Giddens, and Harvey—we conceive of globalization as a specifically modern or postmodern phenomenon, we would focus primarily on the literatures of the late nineteenth and the twentieth centuries. Which of these points of view is correct? While the arguments Appadurai, Giddens, and Harvey make about the acceleration of globalization in the late twentieth century are important, it seems to me that Robertson's approach is the more nuanced one and that it offers wider opportunities for those of us in literary and cultural studies interested in the intersection of globalization and literary and cultural production. Although it would be a mistake not to acknowledge that a set of explosive forces unleashed in the last half of the twentieth century related to what Jenkins has called "convergence culture" have radically revised transnational exchange, it would be an even bigger mistake not to contextualize these changes in a longer historical view of globalization such as the one Robertson offers. Globalization can certainly help us map the future of literary and cultural studies, but it also provides an important way to rethink our approach to the study of literature across a range of historical periods.

Perhaps more important, the long historical view Robertson takes toward globalization helps dispel the commonplace yet inaccurate idea that globalization is a Western phenomenon fueled by capitalism. Such an argument can only be sustained by viewing globalization narrowly as a late twentieth-century phenomenon. Understood as a longer historical process, however, the phenomenon we call globalization cannot simply be viewed as a product of the West. Critics as disparate as the Nobel Prize–winning economist Amartya Sen and the sociologist Janet Abu-Lughod have quite rightly insisted that globalization long predates the twentieth century and has its roots as much in the East as in the West. Abu-Lughod dates the emergence during the thirteenth and fourteenth centuries of what she calls the first "world system" well before European hegemony. Her 1989 book *Before European Hegemony: The World System A.D. 1250–1350* details the emergence of an economic system linking Europe, the Middle East, and China. Not only was this system *not* dominated by Europe, but many technological and economic advances that developed during this period and which later fueled dramatic expansion in the West came out of China and the Middle East. Sen makes the same point in his 2002 article, "How to Judge Globalism," but pushes the origins of what we now call globalization back to at least 1000, when "the global reach of science, technology, and mathematics was changing the nature of the world" in a trajectory that ran, not from West to East, but from East to West (1). Sen points to a "chain of intellectual relations that link Western mathematics and science to a collection of distinctly non-Western practitioners" (2) and points out that "the printing of the world's first book was a marvelously globalized event," since the technology was Chinese, the book an Indian Sanskrit treatise, and the translation the work of a half-Turk (2). For Sen, "the agents of globalization are neither European nor exclusively Western, nor are they necessarily linked to Western dominance" (2).[3] Such a nuanced and capacious view of globalization can only come from taking a long historical view of its processes. To see globalization as a recent eruption is to mistake not only the date but the nature of its emergence, for it leads us to miss the extent to which earlier world systems outside the West produced forms of knowledge and technology integral to the later phases of globalization. It is important that we not downplay how globalization has accelerated dramatically in our own time in the ways Appadurai and Jenkins have tried to capture, but in the final analysis this acceleration has to be contextualized within a longer history of technological developments and convergences.[4]

Globalization and Postcolonialism

We cannot consider the historical nature of globalization without thinking of its history in relationship to the histories of colonialism, decolonization, and the era we call "postcolonial." Indeed, the last few years have produced a spirited debate about the historical, theoretical, and strategic relationship between postcolonialism and globalization. Although postcolonialism and globalization studies have clearly worked in concert to transform the substance and geography of both English and comparative literary studies, many critics consistently see their relationship as troubled. Some argue, for example, that postcolonialism as a strategically politicized area of study is threatened by a generalized (and sometimes overly enthusiastic) form of globalization studies, that globalization studies simply represents the newest phase of colonial domination by the West, so that both postcolonial nations themselves and academic fields related to subaltern studies are threatened by the growing hegemony of a thoroughly Westernized brand of economic, cultural, and academic globalization. As we have seen, in Said's view globalization looks like a direct threat to the postcolonial condition and its study. Indeed, it may be that academic forms of globalization simply duplicate the worst effects of economic and cultural globalization. Other critics are more comfortable with trying to accommodate postcolonial studies to the emerging field of globalization studies, which they see offering a new rubric for the transnational study of literature whose historical point of view and dual focus on cultural and economic issues can be an antidote to the narrow textualism and culturalism of the field of postcolonial studies. Viewed together at this particular moment, postcolonialism and globalization seem to offer two somewhat conflicting approaches to the transnational study of literature and culture. How we reconcile the historical relationship between colonialism, postcolonialism, and globalization has a lot to do with the wider question of how we historicize, and thus define, globalization.

It seems to me there are two basic positions one can take on the question of the relationship between postcolonialism and globalization. The first would be to mark a clear historical distinction between the eras of postcolonialism and globalization based on an understanding that, while globalization is a postnational phenomenon, postcolonialism is linked to modernity and the long epoch of the nation-state. The second, however, would insist on a fundamental connection between postcolonialism and globalization, one based on an understanding that both colonialism and postcolonialism are integral to the very history of globalization. The first view separates postcolonialism and globalization historically, connecting postcolonialism to the rise of modernity and the epoch of nationalism, while seeing globalization as fundamentally postnational and postmodern. The second view recognizes that postcolonialism marks a break in the history of colonialism and the exercise of colonial power, while insisting that postcolonialism belongs nevertheless to the late history of the nation-state. From this point of view, postcolonialism marks a break in the history of the nation-state but not a break *from* that history. The second point of view rejects the idea that globalization is a contemporary, or postmodern, phenomenon. It insists that globalization actually has a long history and that the whole arch of European imperial expansion, colonization, decolonization, and the establishment of postcolonial states figures prominently in that history. Instead of drawing a clear line between the modern age of the nation-state and the postmodern emergence of a transnational, global economic and cultural system, this point of view sees globalization as a long historical process unfolding in ever-accelerating phases. To be sure, in the earlier phases of globalization, the nation-state linked colonization and economic exploitation in the interests of its own expansion, while in its more recent phase multinational corporations and the mass media have begun to challenge the power of the nation-state (though questions of domination and exploitation persist). But such observations from this point of view do not undermine the basic argument that colonialism, postcolonialism, and globalization are historically linked in important ways. They simply suggest how the long history of globalization might be written.

The first point of view sees postcolonialism and globalization as largely at odds with each other, and so it does not provide a very productive context for thinking about how the two approaches to transnational literary and cultural studies they inform can be reconciled. From this point of view, the postcolonial state is relegated to the fading epoch of modernity, while the structures and cultures of globalization are associated with postmodern convergence culture and with a future in which the nation-state plays an increasingly peripheral role. Moreover, the violent history of colonialism threatens to get lost in the rush to understand the impact of contemporary economic and cultural globalization in postcolonial states and elsewhere. The second view is more helpful than the first, recognizing as it does that the histories of colonization, decolonization, and postcolonialism are part of the long history of globalization. This view can productively connect the two by questioning the whole idea of a historical break separating postcolonialism from globalization. Indeed, it suggests that there will be some level of continuity between the issues taken up by both postcolonial and global literatures.

Critics who have written about the tensions between postcolonialism and globalization have taken a number of different strategies in sorting out their relationship. Writing in a 2000 article on postcolonialism and globalization, Simon During draws what he calls a "schematic distinction" between the two. In his view postcolonialism is "an intellectual effort at managing the aftermath of the colonial past in an era when official political relations of colonialism had all but ended." It is largely concerned with "rescuing the 'non-modern' and subaltern agency from Western presentist universalism without turning towards transhistorical, participatory myths of origin and continuity." "Globalization theory," in contrast, "has been mainly addressed to the effects of geosynchronous communication technologies and massified transcontinental mobility to the formation of collectivities...bound together by neither history nor geography" and to the "triumph of the 'world economy' over local and national ones" (388–89). On the face of it, During seems to reject the idea that the histories of postcolonialism and globalization intersect or overlap. However, his position is more complicated than that, for rather than treating postcolonialism monolithically he distinguishes between two kinds of postcolonialism, "reconciliatory" and "critical" (385):

> Reconciliatory postcolonialism figures colonialism as a kind of tragedy with a happy ending—tragic because it was partly based on destruction and ethnocide; happy in the sense that the world-historical outcome—which we now name globalization—unifies and de-spatializes the world in ways which supposedly render colonial repression obsolete. From this postcolonialist perspective, colonialism in effect becomes an episode in the longer sweep of globalization, and all events that once fell under the rubric colonialism are ripe to fall under the rubric globalization. (392)

This is a helpful distinction up to a point, but it is ultimately too reductive and simplifying. It tacks a rather spurious conclusion (colonial repression has happily become "obsolete") onto the otherwise quite logical assertion that colonialism can be understood in the context of "the longer sweep of globalization." Does any serious critic really see this as constituting a "happy ending" for colonialism, one in which "colonial repression" becomes "obsolete?" I don't think so.[5] Beyond this, there is a problem with the episodic structure of this formulation. Colonialism, postcolonialism, and globalization are not successive episodes. They have to a significant degree unfolded simultaneously. So, During's "reconciliatory postcolonialism" is a bit of a straw man. It represents a position very few people actually take and is based on the assumption you cannot construe colonialism, postcoloniality, and globalization in relation to one another without taking a politically retrograde position toward the historical and contemporary violence committed by colonialism. This is just plain wrong.

To some degree During has intentionally set up "reconciliatory postcolonialism" as a kind of foil for "critical postcolonialism," which he somewhat ambiguously defines as a practice that "names the seizing of an opportunity to recover or construct differences and marginalized pasts by activists and intellectuals against the West, as the West was being emptied out into, or diffused through, the global system" (392). Critical postcolonialism recognizes the relationship between colonialism and the development of a global system and understands "reconciliatory postcolonialism" as complicit with a Western-dominated modernity bent on normalizing the Other through economic and cultural assimilation. (Again, if "reconciliatory postcolonialism" is defined by a view that the history of colonialism is part of the history of globalization, it is not clear why it also has to be "complicit" with modernity's domination of the Other.) Since critical postcolonialism is by definition looking for new paradigms and a new language with which to critique traditional approaches to the study of colonization and the postcolonial condition, it is, according to During, much more open to a dialogue with globalization studies. Indeed, he goes so far as to suggest that globalization has begun to supersede postcolonialism as a critical rubric for the historical study of colonization and decolonization (387). In his view, if one affirms a "dialectical relation between postcolonialism and globalism it becomes more difficult either to claim intellectual radicalness and subversion while preparing the way for a happy globalism, as reconciliatory postcolonialists do, or to make claims for the strict autonomy and continuity of identities rooted in pre-colonial pasts as some indigenous groups do" (393). Critical postcolonialism, then, rejects the idea there is an episodic relationship between postcolonialism and globalization, and reconceives the relationship in dialectical terms. During is generally upbeat about the role a critical discourse about globalization can play in the study of postcoloniality; but he warns globalization must not be seen as "the end of ethnic and colonialist struggles" but as a "force through which these struggles are continually re-articulated and re-placed, and through which the transitivity of relations like colonizer/colonized, centre/local is continually proved" (402). In this sense, globalization emerges as something like a discourse for redescribing the entire history of colonization, decolonization, and postcoloniality. But During has a final caveat: "If the colonial era is going to be remembered in the era of globalization as always already global, that analytic and commemoratory move does not have to be set against the local and indigenous politics of self-determination upon which critical postcolonialisms finally rest" (402).

During's concerns here are reminiscent of Miyoshi's complaint about the turn toward difference and the local in contemporary criticism and his advocacy of a totalizing critical system. Where Miyoshi rejects outright the idea that globalization studies offers an appropriate totalizing system, During suggests that it does, but his concerns are diametrically opposed to Miyoshi's. Where Miyoshi worries that a focus on the local, the indigenous, and on difference undermines our ability to articulate the kind of totalizing system he advocates, During worries that any totalizing system runs the risk of setting the needs of a global picture "against the local and indigenous." Their different positions underscore a basic dilemma for any transnational critical practice: how to balance a global or macro view that tries to take the kind of totalizing approach Miyoshi advocates with one that focuses, as During insists it must, on local histories, economies, subjectivities, and cultural practices.

Where During and Miyoshi worry about the balance of emphasis in the transnational study of literature and culture between the global and the local, other critics, such as Simon Gikandi, Revathi Krishnaswamy, and Harry Harootunian, are concerned about the extent to which postcolonial theory has fostered an excessive interest in culture at the expense of material and economic conditions among contemporary globalization critics. In his discussion of the somewhat vexed relationship between postcolonial and area studies, Harootunian notes in the 2002 essay "Postcolonality's Unconscious/Area Studies' Desire," that while "postcolonial studies resembles the older practices of area studies programs with their intellectual and scholarly divisions of labor into regional subsets like East Asia, Middle East, South Asia, [and] Africa" (150), it is predicated on a critique of the very neocolonialism that area studies helped prop up.[6] However, he laments that "postcolonial studies has strangely converged with area studies in recuperating the privilege of culture and cultural values" (169) rather than paying attention to economic and material conditions, to "the role played by capitalism throughout the globe and to the relationship between the experience of everydayness and the relentless regime of the commodity form" (173). Because the implications of Said's *Orientalism* got taken up by literary studies rather than by areas studies, postcolonial criticism, in Harootunian's view, was forced "to appeal to culturalism" (154) and the "textuality" of the "literary/semiotic disciplines" (155). For this reason, one effect of the monopolization of colonial discourse by English studies and its gradual transformation into postcolonial theory is that the migration of colonial discourse to English studies meant that its emphasis would be textual, semiotic, and generic, whereas if area studies had confronted the challenge posed by the Saidian critique, there would have been greater concern for the social sciences and the role played by political economy, that is to say, materiality (167).

In making this argument, Harootunian exaggerates the extent to which post-colonial criticism has come to dominate literary studies in general and English in particular. In the interests of indicting postcolonialism for its complicity with literary studies (as over against "functionalist social science" [155]), Harootunian seems to forget that Said was a literature professor who wrote important books on Joseph Conrad and the English novel. It is, therefore, no surprise that postcolonialism found literature departments hospitable. But surely it is an exaggeration to claim, as Harootunian does, that "English studies became postcoloniality" (168). For this reason, Harootunian reduces postcolonial studies to a form of textualized culturalism and then laments its inattention to material and economic conditions. Harootunian would have area studies supplanted by a new form of postcolonial studies that eschews textualism and culture and instead incorporates social science methodology in the analysis of political economy and materiality.

Harootunian's argument, it seems to me, is based on a false distinction between economies and cultures. His emphasis on material conditions makes sense until it is used as a club to beat "culturalism" over the head. For no contemporary approach to economic flows of power under the forces of globalization can do without a clear historical understanding of how cultures and commodities are embedded within each other. (Appadurai does an effective job making this link, as we have already seen.) It seems to me that any transnational or global approach to literary and cultural studies has to find a way to link cultural and textual analysis to an analysis of material conditions and economic forces. Surely, it is clear by now that culture and textuality are embedded in economic and social relations, and that material economies are inextricably connected both to cultural forms and to structures of discourse and representation that are open to textual analyses. My argument here is that *both* culturalist and materialist positions, when they are articulated too narrowly, are mistaken. Culture *is* a set of material practices linked to economies, and economic and material relations are always mediated by cultural factors and forms. We need to avoid taking methodological or theoretical positions that imply that they are separate. (Indeed, in part 2, we see by analyzing selected novels that contemporary literature dealing with globalization often takes this more nuanced position.)

Like Harootunian, Gikandi in *Maps of Englishness: Writing Identity in the Culture of Colonialism* sees the contribution postcolonial studies makes to our thinking about globalization in primarily cultural terms. He points out that "when social scientists try to differentiate older forms of globalization...from the new forms" they often "fall back on key words borrowed from postcolonial theory" such as "hybridity and difference" (631). This borrowing, in his view, is linked to a general claim among such critics that "culture, as a social and conceptual category," is at the center of contemporary globalization because it is culture, more than anything else, that has "escaped 'the bounded nation-state society' and has thus become the common property of the world" (631).[7] Appadurai and Homi Bhabha serve as Gikandi's main examples of this trend, which includes a tendency to make "rather optimistic claims that the institutions of cultural production" under contemporary globalization "provide irrefutable evidence of new global relations" (631–32), relations that are used to authorize a liberatory conception of the effects of global cultural hybridity. According to Gikandi, critics like Appadurai (and Bhabha) tend to see "global images" as a "substitute for material experiences" and privilege "literary texts—and the institutions that teach them—as the exemplars of globalization" (632). In Gikandi's scenario, "older forms of globalization based on the centrality of the nation and theories of modernization" (636) have been displaced by a "postcolonial perspective on globalization" (636) that sees it as characterized by a "new mode of global cultural, and social relations" defined "by its transgression of the boundaries established by the nation-state, the structures of dominant economic and social formations," and by a "Eurocentric sense of time" tied to theories of modernity (635). Earlier conceptions of globalization in sociology and political science tended to see globalization as an extension of modernity dominated by nation-states and as fundamentally economic in nature, while the new conceptions of globalization developing in postcolonial studies tend to see globalization as a fundamentally cultural phenomena that transcends nation-states and is distinguishable from economic globalization. The dangers of an exclusively culturalist approach are that a narrow focus on access to popular cultural forms in convergence culture that are too glibly seen to be liberatory can obscure the extent to which the material reality of economic globalization remains asymmetrical and unfair.

Gikandi ties this newer culturalist approach to what at the beginning of his essay he identifies as a positive, upbeat narrative about globalization (629) embraced by critics like Bhabha and Jan Nederveen Pieterse. In this narrative, contemporary globalization ushers in something like a "cultural world order" markedly different from the one defined by modernity (629). In this new order the power of the nation-state to regulate culture and its constitutive role in constructing subjectivity and agency is replaced by one in which both are constructed across old borders and boundaries in strikingly appropriative and imaginative ways by individuals and groups. In this scenario, globalization looks less like a dominating homogenization or westernization and a lot more like a chaotic but ultimately liberating context for constructing new subjectivities that are essentially "hybrid," relatively free of the constraints of nationalism and the power it wields over its subjects. Gikandi contrasts this positive narrative about globalization to one that views globalization as a crisis. This narrative of crisis, again a fairly familiar one in debates about globalization, focuses less on culture than on the uneven or detrimental effects of economic globalization, insisting that there is a stark reality of material conditions that is not reflected in the global cultural imaginary conjured up by critics like Appadurai and Bhabha. In this view, global images (especially in literature) are no "substitute for material experiences" (632), and the material experience of globalization by populations outside metropolitan centers (and a good many within them) do not correspond to the liberatory narrative of the culturalist critics Gikandi discusses.[8] He insists that those who celebrate the liberatory effects of globalization in effect have to "forget the nation," where those effects are hard to find, and focus on an amorphous, metropolitan, and highly westernized sphere of the "global," where it is mainly elite migrants who enjoy the supposed benefits of hybridity and difference (639).[9] From this point of view it is important to "recognize that although almost all theories of globalization are premised on the assumed marginalization of the nation-state in the domain of culture and the imaginary, there is scant evidence that the same processes are at work in the politics of everyday life, where the rhetoric of globalization is constantly undermined by the resurgence of older forms of nationalism, patriotism, and fundamentalism" (640).[10]

The possibility that the critical discourses of postcolonialism and globalization can somehow be integrated is dogged by a pressing problem linked to Gikandi's insistence that a narrative of "crisis" dominates contemporary forms of globalization, for he is certainly right that the forces of economic and cultural globalization have been, at the very least, a double-edged sword for postcolonial nations and the cultures they seek to sustain. (We need only recall the stress Stiglitz puts on the West's clumsy attempts to control and manage globalization toward its own ends.) Although in the first phase of globalization the nation-state harnesses colonization with capital development in the interests of its own expansion, in globalization's later phases multinational corporations and the mass media begin to outpace the colonizing state's power, but too often with the same asymmetrical economic results. The late postcolonial phase of this first stage suggests a historical epoch in which the formerly colonized achieve a measure of power and autonomy through the creation of postcolonial nation-states. However, the forces of globalization represent something of an ironic moment for such states. One irony, as Ania Loomba points out in her discussion of Benedict Anderson's work in *Colonialism/Postcolonialism,* is that the nation-state itself is based on a European, colonial model, so that "anti-colonial nationalism," as represented by the emergence of the postcolonial nation-state, "is itself made possible and shaped by European political and intellectual history" (189). The structure that colonizes becomes, ironically, the vehicle of liberation. A second irony, as Loomba points out, is that at the very moment of the postcolonial state's constitution, the power and autonomy of the nation-state itself get called into question by transnational forces that threaten its demise. Worse yet, economic globalization demands participation in a transnational economic system that threatens the economy, sovereignty, and cultural identity of all nation-states, especially newly emergent ones. The paradox here is painfully clear. Economic development is tied to investment in a global economy, but that economy also brings with it a potentially homogenizing, westernizing set of cultural forces that threaten both the economic and cultural autonomy of the nation-state. The combined economic and cultural force of globalization seems poised to take control of the very economy it might liberate. And, too often, "liberation" is cast by academic critics as a function of cultural consumption.

This quandary underscores the central challenge in constructing a working relationship between postcolonialism and globalization. On the one hand, it is not that difficult to see how the histories of colonization, decolonization, and postcolonialism are integral to the history of globalization, and that for this reason the two processes or epochs ought to be studied in interconnected ways. But how can globalization studies contribute to the project of postcolonial studies when globalization itself is now a central threat to the postcolonial nation-state? And, after all, isn't postcolonialism grounded in resistance to, and autonomy from, the kind of colonization the forces of globalization represent? (Such resistance is central to During's "critical postcolonialism.") Doesn't globalization, as a historical, political, economic, and cultural force, threaten the distinct political structures and cultural identities of postcolonial nation-states that are deeply committed to the process of recovering and enriching forms of cultural expression nearly obliterated by colonization? Don't we have to take seriously the argument that globalization is a fundamentally homogenizing force, one that inexorably spreads Western foods, fashions, music, patterns of consumption, and values wherever capital expansion and the media go, laying waste to local forms of identity and cultural expression? Finally, don't academic globalization studies represent the return of the repressed, the colonizing machinery of critical paradigms (whether culturalist or materialist) that in their most benign forms assimilate Otherness to Western disciplinary forms, and in their more insidious ones, as Loomba has put it, celebrate globalization "as the producer of a new and 'liberating' hybridity or multiculturalism, terms that now circulate to ratify the mish-mash of cultures generated by the near unipolar domination of the western, particularly United States, media machine?" (256).

These are hard questions to answer, especially for academics in the West who are deeply interested in postcolonial literatures and cultures yet also fascinated by the processes of globalization and the hybrid cultural forms it is creating. We can begin to deal with them, however, by acknowledging that there ought to be two sides to Loomba's warning. We do need to guard against making a fetish of hybridity and multiculturalism when it simply represents a "mish-mash" of homogenized cultural forms shaped and dominated by mass media outlets in the West. We also need to be wary of celebrating the liberating effects of this "mish-mash" when it may be obliterating deeply felt and long-standing forms of cultural and economic behavior. We need to take care not to obscure the asymmetrical nature of economic and cultural change under the regimes of colonialism *and* contemporary globalization. The kind of hybridity Loomba references is too often produced in a fundamentally oppressive context, even if the exchanges are reciprocal. As Stiglitz points out, although the developing world generally has more agency under globalization than it did under colonialism, agency is still too often restricted, and syncretism can be imposed through hierarchical structures dominated by the West.

With respect to cultural autonomy, no matter where we come from or what our cultural roots, we also need to guard against insisting that whole regions of the world, and their sometimes impoverished populations, must preserve their traditional economic and cultural characters and resist accommodation with a global economy and the cultural changes it brings simply because we in the West enjoy their traditional economic practices or what their ways of dressing, eating, or making music represent (as if these cultures exist for the West as a kind of anthropological museum or living diorama). It is nearly impossible to question this impulse without seeming to side with Western capitalist forces of exploitation and sameness, but I think we need to find a way to try. There has to be a more complicated, nuanced, and carefully thought-through position on the relationship between postcolonialism and globalization than the polar ones suggested by Loomba and other critics, that is, one that sees all forms of cultural hybridity or cultural experimentation and transformation as the evil result of globalization, and the position that unthinkingly celebrates hybridity and multiculturalism as paths to liberation from the paralyzing effects of cultural fundamentalisms wherever they may be. The first position makes a fetish of purity and stasis, ignoring the fact that cultures all over the world have always evolved syncretically in the context of complicated interactions, and it plays down the extent to which people subject to contemporary Western cultural forms translate and appropriate them in complex ways (a position that ought not to play down the history of cultural and political violence perpetuated in the name of colonization). The second position runs the risk of making a fetish of cultural syncretism and hybridity for its own sake, as if culture only liberates when it renounces tradition and embraces syncretism and change, as if cultural forms of liberation somehow compensate for continued economic exploitation. This position can represent too enthusiastic an embrace of globalization without a recognition of the price it exacts.

It seems to me that transnational literary and cultural studies, whether they present themselves as postcolonial or global, have to begin with a recognition that cultures have always traveled and changed, that the effects of globalization, dramatic as they are, only represent in an accelerated form something that has always taken place: the inexorable change that occurs through intercultural contact, as uneven as the forms it takes may be. Here we need to return to the helpfully complicated analyses of Abu-Lughod and Sen, who reject the idea that globalization is simply a Western imperializing or colonizing phenomenon, arguing that it represents a set of developmental processes that cannot be reduced in any politically vulgar way to "westernization," that problems related to globalization require not that it be rejected outright but that we develop just and ethical processes for its regulation (the position Stiglitz endorses). It ought to be possible to take such a totalizing view of social and cultural change without ignoring obvious differences in how such changes occur, without, that is, collapsing benign forms of change into those resulting from violence and domination (a position During rightly or not ascribes to reconciliatory postcolonialism) or mistaking imaginative cultural appropriations for the achievement of economic autonomy and power. To say that all cultures are always hybrid, or to draw a link between cultural change under economic globalization to cultural change under colonialism, should not mean ignoring the differences between relatively benign and openly violent forms of change, and it should not inhibit the development of a historical and contemporary critique of the negative effects of such forms of change. And, most certainly, it does not necessitate our seeing colonialism as having come to some happy resolution in the age of globalization, as During asserts. Sometimes cultural change comes in the context of trade and commodity exchange, which often creates deeply institutionalized forms of economic oppression, but which can also facilitate fascinating forms of cultural improvisation in terms of social behavior or the production of anything from food to fashion, music, and literature.[11] But such change, as Abu-Lughod, Sen, and Appiah emphasize, has always happened, and it is hard to find a place on the globe where what we might want to celebrate as local or indigenous culture is either local or indigenous.

This is certainly the case with respect to the geographical areas central to my own work on transnational literatures in English: the Caribbean, South Asia, and the border zone of the United States and Mexico. One would be hard put to identify cultural forms that are "indigenous" to any of these regions. Culture and identity in these areas are the complex result of the long history of what we now call globalization. There are, lamentably, no "indigenous" Caribbeans in anything like the strict sense of the word. The literatures of the Caribbean are therefore deeply engaged with the complex interaction of indigenous, African,

Asian, and colonial populations and cultures, all of which have contributed to the creation of a radically syncretic set of Caribbean populations.[12] The Indian subcontinent, where so much new literature in English has its roots, has been swept by Greek, Persian, and Islamic invasions that forged a deeply hybrid cultural mix in what became modern India, Pakistan, and Bangladesh, well before the establishment of the East India Company and, later, the British Raj. And the border regions of the American Southwest are characterized by a dizzying mix of Native American, Hispanic, and African American populations and cultures (from Florida and New Orleans all the way to Southern California) that make the whole notion of the indigenous almost obsolete.

In the final analysis, any integration of postcolonial and globalization studies in the interests of transnationalizing literary studies must be based on a critical postcolonialism like the one During articulates, and it must be committed to his view that the relationship between postcolonialism and globalization is dialectical. To the extent such a project attempts to "reconcile" the two forces, it need not, as During suggests it is fated to do, turn attention away from analyzing the violent and oppressive nature of colonization (including the ways in which those forces extend well into the era of postcolonization). Understanding that globalization is not just a contemporary phenomenon, but that it has a long history that incorporates the epochs of colonization, decolonization, and postcolonialism, can help us deal with the complexity of literary and cultural production without taking either of the polar positions. Globalization can provide a comprehensive historical framework through which we can analyze more carefully forms of political colonization and cultural syncretism created by the long history of cross-cultural contact and how these forms have directed the struggle of both "indigenous" and diasporic populations to develop forms of political and economic autonomy.

For literary studies, this framework suggests a context in which the literatures of postcolonialism and globalization ought to be studied in relationship to each other. Indeed, if we accept the idea I have been advocating here that globalization has a long history in the East as well as the West, encompassing the various epochs of colonization, decolonization, and postcolonialism in all their historical complexity, it becomes difficult to draw clear distinctions between postcolonial literature and literature engaged more specifically with the contemporary effects of globalization. We ought to recognize that globalization in the eras of conquest and colonization was tied to the long epoch of modernity and the rise to dominance of the nation-state, and that globalization in a postcolonial and postmodern era complicates the power of nation-states and facilitates the creation of radically unpredictable and transnational cultural forms and hybrid subjectivities. As I have stressed, it is important that we draw distinctions between the forms of economic and cultural exchange produced (and to some degree, enforced) by colonialism and its demise and those produced since then—through the convergence of new technologies of communication and travel; the circulation of commodities, people, knowledge, and cash characterized by Appadurai's "financescape"; and the advent of globalization as an institutional practice as charted by Stiglitz. However, we also need to recognize that the continuities between these historical eras are at least as important as their differences. If they are worth distinguishing, it is in order to underscore the dialectical relationship they have with one another.

Economies, Cultures, and the Politics of Globalization

While the economic and cultural dimensions of globalization are inextricably linked across the various phases of its development, we cannot understand the acceleration of globalization without recognizing its development first as an economic phenomenon, especially in the twentieth century, when trade and capital exchange across national borders dramatically expanded in response to the increasing modernization of technologies of transport and communication. Here it will be instructive to return to Stiglitz's definition of globalization: "What is this phenomenon of globalization that has been subject, at the same time, to such vilification and such praise? Fundamentally, it is the closer integration of the countries and peoples of the world which has been brought about by the enormous reduction of costs of transportation and communication, and the breaking down of artificial barriers to the flows of goods, services, capital, knowledge, and (to a lesser extent) people across borders" (9). For Stiglitz, globalization is fundamentally related to economic flows, but more important, it is about the *convergence* of expanding markets and communication technologies, and the rapid transport of goods, capital, knowledge, and services. We earlier saw Appadurai emphasize this phenomenon of convergence in his articulation of the various "landscapes" that characterize globalization: ethnoscapes, mediascapes, technoscapes, financescapes, and ideoscapes. Stiglitz focuses on Appadurai's "financescapes," but he defines globalization in a way that recognizes how it is driven by the convergence of forces across the various human, technological, and ideological landscapes Appadurai invokes, forces that transcend economic exchange narrowly defined.

In addition to stressing how this convergence of forces has accelerated globalization in the twentieth century, Stiglitz links contemporary economic globalization to the development of institutional structures aimed at managing and equalizing its impact. His narrative presents globalization as the complex product of dramatically increased and unregulated economic exchanges across national borders and the creation of institutional structures to manage and equalize those exchanges, a process determined and disrupted by a successive series of global crises. To a significant degree, economic globalization for Stiglitz is defined by these institutions and their practices. As an institutional practice, globalization has its origins in the July 1944 UN Monetary and Financial Conference at Bretton Woods, New Hampshire, a meeting that resulted in the creation of the World Bank and the International Monetary Fund (IMF). These institutions originated as part of a concerted effort to rebuild Europe after World War II, but they have successively expanded their regulatory purview in response to a sequence of historical crises beginning with the collapse of colonial rule in Africa, Asia, and the Caribbean, and culminating in the demise of Communism in the late 1980s. Increasingly, as Stiglitz explains, economic stability in an age of expanding markets, global trade, and exploding technologies of communication and transport required "collective action at the global level" to ensure both stability and equality (12). For Stiglitz, globalization can be measured by the expanding complexity of these institutional practices as much as by the expanding economies they seek to regulate.

Many of the debates about globalization I discuss in this book are connected to the fact that these institutions have, on the whole, failed to successfully manage and administer economic globalization and the social and cultural disruptions it can bring. As Stiglitz demonstrates, the failure of global institutions like the World Bank, the IMF, and the World Trade Organization (WTO) to manage globalization have led to widespread protests against globalization in the public sphere, and these failures are clearly connected as well to academic critiques of globalization. In Stiglitz's view, economic "globalization itself is neither good nor bad" (20). "The removal of barriers to free trade and the closer integration of national economies" can "be a force for good," he insists, but the whole process has been managed badly by institutions like the World Bank, the IMF, and the WTO (ix). The problem is not globalization itself but "international bureaucrats," the "faceless symbols of the world economic order" who, in Stiglitz's view,

have badly bungled their jobs (3).[1] As we have seen, a key concern expressed by
many academic critics in the humanities and social sciences is the extent to which
the institutional regulation of globalization has been conducted as a colonialist
practice. Stiglitz, too, sees this as a significant problem. The World Bank and
the IMF, for example, came into being at a time when "most of the countries in
the developing world were still colonies, and what meager economic development efforts could or would be undertaken were considered the responsibility of
their European masters" (11). Moreover, while the original mandates for regulation came in the immediate aftermath of World War II, the "end of colonialism
and communism" allowed these international financial institutions "to expand
greatly their original mandates" (17–18) while continuing to conduct themselves
with a colonialist mind-set, implementing Western-dominated policies and practices that have continually impinged on the sovereignty of developing nations.

Although Stiglitz is particularly skilled at analysis of economic globalization,
he also recognizes that one of the failures of globalization as an institutional practice is its blindness to the cultural dimension of globalization. "Finance and trade
ministers," he writes, "view globalization as largely an economic phenomenon;
but to many in the developing world, it is far more than that," for globalization
tends to "undermine traditional values," since rapid economic growth always
results in "urbanization, undermining traditional rural societies" and presenting
a general "threat to cultural identity and values" (247).[2] Although I have been
arguing that we need to make distinctions between cultural and economic conditions and processes—between the semiotic, representational, and imaginary,
on the one hand, and the lived reality of material and economic relations on the
other—Stiglitz recognizes that, in the final analysis, we cannot understand or
manage globalization without acknowledging the synchronicity of its economic
and cultural dimensions.

As the study of globalization has moved from an initial narrow interest in
economic globalization toward an interest in globalization as a cultural phenomenon, it has unleashed (as we have seen) spirited debates about culturalist and materialist models for studying globalization and its effects. The shift
sparking these debates, of course, did not mark a simplistic reorganizing of globalization studies around cultures rather than economies but, rather, entailed
a recognition of the reciprocal relation between the economic and the cultural
spheres, a recognition that cultures are exchanged along with commodities. One
of the central points of globalization studies in the humanities is that cultural
forms (literary narrative, cinema, television, live performance, etc.) are commodities, a position that counters older notions of the literary as purely aesthetic
and somehow beyond the world of commodities, economies, and even history.
We can no longer make a clear distinction between exchanges that are purely

material and take place in an economy of commodities and exchanges that are purely symbolic and take place in a cultural economy. Indeed, that these two forms of exchange have always overlapped (and that they are becoming increasingly indistinguishable) ought to be a central component in any comprehensive study of globalization.

Indeed, economic and cultural systems have become so intertwined that it makes little sense to advocate for a strictly materialist or a strictly culturalist model for studying the effects of globalization. One might complain such a point of view is symptomatic of the worst elements of postmodern or poststructuralist theory, but too much important work in the fields of deconstruction, poststructuralist Marxism, the New Historicism, feminism, and psychoanalysis would have to be rejected out of hand to invoke a schematic distinction between the economic and the cultural. It makes more sense to avoid culturalist approaches that ignore material and economic conditions or privilege the cultural over the material as if all material conditions and so-called everyday experiences were mediated by representation to the point the real was irrecoverable. And, of course, the same caution should be extended to materialist approaches. The importance of such approaches ought not to be established through a denigration of culture or of textuality and representation based on the idea that economic and material conditions exist apart from and determine cultural ones (as I argued, Miyoshi and Harootunian veer too close to this position) or that cultural objects do not have anything to tell us about economic and material conditions. The danger here is that we reintroduce something like the old and largely discredited Marxist distinction between base and superstructure.

The position I have been endorsing understands economic and cultural flows as interdependent systems of exchange. Here I follow the sociologist Malcolm Waters, who insists that globalization studies ought to center on the "types of exchange that predominate in social relationships" in and across economies, political systems, and forms of cultural discourse. In his view each of these "arenas" facilitates forms of exchange contributing to globalization: economies facilitate material exchange; politics facilitate exchanges relative to the maintenance and support of power; and culture facilitates "symbolic exchanges" through "oral communication, publication, performance, ritual, entertainment," and narrative (8). Breaking with Giddens's economism, Waters rejects the simplistic view that "the driving force for global integration is restless capitalist expansionism" (10) and insists that symbolic exchange facilitates globalization more quickly than either of the other two arenas. He argues that globalization is tied to the acceleration of symbolic exchanges (the production and dissemination of films, novels, advertisements, music, even fast food—cultural forms that are circulated, adopted, and revised in a myriad of locations), since "symbols can be produced anywhere and at any time and there are relatively few resource constraints on their production and reproduction" (9).

This approach to the complex economic and social effects of symbolic exchange has already been explored by cultural studies critics, especially those associated with the Birmingham school, where a decidedly Marxian cultural materialism helped inspire a commitment to the study of culture and its relationship both to commodification and the construction of national identities. Thus the relatively new culturalist orientation to globalization theory, which sees the products of culture as integral to the more general flow of economies and commodities, represents the intersection of globalization theory (with its roots in the social sciences) and cultural studies (with its roots in the humanities), and produces a practice that has come under the kind of criticism we have seen from Said and Miyoshi, who both advocated a more materialist approach to the study of globalization. This convergence is connected, on the one hand, to the redefinition of culture, following the lead of Raymond Williams, as the "whole way of life" of a people and our more current interest in culture as a fluid, mobile, transnational phenomenon that predates and often ignores nation-state boundaries. (British cultural studies has remained interested in culture's relationship to national identity, while the interest in culture as a set of transnational flows is more characteristic of globalization studies.) In his essay "Traveling Cultures," for example, James Clifford questions the conventional anthropological model of culture as something fixed and local. This model, in which local cultures are studied by objective scientists from other cultures who dwell in them, elides "the wider global world of intercultural import-export in which the ethnographic encounter is always already enmeshed" (100). In effect, the observer, operating in a complex network of mobile forms of exchange and translation (technologies of travel facilitating the encounter in the first place, the international context of such encounters, the degree of "translation" that takes place in cross-cultural exchanges, etc.), "coproduces" the culture studied:

> Once the representational challenge is seen to be the portrayal and understanding of local/global historical encounters, co-productions, dominations and resistances, then one needs to focus on hybrid, cosmopolitan experiences as much as on rooted, native ones.... The goal is not to replace the cultural figure "native" with the intercultural figure "traveler." Rather the task is to focus on concrete mediations of the two, in specific cases of historical tension and relationship. (101)

Clifford's focus on the mobility of culture echoes Waters's insistence on the ease of symbolic exchange under the forces of globalization. However, Clifford stresses the dislocation of culture, that in an age of accelerating globalization culture has become deterritorialized and diasporic. The dislocation of cultures requires that we rethink where and how cultures are located. "We need," Clifford insists, to "conjure with new localizations like 'the border,'" specific places of "hybridity and struggle, policing and transgression" (109), which is something I pursue in our discussion of Paul Gilroy's concept of the "black Atlantic" in chapter 4. An important development contributing to this new approach to culture is the rise of diasporic communities, an important feature of globalization connected to increased migration and to the proliferation of electronic media that permit instantaneous communication between diasporic communities and between these communities and their nations of origin. The proliferation of electronic media adds another dimension to the phenomenon of "traveling cultures," for in the twenty-first century literal travel is increasingly facilitated by "virtual" travel, so that "travel, or displacement, can involve forces that pass powerfully through cultures—television, radio, tourists, commodities, armies" (Clifford 103). Appadurai, building on Clifford's contrast between literal and virtual travel, approaches globalization as a dual function of increased migration and the rise of new electronic media. Like Readings, Appadurai suggests that globalization represents a profound weakening of the nation-state:

> The wave of debates about multiculturalism that has spread through the United States and Europe is surely testimony to the incapacity of states to prevent their minority populations from linking themselves to wider constituencies of religious or ethnic affiliation. These examples, and others, suggest that the era in which we could assume that viable public spheres were typically, exclusively, or necessarily national could be at an end. Diasporic public spheres, diverse among themselves, are the crucibles of a postnational political order. (22)

Appadurai's remarks underscore globalization's profound potential for disrupting traditional nationalist paradigms for literary study, something I explore in more detail in chapter 4. However the changes Appadurai reviews here, while profound at the cultural level, do not in my view necessarily portend the arrival of a "postnational political order." The United States has done a fairly good job so far of accommodating itself politically and militarily to cultural change, and in many western European countries there is significant resistance to the effect immigration is having on the national cultural fabric (witness, for example, the civil unrest among citizens of Arab descent in France in 2005, and again in 2007 and 2009, and the widespread protests that developed in Denmark and elsewhere in response to editorial cartoons depicting Muhammad in a Danish newspaper). Given all this, Appadurai's prediction here strikes me as a bit premature. Certainly the deterritorialization of culture will continue to elude the policing capabilities of the nation-state, and the religious, ethnic, and cultural affiliations of mobile populations will continue to transform and reconstruct national and cultural identities, but it is still too soon to argue that we've entered the era of a postnational order.

For Appadurai this development can be culturally empowering in a way that can lead to economic empowerment. His *Modernity at Large* (1996) articulates a *culturalist* theory of globalization and agency that is worth exploring in the larger context of our discussion of how to balance culturalist and materialist approaches to the study of globalization. Whereas Clifford stresses how cultures travel, become deterritorialized, and tend to hybridize under globalization, Appadurai insists on the importance of what he calls "culturalism . . . the process of naturalizing a subset of differences that have been mobilized to articulate group identity" (15). While culture has been traditionally conceived as a "property of individuals and groups" deployed "to articulate the boundary of difference" (13) connected to the needs of nation-states and to the nationalist ideologies they require, *culturalism* denotes a concern with identities constructed across national boundaries. As Appadurai thinks of it, culturalism is "the conscious mobilization of cultural differences in the service of a larger national or transnational politics" (15). It is often based on identity politics and deployed to fashion diasporic identities imaginatively and to assert the rights of deterritorialized groups in nation-states. As such, culturalism represents an "instrumental conception of ethnicity," whereas culture is grounded in a "primordial" myth of ethnicity or other traits in which a carefully constructed group identity has been "naturalized" into something substantive, inherent, primary, or originary (14).[3]

Appadurai links culturalism to processes of identity formation influenced by the media and by the rise of mass consumer culture. Deterritorialization, as he points out, "creates new markets for film companies, art impresarios, and travel agencies, which thrive on the need of the deterritorialized population for contact with its homeland" (38). This contact is not simply a matter of keeping up with the news at home. In Appadurai's view, it enables transnational subjects or members of diasporic public spheres to imagine or improvise new postnational identities.[4] Opportunities for mobility and self-fashioning are increasingly worked out in a social imaginary in which the kinds of symbols and imagery we usually associate with narrative and the performing arts engage the imagination in the complex re-formation of subjectivity (reflecting the kinds of symbolic exchange Waters insists is a central factor in globalization). To the extent global culture is a function of this "mass-mediated imaginary," what Appadurai calls the "social work of the imagination" lies at the heart of culturalism, construed as the conscious construction of individual and communal identities that are always making and remaking themselves in response to new localities, social and political pressures, and transnational cultural discourses (31). Global mass culture creates a postnational context for reimagining, organizing, and disseminating subjectivity through all the devices formally associated with literary (or cinematic) narrative. National scripts regularly give way to globally disseminated media scripts that engage the imagination complexly. Crucially, all of this happens in ways that are simultaneously economic and cultural. It makes no sense, following Appadurai's approach to studying globalization and its effects, to separate out global economic from global cultural flows. The two are inextricably connected.

Appadurai's view that globalization provides a productive context for the reimagining and construction of new hybrid identities and cultures is directly at odds with the much bleaker assessments of globalization of those such as Miyoshi and Harootunian who have insisted on a narrowly materialist approach to globalization based on a critique of culturalist models like Appadurai's. Appadurai's approach resists the idea that the proliferation of Western styles, products, and tastes under the forces of globalization extinguishes cultural difference and that economic globalization is always an uneven and oppressive process. He rejects the simplistic idea that globalization is always synonymous with homogenization or westernization, insisting that "there is growing evidence that the consumption of the mass media throughout the world often provokes resistance, irony, selectivity, and, in general, agency.... T-shirts, billboards, and graffiti as well as rap music, street dancing, and slum housing all show that the images of the media are quickly moved into local repertoires of irony, anger, humor, and resistance." For Appadurai the dissemination of Western or American culture provides a context for the exercise of power, for "action" rather than "escape" (7). The local appropriation and transformation of Western cultural forms and behaviors works against homogenization, since "different societies appropriate the materials of modernity differently" (17). In this logic, the United States "is no longer the puppeteer of a world system of images but is only one mode of a complex transnational construction of imaginary landscapes" (31). While Appadurai's analysis is open to the accusation that, at the very least, it tolerates the unevenness and inequities of economic globalization in a naive celebration of its liberatory possibilities in mostly urban pockets around the world, and at its worst actually works in concert (as Miyoshi feared globalization critics always will) with its exploitive ends, it seems to me his position is a nuanced one that understands the contradictory forces at work under globalization and works with the assumption that economic and cultural forces are linked.[5] Moreover, he resists the tendency to view globalization as Western capitalism's triumphant commodifying and exporting of its own cultural forms and practices in a ruthless effort (conscious or otherwise) to create new markets for them, an effort that leads inexorably to the collapse of local cultural forms. This is clearly a major effect of globalization, but I think Appadurai is correct in suggesting there is more going on beneath the surface, that we need to pay attention to the opportunities for self-fashioning and positive economic transformation offered under globalization, and that we need to guard against romanticizing "other" cultures in a way that both belies the nature of cultural development and locks them into economic paralysis.

In *Cosmopolitanism* (2006) Kwame Anthony Appiah has followed Appadurai's lead in arguing against the idea that globalization is having a new and dramatically homogenizing effect on cultural forms and identities, insisting that the effects of globalization on both subjectivity and culture ought to be understood in connection with a long and perfectly normal set of historical adaptations. He links this argument to the endorsement of "cosmopolitanism" as both a social and a critical position. There are some fundamental differences behind Appadurai's endorsement of culturalism and Appiah's cosmopolitanism. Appadurai's culturalism, as we just saw, is related to "the process of naturalizing a subset of differences that have been mobilized to articulate group identity" (15). It refers to the *conscious mobilization* by groups "according to identitarian criteria" and, "put simply, is identity politics mobilized at the level of the nation-state" (15). Culturalism is therefore philosophically and strategically at odds with cosmopolitanism, for while cosmopolitanism wants to look beyond cultural and "identitarian" differences in the interests of fostering a view of identity organized around shared human traits, values, and rights, culturalism tends to see both rights and power as a function of discrete and specifically articulated cultural differences. Although the cosmopolitanism he endorses is difficult to reconcile with Appadurai's culturalism, Appiah shares Appadurai's rejection of the idea that contemporary forms of globalization disrupt cultural authenticity and lead to homogenization, because cultural authenticity is always a product of what he calls "contamination," and cultural homogenization is always localized. In his view, the traditional distinction between authenticity and contamination does not hold, because cultural forms and practices often deemed to be authentic are in fact the product of contamination.

> Trying to find some primordially authentic culture can be like peeling an onion [since] the textiles most people think of as traditional West African cloths are known as java prints, and arrived with the Javanese batiks sold, and often milled by, the Dutch. The traditional garb of Herero women derives from the attire of nineteenth-century German missionaries, though it's still unmistakably Herero, not least because the fabrics they use have a distinctly un-Lutheran range of colors. And so with our *kente* cloth: the silk was always imported, traded by Europeans, produced in Asia. This tradition was once an innovation. Should we reject *it*

for that reason as untraditional? How far back must one go? ...Cultures are made of continuities *and* changes, and the identity of a society can survive through these changes. (107)

Appiah embraces what he calls "cosmopolitan contamination" (101) because he rejects as inaccurate in the first place the distinction between authenticity and contamination. All "authentic" cultures, he insists, are the products of contamination, so what critics of "cultural imperialism" see as the contemporary disruption of traditional cultures by the forces of globalization is in fact part of the long history of normal cultural development. "Cultural purity," he insists, "is an oxymoron" (113). Again, the absence of cultural purity according to Appiah is not a recent phenomenon:

> [The] migrations that have contaminated the larger world were not all modern. Alexander's empire molded both the states and the sculpture of Egypt and North India; first the Mongols then the Mughals shaped great swaths of Asia; the Bantu migrations populated half the African continent. Islamic states stretch from Morocco to Indonesia; Christianity reached Africa, Europe, and Asia within a few centuries of the death of Jesus of Nazareth; Buddhism long ago migrated from India into much of the East and Southeast Asia. Jews and people whose ancestors came from many parts of China have long lived in vast diasporas. The traders of the Silk Road changed the style of elite dress in Italy; someone brought Chinese pottery for burial in fifteenth-century Swahili graves. (112)

For all of these reasons, Appiah insists that globalization, conceived as a long historical process in a way quite consistent with Robertson, does not produce cultural homogenization in any conventional sense of the term. Here Appiah's position echoes the stress in Appadurai on the idea that Western cultural forms and products are appropriated in myriad and imaginative ways by people in different places, so that while it might be accurate to think of the West as exporting homogenous cultural forms, it is inaccurate to think of their *reception* by different cultures as homogenous. Appiah goes so far as to insist that globalization is actually "a threat to homogeneity" (101). The city of Kumasi, in the Asante region of Ghana, is thoroughly "integrated into the global markets," but "what it isn't, just because it's a city, is homogeneous" (101). Because different people in different places adopt Western cultural products differently,[6] and because those products, and the behaviors that come with them, are integrated into different languages and cultural styles in different localities, we end up with something Appiah sees as "homogeneity" of a "local kind" (102). Following his logic, globalization facilitates the proliferation of similar products around the world, but those products have a localized reception and adaptation and therefore do not produce homogeneity. Appiah's version of cosmopolitanism, to a large extent, involves recognizing this fact and avoiding what he insists is the "deeply condescending" insistence by Western critics of "cultural imperialism" that so-called traditional cultures ought to resist forms of innovation and change linked to the global flow of capital and commodities, even if they offer a way out of grinding poverty and perpetual disease.

It seems to me Appiah's approach to culture in *Cosmopolitanism* is fundamentally sound, accurate both in theoretical and historical terms and essential to analyses of how the long history of globalization is related not just to cultural change but to the nature of culture itself. However, before I explain why, I want to pause a moment to look at Appiah's much more problematical attempt to rehabilitate cosmopolitanism. Appiah is generally interested in how we manage difference in an increasingly globalized world, but as a philosopher his particular interest is in developing "ethics in a world of strangers" (the subtitle of his book). He wants to tackle the practical "challenge" of equipping people rooted in the local with "ideas and institutions that will allow us to live together as the global tribe we have become" (xiii). Choosing a "rubric to proceed," he rejects "globalization" (no good because it seems to encompass "everything and nothing") and "multiculturalism" (no good because it "designates the disease it purports to cure") in favor of "cosmopolitanism" (xiii). Appiah acknowledges the negative baggage the term carries, noting that it can "suggest an unpleasant posture of superiority toward the putative provincial" and border on "kindly condescension." But he believes the term can be "rescued" from these associations (xiii–xiv), that it can provide a framework for understanding "what we talk about when we talk about difference" and "what we owe strangers by virtue of our shared humanity" (xxi).

This is a laudable project, but Appiah does not take the time to adequately explore the problems attending his rescue operation, nor does he acknowledge the spirited academic arguments about cosmopolitanism that had been going on in the years preceding the publication of his book. Notable here is Timothy Brennan's *At Home in the World: Cosmopolitanism Now* (1997), the special issue of *Public Culture* (2000) devoted to cosmopolitanism, and the essays collected by Simon Learmount and Robin Cohen in *Conceiving Cosmopolitanism: Theory, Context, and Practice* (2003). Together this work explores the challenges and pitfalls of redescribing cosmopolitanism in a way that makes it tenable for our own age, and by avoiding any reference to it Appiah skirts a set of important challenges.

These challenges are presented in a telescoped fashion by Walter Mignolo in his 2000 essay, "The Many Faces of Cosmo-polis: Border Thinking and Critical Cosmopolitanism." Mignolo provides a sweeping historical analysis of the development of various cosmopolitanisms, both religious and secular, dating from the early Renaissance, one that is much too detailed to review here. The key point is that his historical analysis details the complicity of cosmopolitanism as a social and philosophical project with colonialism, imperialism, and "neoliberal globalization," and it insists on the need for what he calls a "critical cosmopolitanism" (723). Mignolo links cosmopolitanism per se to the *interiority* of modernity and calls for a critical cosmopolitanism *exterior* to modernity and grounded in what he calls "colonial difference" (724). Here Mignolo follows Enrique Dussel in "World-System and 'Trans'-Modernity" (2002) in connecting traditional forms of cosmopolitanism to a Eurocentric modernity, invoking what Dussel has called a "transmodernity" that counters the "universal perspective" of cosmopolitanism with a perspective linked to "colonial difference" (Mignolo 733). Thus, traditional European forms of cosmopolitanism dating from the Enlightenment, like the one invoked by Appiah, can only be "thought out from one particular geopolitical location: that of the heart of Europe, of the most civilized nations" with their ideals of "justice, equality, rights, and planetary peace" (735–36). However, he insists, "it remains difficult to carry these ideas further without clearing up the Renaissance and Enlightenment prejudices that surrounded concepts of race and manhood. One of the tasks of critical cosmopolitanism is precisely clearing up the encumbrances of the past. The other is to point toward the future" (736).

For Mignolo the project of a critical cosmopolitanism engaged with the future must evolve from formerly "silenced and marginalized voices . . . bringing themselves into the conversation" that has been called "cosmopolitanism" in order to change that conversation, enacting a "transformative project that takes the form of border thinking or border epistemology . . . the recognition and transformation of the hegemonic imaginary from the perspectives of people in subaltern positions" so that "border thinking" becomes a "'tool' of the project of critical cosmopolitanism" (736–37). I will have more to say about Mignolo's concept of border thinking in chapter 4, but for now I want to call attention to the vexed relationship Appiah has with Mignolo's critical cosmopolitanism. On the one hand, as a "subaltern" himself (he was born and raised in Ghana, the son of an African father and an English mother), Appiah can be understood as rewriting the discourse on cosmopolitanism from a formerly marginalized or subaltern position. But, on the other hand, the high-academic philosophical perspective Appiah takes comes off as thoroughly Western, dominated in its philosophical discursivity by just the kind of Eurocentricity critical cosmopolitanism is supposed to clear up and move beyond. (And, as I have indicated, it pays insufficient attention after a brief nod in the introduction to the decidedly negative aspects of cosmopolitanism and the drag they put on using the term strategically in our own time.) Appiah himself represents what Mignolo calls "colonial difference," but in my view his discourse about cosmopolitanism is too rooted *within* European modernity. If Appiah had acknowledged the current debates about cosmopolitanism out of which his book emerged, and if he had aligned his attempt to rescue cosmopolitanism with Mignolo's concept of critical cosmopolitanism, his rubric for managing difference and developing an ethics in a world of strangers would have been more critically compelling. As it stands, Appiah's theory of culture and contamination is, I believe, philosophically sound and ought to guide any attempt to analyze the cultural effects of globalization. However, the culturalist position he calls "cosmopolitanism" is too narrowly articulated and pays insufficient attention to the historical problems with its own position.

Finally, a key problem with the discourse of cosmopolitanism Appiah endorses is its complicity with the failures of economic globalization as enumerated by Stiglitz. Indeed, globalization as an institutional practice is governed by the traditional kind of cosmopolitanism Appiah endorses. We need only recall Stiglitz's condemnation of this practice as a fundamentally colonialist one to see this connection. For Stiglitz, the problem with globalization is its governance by a narrowly Western (and self-protective) "free market" ideology, an ideology imposed on the rest of the world by international bureaucrats in institutions that regularly ignore national sovereignty. The fundamentally colonialist structure of globalization as an institutional practice reflects its reliance on the kind of traditional cosmopolitan ideology Mignolo critiques. Appiah's discussion of cosmopolitanism focuses on cultural matters almost to the exclusion of economic ones, but it is not hard to see how what he calls cosmopolitanism will continue to work to the economic advantage of the very Western elites Stiglitz sees as responsible for the failures of globalization.

In spite of these problems, I think Appadurai and Appiah are fundamentally correct that globalization cannot be reduced to Westernization or Americanization, and that the dynamics of reception and appropriation within globalization have a complexity that belies such simple labels. Theories of cultural change under the pressures of globalization (keeping in mind that cultural forms are economic commodities and that cultural systems work like economies) have to be complex enough to acknowledge how local cultures are transformed by the products and styles of the West *and* how those cultures appropriate Western materials in a way that transforms both those products and styles and the cultures from which they come. The economic and cultural effects of globalization, that is to say, are increasingly reciprocal. Moreover, as Appiah rightly insists, we need to let go of the romantic and erroneous notion that there are such things as pure, indigenous, and timeless social communities uncontaminated by long and complex histories of cultural exchange and perpetual transformation. A Big Mac in Venice or Tokyo is pretty much a Big Mac, but American soul music of the 1960s as it is assimilated and transformed by musicians in Soweto or the Caribbean and then sent back to the United States, where it in turn influences the production of new musical idioms, participates in a much more complicated and less hierarchical process.[7] This process is certainly at work in the global production of English, which is increasingly influenced by South Asian and Latin American writing, a Latina/o tradition grounded in the borderlands of the United States and Mexico, African American literary idioms, and any number of cultural traditions specific to diaspora communities in the United States (Asian, Puerto Rican, Dominican, South Asian, African, etc.). The culture we call "English" is so thoroughly hybridized, so inexorably based on complex exchanges among these various cultural traditions that it is getting ever more difficult to identify a dominant Western discourse that is not being subordinated to, and shaped by, this accelerating mix of sources and discourses from outside Britain and the United States.

While it may make little sense from this perspective to worry that cultural forms produced under the pressures of globalization will simply replicate Western ones, we ought to pause a moment to consider the economic and class differences that mark these cultural flows and transformations (something Appadurai and Appiah pay too little attention to). For example, while Appadurai may be right that the appropriation of Western cultural forms can be a potentially liberating exercise of power, we need to recognize that this power is inherently uneven for economic reasons. Well-off secular youth in Dubai, Kingston, Mumbai, or Nairobi may have the privilege of exercising this power through cultural consumption and appropriation, but the poor in such cities and in rural populations do not. The kind of transnational cultural hybridity Appadurai and Appiah write about and that we can trace in the literary production of global English is potentially liberating in a cultural way for plugged-in urban youth, but it may not have much to do with their economic lives, or the lives of rural poor who are still caught in the stratifications of a global economy that leaves their material existence relatively unchanged. Globalization, and the kind of cultural hybridity it may foster, is much more readily available to elite postcolonial academics than it is to poor migrants working at menial jobs in the metropolitan West.[8]

I noted earlier that while Appadurai and Appiah sketch out the kind of culturalist approaches to globalization criticized by materialist critics such as Miyoshi and Harootunian, it seems to me they pay more attention to the link between material and cultural forces than their critics acknowledge. As I indicated in discussing Miyoshi and Harootunian, their criticisms are too often predicated on a distinction between economic and cultural products and processes that is untenable. Their positions also tend to fragment and hierarchize the study of globalization by privileging "economic" approaches over "cultural" ones, implying that economic approaches have a kind of priority that render cultural ones secondary. At its worst moments, this view seems to imply that "culturalist" approaches to

globalization are inherently flawed. Again, I believe the problem lies in drawing too clear a line between the economic and the cultural. Surely, approaches
to globalization that focus on cultural matters ought to demonstrate an awareness of how culture is always implicated in—and often helps foster—economic
interests, but such approaches ought not to be rejected out of hand because they
deal with culture.

To argue that globalization represents the disastrous triumph of the West
over the rest suggests that globalizing literary studies might amount to Ameri-
canizing or westernizing global literature in the ways that Said worried about.
Just as in globalization per se homogenization is tied to the export and rapid
proliferation of Western commodities, the kind of homogenization that may become associated with the globalization of literary studies is linked to the export
of Western critical categories, terms, theories, and practices, all of which threaten
to create a Western critical context for the local literatures studied. It may be
that English is expanding its dominance of literary study in the same way that
Western capitalism has come to dominate world markets in the contemporary
age of globalization. In this analogy critics from the United States and Britain,
having used up their own literatures and feeling guilty about its complicity with
the various oppressive practices of patriarchy, slavery, imperialism, and colonization, have turned for new material to the literature of the Other. The danger
here is that in globalizing literary studies we may replicate the same oppressive
structures and practices many critics associate with the homogenizing effects of
cultural globalization (or the colonizing practices of institutionalized economic
globalization), structures and practices that further the dominance of expansionist cultures at the expense of local ones. It is crucial, then, that we find a way to
supplement the traditionally nationalist orientation of "English" with a transnational one without seeming to colonize the study of global literature within
English departments. For, as I have indicated, we will not have got anywhere if
we end up reconstructing the paradigm of English as the privileged center of a
transnational approach to literary studies.

One way to negotiate the transnational turn in literary studies in a way that
is sensitive to these problems can be found in the work of feminist critics like
Caren Kaplan and Louise Yelin. Such a perspective is too often ignored in what
remains a largely male-dominated discourse about globalization.[9] Like Clifford
and Appadurai, Kaplan is interested in the cultural effects of displacement,
especially in how the emerging global "world system" (58) is linked to tourism.
However, she is interested less in how theories travel than in the pitfalls of travel
as a mode of theorizing, pitfalls she locates in the critic as nomad, the fantasy of
being "the one who can track a path through a seemingly illogical space without
succumbing to nation-state and/or bourgeois organization and mastery." Linking

her discussion of the nomad to Gilles Deleuze's and Felix Guattari's concept of deterritorialization, Kaplan "caution[s] against critical practices that romanticize or mystify regions or figures" and ultimately represent them "through the lens of colonial discourse" (66). This cautionary tale is worked out in her critique of Jean Baudrillard, whose "theoretical peregrinations [in *America (1988)*] adopt the codes and terms of colonial discourse, producing Euro-American modernist aesthetics in the face of postmodernity's transnational challenges to those values and forms of culture" (82). While the critic expands his territory, his theorizing of it subordinates its difference to his Eurocentric critical categories (a problem I highlighted with Appiah's cosmopolitanism). Kaplan sees the same problems in Deleuze and Guattari, where "becoming minor" is all too often a "strategy that only makes sense to the central, major, or powerful" critic, a strategy wherein "the Third World functions simply as a metaphorical margin for European oppositional strategies, an imaginary space, rather than a location of theoretical production itself" (88). The concepts of Deleuze and Guattari regarding deterritorialization and becoming minor represent the dark side of Appadurai's vision of agency and liberation, for in Kaplan's view "deterritorialization itself cannot escape colonial discourse. The movement of deterritorialization colonizes, appropriates, even raids other spaces" (89).

Kaplan counters this Eurocentric tendency with a feminist stress on the local, one that aims to reverse the power relations between what globalization theorists call the center and the periphery. (Her congruity with Stiglitz is striking, given his stress on the importance of returning sovereignty in economic matters to the local countries that are supposed to benefit from globalization.) For Kaplan the "privileging of the local" (146) by critics like Adrienne Rich and Chandra Mohanty requires that we view local cultures as sites of resistance to globalization and underscores the danger that globalizing literary studies will colonize world literatures for Western academic consumption by channeling them through its own normalizing vocabulary. Other feminist critics of globalization share Kaplan's concern about how often globalization theorists ground their analyses in master narratives in which the mapping of core-periphery relations seems to replicate an older Eurocentrism. For example, Janet Abu-Lughod, who is "uncomfortable with the high level of abstraction of much of the discourse" about globalization (131), complains that critics like Ulf Hannerz treat the cultural flow between core and periphery as essentially unidirectional ("global" culture, produced in the West, is exported to a passive, consuming Third World). She argues that more attention has to be paid to specific localities in which cultural products from core cultures are appropriated and transformed in a "two-way process" (132). (Her examples come from a bazaar in Tunis and the syncretic relation between "Oriental" and Western musical idioms [133]).

Barbara Abou-El-Haj also worries about the tendency of major globalization critics to "emphasize the center in cultural analyses...premised on the core-periphery model.... In this model the remnants of Eurocentrism lurk in the un-equal attention given to the local stake in the reception and alliance with global powerbrokers." These critics see the periphery as the site of "homogenization and corruption," but they ought to concentrate more on "reciprocity and syn-thesis" in global cultural flows (140–41). Likewise, Janet Wolff sees too much "grand sociological theory" and not enough "concrete ethnography" focused on the local in the work of major critics on globalization (163). For Kaplan, Abu-Lughod, Abou-El-Haj, and Wolff, globalization theory as it has been domi-nated by male critics too easily colonizes discrete local cultures, subordinating them to sweeping formulations that are often Eurocentric.

Valuable as these criticisms are, they run the risk of rigidifying the distinc-tion between the privileged core and the marginalized periphery by insisting on the power and the autonomy, even the privilege, of the local. There is a danger in any discussion of the relation between dominant and dominated cultures of characterizing the local as a pure (or gendered) space in need of protection, as if local cultures were not already contaminated in the sense Appiah has in mind. The danger of ceding dominant economic and/or cultural power to the core so-cieties of the West may be matched by the danger of making a fetish of the local in its resistance to global cultures and treating that resistance as more impor-tant than the detrimental effect it might have on the inhabitants of the so-called periphery. Feminist critics such as Louise Yelin and Carla Freeman have been making this argument for a number of years. In her 2004 essay, "Globalizing Subjects," she discusses the relative absence of gender and women's issues as cat-egories for analysis in studies of globalization, Yelin endorses what she calls the "bracing corrective" in Hardt and Negri's *Empire* "to the nostalgic mystification of the 'local' as antidote and site of resistance to processes of globalization" (441), but she rightly complains that their complete inattention to gender as a concep-tual category for analyzing identity and difference under globalization is symp-tomatic of a tendency to ignore "women as actors on the global stage and gender as a component of global modes of political, social, economic, and cultural or-ganization" (440). Yelin's argument builds on Freeman's earlier article on the dominance of male critics in globalization studies, and on the general tendency to equate male experience with the public sphere and women's with the local:

Not only has globalization theory been gendered masculine but the very processes defining globalization itself—the spatial reorganization of production across na-tional borders and a vast acceleration in the global circulation of capital, goods, labor, and ideas, all of which have generally been traced in their contemporary form to economic and political shifts in the 1970s—are implicitly ascribed a masculine gender. Indeed, two interconnected patterns have emerged: the erasure of gender as integral to social and economic dimensions of globalization when framed at the macro, or "grand theory," level and an implicit masculinization of these macrostructural models. (Freeman 1007)

One of these macrostructural models, in Freeman's view, is the one that has "construed the global as masculine and local as feminine terrains and practices" (1007). Freeman insists that we need to reconceive the "local" by understanding that the local and the global are "mutually constitutive, and bound up in modes of gender at all levels" (1012). This leads her to "challenge the portrayal of the local as contained within, and thus defined fundamentally by, the global," so that we can decouple "the link that has fused gender with the local and left the macropicture of globalization bereft of gender as a constitutive force" (1012).[10]

It seems to me that by its very nature globalization complicates the distinction between the indigenous or local, on the one hand, and the transnational or global, on the other. Certainly, we can isolate specific, local, cultural practices, commodity forms, economic and political systems, and the like, but as we have already seen, almost always those practices, forms, and systems are not indigenous in any traditional sense of the word but the product of cross-cultural contact, appropriation, and transformation. This, of course, is central to the argument Appiah makes about culture and identity in *Cosmopolitanism,* that they are always products of contamination. So the whole category of the "local" or "particular" is suspect at the outset. The same holds for the category of the "global," for there are no global forms that are not made up of particulars from this culture and that. While Miyoshi may be correct that to study transnational "areas" or global economic and/or cultural flows we need some kind of totalizing system, such a system cannot do without attention to local histories and particular cultural and commodity forms, since these histories and forms are the product of a dialectical relationship between localities and totalities (however that term is defined).

The questions raised by Kaplan, Yelin, Freeman, Abu-Lughod, Abou-El-Haj, and Wolff ought to give us pause. However we proceed in our efforts to deal with literature and its production in a transnational context, we need to avoid the problems these writers enumerate. As Susan Stanford Friedman has written, we need to resist "simplistically universalist and binarist narratives" as we think about globalizing the study of literature; we must undertake the more "difficult negotiation between insistence on multidirectional flows of power in [a] global context and continued vigilance about specifically western forms of domination" (6). This would clearly involve looking at local cultures outside the West, not as the passive recipients of mass culture, but as sites of transformation or even active resistance. However, this does not mean simply reasserting the autonomy of the local over and against the global. The trap here is that we may perpetuate a simple-minded binarism that facilely and uncritically celebrates the local as pure culture opposed to rapacious and homogenizing westernization. The stress, rather, ought to be on the multidirectionality of cultural flows, on the appropriation and transformation of globalized cultural forms wherever they settle in, with close attention to how those forms are reshaped and sent off again to undergo further transformations elsewhere. This work will take on increasing urgency as globalization accelerates and these processes remake English into something altogether new and more complicated.

The transnational turn in literary and cultural studies, which mirrors similar shifts in disciplines throughout the humanities and social sciences, will by definition have a culturalist orientation, given the objects it studies. The question is not *whether* it will have this kind of orientation but *how* culturalist models for the study of globalization are informed by materialist approaches that consider the relationship between economies and cultures and pay particular attention to how economic forces both enable and restrict forms of cultural production. This is particularly urgent for critics interested in how literary texts engage issues related to globalization. Any analysis of literature's engagement with how subjectivity, social relationships, and forms of economic and cultural production get constructed under globalization has to pay attention to the representation of economic inequities and class relationships in the texts we study and to how material conditions mediate what we call "cultural" (and "personal") relations. Our work ought to be grounded firmly in an understanding that the realms of the cultural and the economic are inextricably linked, that no analysis of cultural relations or production (including analyses like Appadurai's or Appiah's of subjectivity and agency) can proceed without simultaneous attention to how economic and material conditions contribute to and even determine the opportunities and limits of such production. The transnational turn in literary studies is predicated on the idea that cultural forms (literary narrative, cinema, television, live performance, etc.) are not purely aesthetic objects but forms of production rooted in the historical world of commodities and economies. A narrowly aestheticized culturalist approach rooted in the old Arnoldian notion that we ought to be studying great literature defined in terms of its capacity to transcend local historical forces as it embodies timeless universal truths will not do for such projects, a truth that ought to be absolutely clear at this point in the history of contemporary literary studies. At points I have argued that the kind of materialist critiques of "culturalist" approaches developed by critics like Miyoshi and Harootunian seem to be tilting at windmills, for in fact there are very few critics trying to practice this narrow kind of culturalism. Rather, the best culturalist criticism, whether it focuses on an analysis of the impact of globalization on literary production per se or whether it is engaged more broadly with understanding the transnational turn in literary studies itself, will take the more nuanced approach I have been advocating here, one in which cultural production is analyzed within a context that assumes its connection to economic flows, material conditions, and inequities related to class relations. This is an approach I model in part 2 when I turn my attention to the analysis of a set of contemporary transnational novels that themselves embody this nuanced way of dramatizing the nature and effects of globalization. But before I do this, I want to look at how our treatment of place and location is getting reconfigured as we begin to complicate—and move beyond—older national paradigms for the study of literature.

4

BORDER STUDIES

Remapping the Locations of Literary Study

One of the most important lessons contemporary theory about space, place, and location has taught us is that, to a significant degree, we construct the locations we study. It is true that the national model for literary studies is the product of a focus on literature produced in countries that have an empirical existence. These nations are not, strictly speaking, locations that have been constructed by scholars and critics.[1] My point, however, is that we make a *choice* to study literary texts and other cultural forms as national productions, and that organizing literary studies around departments of English, Spanish, German, Japanese, or French literatures is in some senses an arbitrary decision. In advocating an aggressive approach to developing theoretical, methodological, and disciplinary structures for studying literature and culture in a transnational framework linked to the history of globalization, I am *not* insisting that we abandon older national models, but that they be supplemented, complicated, and challenged by newer approaches. These newer approaches must be based in part on reimagining and reconstructing the locations we study. Here I want to explore some recent theoretical approaches to location characteristic of the transnational turn in literary and cultural studies, the collective conjuring of new, more fluid, historically innovative, and heterogeneous locations in which to situate literary and cultural analysis. While in this chapter I focus on new approaches to location in American studies because I think they provide, collectively, a helpful model for such work, at the end of the chapter I gesture toward other fields that have offered scholars in the age of globalization an opportunity to reconfigure the spaces we study in ways that both predate and transcend traditional nation-state boundaries.

A key challenge in locating transnational forms of literary and cultural analysis is how to map relationships between the local and the global. Here we can begin by recalling James Clifford's reference to the "representational challenge" involved in "the portrayal and understanding of local/global historical encounters" and how in meeting this challenge we need to "conjure with new localizations like 'the border,'" specific places of "hybridity and struggle, policing and transgression" (109). Globalizing literary studies must involve a radical dislocation of the traditional geographical spaces we have been using to organize work in both the humanities and the social sciences. It begins with a recognition that we create the spaces we study, that there is a reciprocal, constitutive relationship between locations and the act of locating. The locations we study do not exist apart from the human act of measuring, delimiting, identifying, categorizing, and making boundaries and distinctions. As we complicate the traditional attention we pay to nation-state locations by paying attention to transnational spaces and regions, it is important that we develop a clear sense of the constructedness of these regions.

How *do* geographical spaces get localized when we study them? A good example can be found in Rob Wilson's essay, "Imagining 'Asia-Pacific' Today." Discussing the successive shifts from Asian studies to Pacific Rim studies to Asia-Pacific studies, Wilson emphasizes how geographical areas are regionalized by critics and funding agencies in response to shifting political, economic, and cultural exigencies, and by our critical response to those shifts. It is one thing to study the nation of Japan, but quite another, Wilson argues, to "regionalize a space" called "Asia-Pacific" so that it constitutes a "porous" area of "cross-border flows of information, labor, finance, media images, and global commodities" within which the nation of Japan is situated (233). Regionalizing a space involves an "act of social imagining" that has to "be shaped into coherence and consensus" (235). To be sure, Wilson is wary about such operations, insisting that "'Asia-Pacific' reeks of the contemporary (transnational/postcolonial) situation we are living through" (235). While it replaces "Cold War visions of the 'Pacific Rim' as the preferred global imaginary in the discourse of transnationalizing and de-nationalizing corporate Americans," the regionalized space of "Asia-Pacific" strikes Wilson as "the utopic dream of a 'free market,'" the "post–Cold War trope of First World policy planners and market strategists" (235). However, the concept he develops here of regionalizing spaces by imagining them is powerful. Wilson insists on distinguishing the concept of "'imagining-Asia Pacific' as region" from the "act of liberal consensus" or the "postcolonial construction of transnational 'hybridity'" (236). He uses the verb "imagining" in the sense of "articulating a situated and contested social fantasy" that "involves ongoing transformations in the language and space of identity by creating affiliated representations of power, location, and subject...expressing the will to achieve new suturings of (national) wholeness within 'the ideological imaginary' of a given culture" (236). This is a very useful model for thinking about how we identify and organize the locations we study, since it puts the stress on how the locations we analyze are fluid imagined spaces structured and demarcated in the context of political debates in which reimagining new places is understood as integral to the (re)constitution of identities, cultures, and power. Wilson's stress on the work of the imagination in constructing places in relationship to identities and cultures is reminiscent of Appadurai's insistence on the role the imagination plays in appropriating and transforming globalized cultural forms in the context of remaking personal and cultural identities. Both critics see geography, identity, and culture as fluid spaces in which both local populations and the critics who study them are involved in a creative activity of appropriation and pastiche.

Wilson's focus on how we regionalize spaces for both economic development and academic study is dedicated to what he calls a "critical regionalism" (248). A critical regionalism analyzes the history and politics of how particular spaces get "regionalized" (how, and when, for example, the "Orient," "the Middle East," "America," or the "West Indies" came into being as cohesive areas for academic study), and it fosters a contemporary revision and reconstruction of regions or areas based on new political and cultural realities and new theories and methodologies in the general field of international studies in both the humanities and social sciences. A good early example of this kind of critical regionalism can be found in the field of U.S. border studies, which in the last twenty years or so has helped turn American studies into a hemispheric and increasingly transnationalized enterprise.[2] The field of border studies began with a commitment to study the production of literature and culture along the U.S.-Mexican border; it contributed dramatically to our understanding of the centrality of Latina/o literature to literature in the United States and helped remap and rehistoricize our understanding of its emergence.[3] Border studies criticism was predicated on the idea that criticism of literature and culture of the United States could best be revitalized by relocating it in a hemispheric context, by paying more attention to locations that are between or that transgress conventional national borders— liminal margins, regions, or border zones in which individual and national identities migrate, merge, and hybridize. This shift in the geographical scope of American studies contributed to a dramatic shift in how we historicize the literature and cultures of the Americas.

In developing what Wilson has called a critical regionalism, the field of border studies has drawn on the work of a range of critics who have been rethinking how we conceptualize and map locations in the Americas and elsewhere. Mary Louise Pratt and Gloria Anzaldúa, for example, helped focus attention on how identities, cultures, and nations are produced, fractured, and continually reproduced within spaces or locations where there are no fixed borders or absolutes, where previously constructed "essences" are deployed, transformed, and reconstructed into cultural spaces whose very nature is defined by their contingency and constructedness. This kind of attention to the politics of location brought with it a proliferating set of terms to designate spaces that exist between, on the margins of, or within traditional national borders. One of the most influential has been Pratt's "contact zone," which "refer[s] to the space of colonial encounters, the space in which peoples geographically and historically separated come into contact with each other and establish ongoing relations, usually involving conditions of coercion, radical inequality, and intractable conflict" (6).[4] This term is meant to "foreground the interactive, improvisational dimensions of colonial encounters" in order to emphasize "how subjects are constituted in and by their relations to each other" (7). The Native American critic Louis Owens drew on Pratt's term to conceptualize the improvisation of individual subjectivity and hybrid cultures in the "American" frontier. He borrowed Pratt's term to help rethink the "colonized space" of European/Native American contact in the United States as a "transcultural frontier" (51). Owens is concerned less with theorizing a context for reading travel writing on a global scale (Pratt's focus) than with theorizing a context for reading Native American literature. He finds Pratt's "contact zone" useful in trying "to achieve a theoretical discourse that might help to illuminate the complexities of multicultural literature," which, in Bakhtinian fashion, he sees as unfolding in a "dialogically agitated space" where "discourse is multidirectional and hybridized" (58). The multidirectional and hybrid quality of experience on the transcultural frontier, characterized as Owens sees it by instability, "heteroglossia," and indeterminacy (59), gives it the improvisational quality Pratt ascribes to contact zones. As such, it contrasts markedly with the historical term, "territory," a "space which is mapped, fully imagined as a place of containment, invented to control and subdue the wild imaginations of imagined Native peoples" (59). Owens's position on cultural contact and cultural change, which emphasizes improvisation over domination, clearly looks forward to the kinds of positions Appadurai and Appiah have come to endorse.

The key terms here are "colonial" and "improvisational." Although the relations of power in Pratt's contact zones are "radically asymmetrical," Pratt starts with the premise that something like a syncretistic third culture evolves within them, since contact zones are characterized by "copresence, interaction, interlocking understandings and practices" (7).[5] Contact zones—and the literatures that come out of them—provide a context for studying the production of subjectivity (and culture) in a historical and geographical space that foregrounds the sometimes arbitrary, syncretic, improvised, and hybrid nature of personal and social forms of expression. The kind of improvisation Pratt calls attention to also operates at a more general level, for "contact zones" in her view not only organize or invent certain forms of subjectivity and culture, they also, literally, organize and invent new worlds. This is why Pratt's study of travel writing and imperialism analyzes how "travel and exploration writing produced 'the rest of the world' for European readerships at particular points in Europe's expansionist trajectory" and how it "differentiated conceptions of [Europe] in relation to something it became possible to call 'the rest of the world'" (5). As a particular type of location, Pratt's contact zones are based, not on the kind of imagined coherence characteristic of a cohesive community or nation-state, but on attention to cross-border flows of information, commodities, and experiences.

Like Appadurai and Appiah, Pratt also resists the idea that sheer domination is at work in center-periphery relations and endorses approaches to cultural development that reject the distinction between authenticity and contamination. Like Pratt's "contact zone," Anzaldúa's "borderland" (*la frontera*) has gained wide usage because it helps emphasize the inevitable processes of contamination and mongrelization writers like Salman Rushdie and, later, Appiah insisted are central to cultural development. Where Pratt's "contact zone" evolves out of her study of imperial travel in Europe's colonies, Anzaldúa's conception of borderlands grows out of her own experience growing up in South Texas and from her study of the radically unstable, migrating cultures of the mestiza/o diaspora in what is now Mexico and the Southwest United States. For Anzaldúa, borders draw violent dividing lines between the "safe and unsafe," between "us" and "them," but at the same time borderlands are "vague and undetermined," in a "constant state of transition." Though different from Pratt's "contact zone," Anzaldúa's "borderland" is also an improvisational space in which languages and identities hybridize and evolve. As such her concept of the borderland is inextricably tied to the production of a "mestiza/o" identity; the borderland is a place whose inhabitants are the "prohibited and forbidden...the squint-eyed, the perverse, the queer, the troublesome, the mongrel, the mulatto, the half-breed...in short, those who cross over, pass over, or go through the confines of the 'normal'" (3). The kind of contact that takes place in such borderlands needs to be distinguished from that which takes place in Pratt's more generalized contact zones, since Anzaldúa's borderland is a specific product of the complex history that links the nations of Mexico and the United States. She is less concerned, that is, with zones of informal contact than with zones organized around very permeable national borders. For Anzaldúa, "borders are set up to define the places that are safe and unsafe, to distinguish us from them. A border is a dividing line, a narrow strip along a steep edge. A borderland is a vague and undetermined place created by the emotional residue of an unnatural boundary. It is in a constant state of transition" (5). Borderlands, as articulated by Anzaldúa, simultaneously organize and disorganize space, identities, and cultures.

The differences between Anzaldúa's geographically specific borderland and Pratt's more generalized contact zone exemplify a tension in border studies between approaching borderlands as geographical spaces, on the one hand, or as a bundle of social, psychological, and cultural issues, on the other. Anzaldúa's borderland is a state of mind as well as a geographical location (the U.S./Texas/Mexican border) where identities, languages, and cultures have become hybrid and syncretic, but border studies critics drawing on Anzaldúa have generalized (and made metaphorical) her concept of borderlands in a way that has become problematical. In what follows I want to explore how the work of border studies critics like Anzaldúa can inform a more geographically complicated hemispheric approach to literature in the Americas, but it is important to recognize at the same time that this work is grounded in the specific geographical and cultural history of Mexicans and Chicanas/os in North America.[6]

We can broaden the hemispheric context of the spaces Pratt, Owen, and Anzaldúa deal with if we connect them to the Martiniquan critic Edouard Glissant's conception of "cultural zones," first developed in an essay in *Caribbean Discourse* called "The Novel of the Americas." Here, Glissant speculates about some of the links between novels written in various parts of the Americas. His point of departure is a historical and experiential distinction that links these zones to the history of modernity, for he wants to insist on a division between the "poetics of the American continent," characterized by "a search for temporal duration," and a European poetics "characterized by the inspiration or the sudden burst of a single moment" (144). In the Americas, he writes, "we do not have a literary tradition that has slowly matured: ours was a brutal emergence that I think is an advantage and not a failing" (146). What distinguishes the literature of the Americas, in his view, is its rapid development out of a "violent departure from tradition, from literary 'continuity'" (146). The novel of the Americas is thus "the product of a system of modernity that is sudden and not sustained or 'evolved'" (149), a form of expression grounded in what he calls a "lived" rather than a "matured" modernity ("matured, here means 'developed over extended historical space,'" and "lived means 'that which is abruptly imposed'" [149]). Within this broad landscape of a hemisphere both marked off and linked together by its irruption out of modernity, Glissant suggests that we can identify specific "cultural zones," spaces where historical, political, social, and religious experiences overlap national boundaries in ways that inform the literature of these zones.

In his brief discussion of U.S. novelists, for example, he distinguishes between the cultural zones inhabited by Henry James, Ernest Hemingway, F. Scott Fitzgerald, and William Faulkner. He argues that it was the "tragedy of those American writers of the 'lost generation' that they continued in literature the European (or 'Bostonian') dream of Henry James," while Faulkner, whose roots were in the "Deep South," was relatively "free" from "the dream of becoming European" (149–50).[7] He suggestively links the cultural orientation of James, Hemingway, and Fitzgerald to the "matured modernity" of Europe, and Faulkner's distinctly Southern preoccupation with racial otherness and difference to the "lived modernity" that characterizes so much of the West Indies, Mexico, and Latin America. All of these writers are linked to modernity, but they write, according to Glissant, in distinguishable zones that relate to it in different ways. The emphasis here is on place, but for Glissant the place is not a metropolitan center but a larger zone with a particular cultural genealogy historicized in terms of different colonial origins and the different concerns that grow out of them.[8]

Glissant's historical link between the United States, Canada, the Caribbean, Mexico, and Central and South America around their collective emergence out of modernity suggests a context for studying their literatures simultaneously—a shift in emphasis that provocatively links American studies, the comparative study of the literature of the Americas, and modernity studies to more recent work on the relationship between globalization and literary production. The concept of "cultural zones" offers a way to at least begin to divide this huge landscape into smaller, more manageable units.[9] Within such a framework the literature of the American West and Southwest—or of New Orleans and the Deep South—would be read in conjunction with literature from Mexico, Spain, and the Caribbean rather than being played off some strained connection to New England; the study of U.S. literature gets both decentered and redirected into a broader historical and cultural framework. The role of "nationalism" and literature's engagement with a set of national ideals does not disappear in this kind of framework, but it does become radically recontextualized.[10] From this point of view, "the nation" is seen as evolving, not just in reaction to British rule and "Englishness," but in relation to social movements and political events in the hemisphere, so that "American experience" and "American identity" are more accurately viewed as structures determined to a significant degree by this North-South relationship, especially in the Southern regions of the country.

Linking the emergence of modernity to the conquest and colonization of the New World rather than to the happy triumph in philosophy and social thought of rationality and the progressive power of secular reason and scientific inquiry de-centers the humanist narrative of modernity as a period that begins with "enlightenment" and leads to unimpeded and dramatic improvement. In this alternative scenario, as John Murrin and Michael Geyer have both suggested, modernity is understood to signal, not just scientific, technological, and political progress, but "catastrophe" and "unsettlement" as well.[11] Modernity from this revised perspective is defined less in terms of the emergence of a certain kind of thought or discourse, marked by a Romantic self-reflexivity Foucault associates with Kant, and more by the development and deployment of maps, ships, money, speculators, and weapons wedded to imperial expansion and religious zeal let loose in the interests of assisting and justifying that expansion.[12] The "Old World," literally unable to contain itself under the pressures of such developments, expands and conquers areas that, when defined as a "new world," revise and reinvent the old one. In this scenario, the very terms "Old World" and "New World" both attend and abet the emergence of modernity. And this expanded conception of modernity links this epoch and its locations to the long history of globalization we saw Robertson outline. Modernity and globalization become coincident developments, providing a set of historical processes for analyzing cultural and literary production that complicate older nationalist paradigms limited to nation-state locations.

The idea that we can date the emergence of modernity from the conquest and invention of the Americas can be traced back to a neglected book by the Mexican philosopher Edmundo O'Gorman, entitled *The Invention of America: An Inquiry into the Historical Nature of the New World and the Meaning of Its History* (1961).[13] O'Gorman argued against the idea that Columbus "discovered" the Americas, not so much to insist on the obvious point that the lands now making up the Americas were conquered, but, rather, to argue that the whole idea that they constituted a "new world" was an invention of Western Europe that was inextricably connected to the emergence of modernity. O'Gorman was less interested in the physical act (or accident) of the conquest than in tracing the unfolding of an interpretive framework that invented the conquered lands as a "new world," and in analyzing how that invention unfolded in the context of a philosophy of history that was itself utterly transformed by its encounter with an unknown landmass and people. Here is O'Gorman's main argument:

> The traditional idea of America as a thing in itself, and the no less traditional idea that because of this previous notion we are dealing with an entity endowed with a "discoverable" being, which in fact was discovered, are, respectively, the ontological and hermeneutical premises on which the truth of that historiography depends. If one ceases to conceive of America as a ready-made thing that had always been there and that one day miraculously revealed its hidden, unknown, and

unforeseeable being to an awe-struck world, then the event which is thus inter-
preted (the finding by Columbus of unknown oceanic lands) takes on an entirely
different meaning, and so, of course, does the long series of events that followed.
All those happenings which are now known as the exploration, the conquest, and
the colonization of America; the establishment of colonial systems in all their diversity and complexity; the gradual formation of nationalities; the movement toward political independence and economic autonomy; in a word, the sum total
of all American history, both Latin and Anglo-American, will assume a new and
surprising significance...its history will no longer be that which *has happened to*
America, but that which *it has been, is, and is in the act of being.* (45–46)

O'Gorman is obviously right in a fundamental way in calling our attention to
the historical, ideological, and political invention of the Americas as a coherent space. Indeed, in so doing he anticipated a number of contemporary critics
who speak of the invention (and reinvention) of the Americas (see, for example,
Dussel's 1995 *The Invention of the Americas*). He also anticipated Glissant in linking that invention to the irruption of modernity, noting that it developed out of a
violent revolution in the West's thinking about the world it inhabited. With the
codification of the "New World" as a "Fourth World" (along with Europe, Asia,
and Africa) "the ancient concept of the world reached its final climax....The archaic notion of the world as a limited space in the universe assigned to man by
God wherein he might gratefully dwell lost its raison d'etre" (128).

With the specific invention of the Americas as the "New World," O'Gorman
argued, humankind began making the transition to a modernity in which "the
universe no longer appears...as a strange, alien, and forbidden reality belonging to God and made for His sake, but as a vast inexhaustible quarry of cosmic
matter out of which man may carve out his world, depending not on divine
permission, but solely on his own initiative, daring, and technical ability" (129).[14]
O'Gorman's analysis here, which sees modernity as the triumph of rationality
and technology over "divine permission," parallels Horkheimer and Adorno's
critique of "the dialectic of Enlightenment" and Habermas's accounts of modernity. However, O'Gorman dates the onset of this "triumph" much earlier and,
unlike the Frankfurt school critics, ties it inextricably to Europe's conquest of the
so-called New World. We can also observe in O'Gorman a stress on the dramatic
importance of "autonomy" in Enlightenment thought, something historians of
modernity like Robert Pippin have rightly put at the center of its emergence.[15]
The "revolution" that attended the conquest and invention of the Americas,
O'Gorman insisted, enabled "man" to "picture himself as a free agent in the
deep and radical sense of possessing unlimited possibilities in his own being, and
as living in a world made by him in his own image and to his own measure.
Such is the profound meaning of this historical process which we have called the

invention of America, a process which implies modern man's contempt for and his rebellion against the fetters which he himself had forged under pressure of archaic religious fears" (129–30).

O'Gorman's analysis is a useful supplement to Glissant's suggestive but sketchy attempt to link the culture and literature of the Americas with their collective origin in the "irruption" of modernity. O'Gorman stresses the reciprocal nature of the relationship between the "new" and "old" worlds; if the "new" world has its birth in the irruption of modernity, the "old" one is redefined as modern in the very act of inventing the other as "new" (and "primitive"). O'Gorman's pre-science comes not just from the attention he pays to the relationship between modernity and the politics of conquest, nor simply from the fact that he begins to think about the "invention" of cultures in ways that look forward to the work of contemporary critics. It also comes from the attention he pays to race and the whole phenomenon of hybridity in the Americas, for in O'Gorman's view modernity is inextricably caught up in the West's confrontation with the Other, specifically, with the challenge indigenous peoples presented to a comfortable European homogeneity.[16]

It is worth pausing for a moment to reflect on the terms "hybridity" and "hybridize," which are often invoked by the critics I have been discussing, keeping in mind that the nation-state locations we have traditionally studied got characterized until quite recently in terms of narrow racialized identities that were often based on spurious notions of purity. The term "hybridity" has become ubiquitous in literary and cultural studies. It is a powerful term, but we ought to acknowledge some problems with it. The concept of "hybridity" has worked effectively to draw critical attention to how colonized and border cultures developed by synthesizing themselves out of elements of multiple cultures. This called attention to what seemed their special or distinguished status vis-à-vis the supposedly monocultural nature of colonial societies, especially to the extent that colonial cultures relied on purist notions of identity and belonging that contributed to the demarcation of discrete political and cultural locations. However, the metaphor of hybridity as an explanation of cultural origins turned out to be so powerful that it very rapidly seemed to deconstruct any kind of purist notion of cultural origins. As Renato Rosaldo points out, once we realize the more general truth about hybridity as an explanation of cultural origins and a map of how identity evolves (that it is "hybridity all the way down" [xv]), the term loses its specific applicability to border zones. If all cultures and identities are at their core hybrid, then two things happen: hybridity loses its value as an explanatory term specific to border cultures, and the term itself becomes essentialized and foundational, since it comes to stand for a general truth about the ontological nature of all forms of subjectivity and identity.

O'Gorman's insistence that we cannot separate the history of the Americas from the history of modernity is a useful supplement to Glissant's point that the novel in the Americas must be seen as the historical product of a sudden "irruption" of modernity. For both writers, the history of the "New World" is marked by discontinuity and rupture; the Americas are not simply conquered by Europe, they are invented by Europe out of a complex web of chance encounter, willful conquest, and the forced importation of populations from Africa and South Asia. In Glissant's view, moreover, this invention creates a fractured space characterized less by the emergence of discrete, unified nations than a set of overlapping cultural zones. The dual stress here on the space of the Americas as an invention of Europe and its long history as a border or contact zone has received sustained treatment by Paul Gilroy, whose book on "the black Atlantic" has important implications for studying the literature and cultures of the Americas. Gilroy's approach to the black Atlantic parallels the work of the revisionist American critics I have been reviewing (with an important and refreshing focus on the economic dimensions of colonialism and the slave trade), and his mapping of the Americas, with some important revisions, can contribute both to the project of transnationalizing American literary and cultural studies and the wider enterprise of understanding how early phases of economic and cultural globalization helped redefine Englishness.

Gilroy is critical of both the historical and ongoing role of nationalism in literary and cultural studies, both in Britain and the United States. He is particularly critical of what he calls "cultural insiderism" among even the most progressive cultural critics in Britain, in which "the ideas of nation, nationality, national belonging, and nationalism are paramount" (3). He is also particularly critical of how New Left and Birmingham school critics consistently treated "culture" in terms of a myth about identity that constructs "the nation as an ethnically homogeneous object" (3), pointing out that in so doing they unconsciously "reproduced" the earlier nationalism of J. M. W. Turner and John Ruskin, a nationalism characterized by an "ethnocentrism" that denies the "imaginary, invented," and "external referents" that have gone into the construction of "Englishness" (14).[17] What we often call "cultural studies," he argues, gains its nationalist coherence by ignoring "the rhizomorphic, fractal structure of the transcultural, international formation" of nation-states like Great Britain and the United States (4). Gilroy's critique was one of the first to insist on taking a transnational approach to the study of national identities. *The Black Atlantic* dislocates the whole geographic and thematic focus of British cultural studies by shifting it to a space between national borders, thus linking his analysis of nationalism to the politics of location informing the work of Pratt, Anzaldúa, Arnold Krupat, José David Saldívar, and the other critics we discussed earlier. Attention to the history and culture of the "black Atlantic," he writes, "challenges the coherence of all narrow nationalist perspectives and points to the spurious invocation of ethnic particularity to enforce them and to insure the tidy flow of cultural output into neat units" (29).

Gilroy insists that attention to the fluid location of the black Atlantic will usefully complicate our understanding of the construction of both "Englishness" and "modernity." On the one hand, by focusing our attention on the history of linked economic and cultural exchange enabled by triangular trade, Gilroy foregrounds the impact of the slave trade and Afro-Caribbean cultural forms on the development of English national identity, emphasizing how "Britain's black citizens...have been produced in a syncretic pattern in which the styles and forms of the Caribbean, the United States, and Africa have been reworked and reinscribed in the novel context of modern Britain's own untidy ensemble of regional and class-oriented conflicts" (3). On the other hand, attention to the history of the "black Atlantic"—from the rise of the slave trade and the establishment of colonial political and economic structures to the eruption of black revolutionary movements like the one led by Toussaint L'Ouverture in Haiti—suggests that we need to fundamentally revise debates in the West about modernity. Like Geyer and Murrin, who want to focus on the emergence of the Americas out of "unsettlement" and "catastrophe," Gilroy wants to displace the narrow understanding of modernity "as a distinct [European] configuration with its own spatial and temporal characteristics defined...through the consciousness of novelty that surrounds the emergence of civil society, the modern state, and industrial capitalism," in order to focus attention on how "the universality and rationality of enlightened Europe and America were used to sustain and relocate rather than eradicate an order of racial difference inherited from the premodern era" (49).

One of the most striking things about Gilroy's influential work is how it redefines space and location. Space in *The Black Atlantic* is, in effect, a borderless location in any conventional sense of the term, characterized as it is by fluidity, mobility, porousness, dislocation, and violent forms of conflict. To analyze the production of subjectivity, national identities, and forms of cultural production in such a location is to radically revise the parameters within which these traditional subjects get treated. His work anticipates the transnational turn in literary and cultural studies I have been analyzing, is consistent with the kind of attention to multidirectional flows of power we have seen Friedman call for, and stands as an example of the kind of critical regionalism Wilson advocates. Gilroy's black Atlantic also constitutes a new kind of location for thinking about the emergence of modernity. He insists on linking such multidirectional flows to a long modernity that parallels the historical processes of globalization we have discussed. Gilroy's work also anticipates and localizes Appiah's point that contamination is at the center of cultural identity. He is not unsympathetic to more traditional critics of modernity like Jürgen Habermas, Marshall Berman, Huyssens, Alice Jardine, and others who have historicized the "crisis of modernity and modern values," but he is rightly troubled by their collective inattention to the "history and expressive culture of the African diaspora, the practice of racial slavery, or the narratives of European imperial conquest," which, in his view, "may require all simple periodisations [sic] of the modern and the postmodern to be drastically rethought" (42)—a project we have seen sketched out three decades earlier by O'Gorman. As Gilroy notes, these topics have not normally found their way into "contemporary debates around the philosophical, ideological, or cultural content and consequences of modernity. Instead, an innocent modernity emerges in the work of these critics from the apparently happy social relations that graced post-Enlightenment life in Paris, Berlin, and London" (44). By shifting our attention to an alternative set of interconnected locations—Africa, England, the West Indies, the American South—and by calling attention to the revolutionary social, cultural, and political events that took place there (enabled by transit over the "black Atlantic") Gilroy literally relocates and helps initiate a "complete revision of the terms in which the modernity debates have been constructed" (46).

Gilroy's black Atlantic proposes a conceptual, historical, and geographical map for rethinking "American" literature in ways that de-center the narrow nationalism border studies critics have been at pains to critique, and it connects in productive ways with Wilson's notion of critical regionalism and the new politics of location that drives much of new work that informs the transnationalizing of American studies that Shelly Fisher Fishkin has discussed. Like Pratt's contact zone and Glissant's cultural zone, Gilroy's black Atlantic constitutes a space between national borders where identity and culture evolve in syncretic patterns traceable in literature and other forms of cultural expression. It is also a space of economic and commodity flows, one in which the kind of convergence we earlier saw Appadurai stress as being a key factor in globalization is at work in a nascent kind of way. Gilroy's black Atlantic is a space of commodity exchange, marked by the economic engine of the slave trade, which did so much to fund modernity, and the development of plantation culture in the Caribbean and the Southern states of the United States. Technologies of travel and communication, crude as they were compared to our own time, converged with the three-way flow of people, knowledge, and commodities to produce early economic forms of globalization that had a profound effect on the production and transformation of personal and cultural identities.[18]

As useful as Gilroy's formulation is, however, it does have significant limitations in terms of conceptualizing a comprehensively global approach to rethinking literature and culture in the Americas, for in the final analysis he does not do full justice to the transcultural and transnational character of the Atlantic during the long historical period he covers. By calling his liminal space "the black Atlantic," Gilroy is able to focus dramatic attention on an African presence in the Americas, and his analysis of how the slave trade and the resulting black diaspora contributed decisively to the creation, not only of hybrid or creolized cultures in the Americas, but to "Englishness" itself, is a major contribution. However, Gilroy pays little, if any, attention to the Spanish conquest of the Americas, to the displacement and migration of indigenous peoples in the Americas, or to the importation of East Indian and Chinese indentured servants to the West Indies, developments absolutely central to the political, cultural, and social history of the Americas.[19] His specific interest is in tracing the influence of Africa on "Englishness," but in doing so he fails to capture the historical complexity of cultural syncretism in the new location he has theorized. These shortcomings are crucial in terms of the applicability of his "black Atlantic" thesis to the study of U.S. literatures in a hemispheric or transnational context, since the Spanish conquest, and its displacement of indigenous peoples—especially from what is now Mexico—had a profound impact on the development of culture and literature in the United States (especially in places like the West, the Southwest, New Orleans, and other areas of the Deep South).[20] Gilroy's black Atlantic suggests a way to remap the geographical and historical origins of literature in the United States, but only if it is expanded to include Spanish/Catholic colonialism and an indigenous diaspora. Revised along these lines, his work contributes in important ways to complicating the origins of "American" literature by calling attention to other, parallel sites of origin (from Spain and Mexico into the U.S. Southwest, and from the Caribbean into New Orleans, for example), and more generally to conjuring up a whole new transnational location for analysis. From this point of view, literature in the United States doesn't simply fan out from New England; it has multiple points of emergence that converge, clash, and reform themselves along and across the borders of various cultural zones.

Gilroy's work can be usefully linked to Mignolo's interest in border thinking, something I touched on in my discussion of cosmopolitanism. Like Gilroy and the other critics I have been discussing here, Mignolo is interested in rethinking both how we locate and conceptualize modernity by linking it to the history of colonialism and the slave trade:

My story begins, then, with the emergence of the modern/colonial world and of modernity/coloniality, as well as with the assumption that cosmopolitan narratives have been performed from the perspective of modernity. That coloniality remains difficult to understand as the darker side of modernity is due to the fact that most stories of modernity have been told from the perspective of modernity itself.... In consequence, I see a need to reconceive cosmopolitanism from the perspective of coloniality.... It should be conceived historically as from the sixteenth century until today, and geographically in the interplay between a growing capitalism in the Mediterranean and the (North) Atlantic and a growing colonialism in other areas of the planet. (723)

These "other areas," of course, prominently include Gilroy's black Atlantic in general and the new world in particular. What Mignolo calls the landmark "macronarratives" of "the modern/colonial world" include "the final victory of Christianity over Islam in 1492, the conversion of Amerindians to Christianity" in the wake of Cortez's conquest of the Aztecs, and the "massive contingent of African slaves" brought to the Americas (726). For Mignolo, the *geography* of the Americas has to be figured in relation to these converging macronarratives, so that "border thinking" involves both critical analyses of these remapped spaces and their intersections, *and* an understanding of what we too easily think of as contemporary "multiculturalism," which has its deep roots in the sixteenth century in the "expulsion of the Moors and Jews from the Iberian Peninsula," the crisis about natural and human rights precipitated by the "Indian doubt" (the debates invoked by Bartolomé de Las Casas and others about the humanity of the indigenous peoples of the Americas), and "the beginnings of the massive contingent of African slaves" arriving in the Americas.[21] In all of this, Mignolo usefully complicates Gilroy by calling attention to the origins of modernity in an "Atlantic commercial circuit that created the conditions for capitalist expansion," the French Revolution, the "emergence of Orientalism," Mediterranean capitalism, and the slave trade (732), an approach that further complicates the transnational map Gilroy draws.

As we have seen, it is precisely the limits of a modernity conceived narrowly without these intersecting and violent histories that leads to the benign forms of cosmopolitanism Mignolo's critical cosmopolitanism is meant to challenge, and it is particularly within this framework that he locates the notion of "border thinking." Border thinking is linked to critical cosmopolitanism because the latter involves a historical stage in which cosmopolitanism "can no longer be articulated from one point of view, within a single logic, a mono-logic" but must be thought in relation to "colonial difference," so that, "instead of cosmopolitanism managed from above," cosmopolitanism emerges "from the various spatial and historical locations of the colonial difference" (741). Mignolo's work is important because it links the various deterritorializing or reterritorializing projects I have been discussing under the rubric of Wilson's critical regionalism with the philosophical/ethical project of cosmopolitanism, a project that is itself linked to the challenge of managing difference in an increasingly globalized age.

The overriding question here has to do with the relationship between culture and *power*. For Mignolo the danger of cosmopolitanism and of thinking within rather than across borders is that it "hide(s) the coloniality of power from which different cultures came into being in the first place." Border thinking is calibrated in particular to enable an analysis of the "coloniality of power and the colonial difference produced, reproduced, and maintained by global designs" (742), a project Gilroy takes up in his study of the black Atlantic. Critics like Gilroy, Glissant, and O'Gorman are most helpful when their work is linked specifically to the kind of critical regionalism Wilson calls for *and* the kind of critical cosmopolitanism, linked to border thinking, endorsed by Mignolo.

Critics like those I have been discussing are committed to theorizing new kinds of locations in order to make their work more responsive to the historical, material, and political realities of the cultures they write about. However, they are also struggling with a methodological or theoretical problem: how to avoid taking either an essentialist or relativist position toward the link between locations, cultures, and identities. (In this sense they anticipate Appiah's version of cosmopolitanism, which, we have seen, also attempts to avoid both.) The "space between" for these critics becomes both a cultural or spatial location and a metaphor that represents a critical or theoretical position. For example, Krupat, in committing himself to analyzing the "shifting space in which two cultures encounter one another" (not a "fixed or mappable" space, but, rather, a culturally defined place that usually cuts across mapped national borders [5]), defines his "ethnocriticism" as a practice "founded upon ethnohistorical descriptions of the frontier," which "must involve a recognition that the topics it takes up from an anthropological, historical, or literary perspective all must be set against the backdrop of a pervasive Western imperialism" (5). Other critics, he acknowledges, have urged a nativist approach to the criticism of tribal literatures, one that takes recourse to specifically "Indian" modes of thinking and analysis (6). However, Krupat (along with Owens) rejects the idea that either Western or native forms of cultural expression and analysis can be purely and absolutely indigenous in the first place. "An ethnocritical frontier orientation," he writes, "soon shows that one of the things that occurs on the borders is that oppositional sets like West/Rest, Us/Them, anthropological/biological, historical/mythical, and so on, often tend to break down" (15), a formulation that looks ahead to Appiah's notion of contamination. The space between, for Krupat, is thus a methodological as well as a geographic one; he sees no choice but to move within and between "native" and "Western" theories and practices. "Ethnocritcal discourse," Krupat writes, "in its self-positioning at the frontier, seeks to traverse rather than occupy a great variety of 'middle grounds,' both at home and abroad" (25–26). It will try to move between "humanist" and "anti-humanist" positions, between what he calls postmodern "fragmentariness" and "social scientific aspirations to cognitive adequacy" (26). The border Krupat wants to inhabit, then, is a double one: the border zone between native and Western culture, and the border zone between what he calls "objectivism" and "relativism" (27).

The work of Gilroy, Glissant, O'Gorman, Mignolo, and the other critics discussed here provide useful models for efforts to simultaneously locate and globalize literary and cultural studies while at the same time paying careful attention to local histories marked by the interaction of particular populations and cultural forms. Collectively, their transnational approach to the study of literature and culture in the Americas helps draw a useful link between literary and cultural production, colonialism, and economic globalization in the hemisphere, while complicating the simplistic center-periphery binary that has overdetermined globalization studies, at least in its early phases.[22] It offers a way to rehistoricize U.S., Caribbean, Mexican, and Latin American literatures in a way consistent with disciplinary shifts away from narrow nationalist frameworks. While some critics complain that such shifts fragment the coherence of disciplines, this kind of "fragmentation" has always been central to disciplinary change, change that in this case will lead to a much more accurate understanding of the multicultural character of identities and cultures in the Americas and elsewhere. Critics like Gilroy, Glissant, and Mignolo open up the way to deterritorializing literary and cultural studies, or at least to reterritorializing these practices in a way that pays attention to the kinds of multidirectional flows of power Friedman has in mind.

In this chapter I have focused on border thinking in the Americas and on Gilroy's work on the black Atlantic because together they present a concrete, useful model for rethinking how we approach the whole question of location in literary and cultural studies. There are, of course, a myriad of other transnational (or prenational) locations that have been or can be treated in this way (see my earlier note about partition studies in India, and border studies in Ireland, for example). Each of these are contact or cultural zones marked by the long history of globalization I discussed earlier. Here, postcolonial studies has paved the way, using the histories of exploration, conquest, colonization, decolonization, and the development of postcolonial identities and cultures to map the study of intersecting locations in transnational and prenational areas as disparate as Africa, the Caribbean, Australia/New Zealand/Micronesia, South and East Asia, and the Middle East. The liminal spaces between these regions constitute contact or cultural zones ripe for literary and cultural analysis following the model Gilroy has provided. The long history of contact, conquest, and cultural exchange across the Mediterranean between what is now Spain and North Africa suggests one such zone, as does the porous territory comprising what is now Iraq, Iran,

Afghanistan, and northeastern India (a space, as we shall see in chapter 6, conjured up in Kiran Desai's novel, *The Inheritance of Loss*). To the south of this region is another fluid space with many of the characteristics of the Pacific Rim or Gilroy's black Atlantic, the cultural zone comprising the nations that rim South India in the areas of the Arabian Sea, the Bay of Bengal, and the Indian Ocean (which includes not only southern India but the Maldives, Malaysia, Indonesia, Burma, and Thailand). All of these locations lend themselves to a globalized, trans/postnational approach to literary and cultural studies, one that could employ Wilson's notion of critical regionalism and draw on Gilroy's conceptualization of the black Atlantic to reconfigure the narrowly national spaces of work in literary and cultural studies, and in the humanities in general.

Part II

Globalization in Contemporary Literature

I began this book by arguing that two intersecting forces are transforming the discipline of English, one operating within academia, the other outside of it. Within academia, work in virtually every major field in literary studies is becoming transnationalized in its theories, practices, and methodologies. This new work is collectively engaged in a sophisticated and multifaceted exploration of how literature across historical periods reflects—and reflects on—a multiplicity of differences grounded in personal, cultural, and political identities across locations where the boundary lines between cultures, races, genders, classes, and sexualities are much more porous than were heretofore acknowledged. Outside of academia, meanwhile, English literature (particularly the novel) is being produced by an increasingly transnational, multicultural group of writers, working in disparate parts of the world, whose work explores the intersecting effects of colonialism, decolonization, migration, and economic and cultural globalization. As in the criticism discussed in part 1, the attention here is on intersecting and sometimes conflicting identities (personal, cultural, political) grounded in forms of displacement endemic to the long history of globalization. Some of this writing might be categorized as postcolonial, but much of it is being produced by what the Pakistani writer Mohsin Hamid has called a "post–postcolonial" generation of writers whose experiences grow out of the postcolonial condition but are informed even more by the forces of globalization.[1] Much of this literature is either situated in the metropolitan West or involves characters whose experience shifts back and forth between the Western metropole and the formerly colonized countries from which their families came. Texts like these have become increasingly popular with readers of contemporary fiction, and many of them have won critical praise. (In Britain, for example, Kiran Desai's *The Inheritance of Loss* won the Man Booker Prize, and in the United States Jumpha Lahiri and Junot Díaz won Pulitzer Prizes for, respectively, *The Interpreter of Maladies* and *The Brief Wondrous Life of Oscar Wao*.) These have become centrally important books in contemporary culture, and they have begun to be taught widely in English literature classes in the United States, contributing to what will clearly be the increasingly transnational nature of English in the twenty-first century.

In the chapters that follow I turn my attention to a group of contemporary literary texts that exemplify the transnational character of this new body of literature, novels that at once transform the nature of the national literatures to which they belong *and* push beyond national boundaries to engage the global character of modern experience, contemporary culture, and the identities they produce.[2] The texts document the transnationalizing of English literature, but more important, they engage the complex range of issues discussed in part 1. That is, they reflect the globalization of English as a mode of literary production, but they also reflect *on* the historical, political, social, cultural, and personal issues of concern to the critics discussed here. It is important to note that the chapters that follow do not attempt to present a geographically or culturally comprehensive range of texts from all over the globe. That would be an impossible task in a book of this size. Rather, I focus on texts from an intersecting set of representative locations in the Americas, South Asia, Africa, and western Europe, texts that fit within the framework of a broadened and more complex version of Gilroy's black Atlantic, or that explore historical, cultural, and social links between India, Britain, and the Americas.

I begin in chapter 5 with an analysis of Arundhati Roy's *The God of Small Things,* Vikram Chandra's *Red Earth and Pouring Rain,* and Mohsin Hamid's *Moth Smoke,* focusing on how each writer deals with the relationship between globalization and the histories of colonialism, decolonization, and postcolonialism. This discussion is designed to explore how these novelists engage in a literary context the debates discussed in part 1. Chapter 6 turns its attention to Kiran Desai's critique of globalization in *The Inheritance of Loss* and the link she draws between globalization and resurgent nationalisms. In chapter 7 I analyze the economic, cultural, environmental, and gender politics at work in Zakes Mda's postapartheid South African novel *The Heart of Redness,* which stages an elaborate and multileveled debate about tradition and modernization in the eras of colonialism and contemporary globalization. Chapter 8 treats Zadie Smith's novel *White Teeth* as a black Atlantic text, demonstrating how Smith both locates her novel in Gilroy's space and complicates it by linking the lives of the black Atlantic characters with others from South Asia, all of whom struggle to live together in a tense and sometimes hilariously multicultural London. Where Smith, Chandra, Hamid, and Mda locate the bulk of their novels in postcolonial settings, Smith locates hers in the metropolitan West (as Desai does in the half of her novel that takes place in New York City), a setting she uses to analyze the construction of new subjectivities in a postcolonial context in which the forces of globalization shape a bewilderingly complex form of "Englishness" in multicultural London. I pay particular attention to how Smith plays multiculturalism and fundamentalism off each other as competing strategic responses to difference. I end with a novel that returns us to Gilroy's black Atlantic, Junot Díaz's *The Brief Wondrous Life of Oscar Wao,* which incisively explores new forms of mobility and migration in the age of globalization and the effect they have on the construction of gendered subjectivities, and which links the transnational histories of the United States and the Dominican Republic in ways that underscore the importance of a hemispheric approach to studying the Americas.

Post–Postcolonial Writing in the Age of Globalization: *The God of Small Things*, *Red Earth and Pouring Rain*, *Moth Smoke*

In part 1 we saw that critics take two general positions on the relationship between postcoloniality and globalization. One group sees conquest, colonization, decolonization, and the postcolonial condition as part of the long history of globalization. The other insists on a strict distinction between the two, and even sees globalization studies as a threat to the political and historical project of postcolonial studies. Where the first position insists on recontextualizing the study of colonialism and postcolonialism within the wider framework of globalization, the second position insists that globalization is a contemporary phenomenon, a dramatic rupture in the history of modernity to which colonialism and postcolonialism belong. The tension between these two critical positions is reflected in contemporary fictional treatments of globalization as well, and my aim in this chapter is to track how the critical debate is played out in three novels published at the end of the twentieth century: Arundhati Roy's *The God of Small Things* (1997), Vikram Chandra's *Red Earth and Pouring Rain* (1995), and Mohsin Hamid's *Moth Smoke* (2000). These texts are in many ways demonstrably different from what we might call classic postcolonial texts, for, while they all allude in some way to the legacy of colonialism, they pay more attention to the contemporary effects of globalization than they do to the imperatives of postcolonial

state making and the construction of specifically *postcolonial* identities and subjectivities. Roy and Chandra have written novels that explicitly link the forces
of contemporary globalization to the history of colonization, while Hamid's
novel treats globalization as a contemporary post–postcolonial moment. Roy and
Chandra tend to reinforce the position we saw Robertson and others take, that
globalization is a long historical process that includes the history of colonialism,
while Hamid insists on drawing a clear line between the history of colonization
and the effects of globalization. Insisting that he belongs to a "post–postcolonial"
generation of writers, he suggests that the category of literature we have been
calling "postcolonial" has become dated in an age of accelerating globalization.

I want to foreground the contrast between these positions, not only to demonstrate the continuity between the critical and fictional treatment of these issues,
but to argue that while Hamid's claim about the post–postcolonial orientation
of his generation is both important and compelling, it underplays the extent to
which contemporary literary engagements with globalization are connected to
an exploration of the ongoing effects of colonialism. I have chosen to look at Roy
and Chandra because they come at this relationship in two different ways. Roy's
novel pays very little overt attention to the history of colonialism and decolonization in India and is much more interested in exploring the contemporary
and disruptive effects of economic and cultural globalization, while Chandra's
novel moves back and forth between the history of colonization in India and the
experiences of its protagonist under globalization in contemporary India and
California. If the category we call *postcolonial* requires a specific, sustained, and
explicitly political engagement with colonial rule, the history of decolonization,
and the practical difficulties of developing a postcolonial nation-state, then *The
God of Small Things* does not to seem to fit. Indeed, it seems to be a new kind of
fiction more akin to Hamid's post–postcolonial fiction. Chandra's novel, however, since it *does* pay sustained attention to the history of colonialism in India,
seems rather easily to fit into the category of postcolonial fiction. But how do
we reconcile the contemporary portions of his book (whose subjects are more
akin to Roy's) with its historical sections on British rule in India? These two
novels, in fact, weave a treatment of colonialism (Chandra overtly, Roy by im-
plication) into their exploration of the effects of globalization, so that the two
histories become linked and continuous in ways consistent with the argument I
have made about recognizing the long history of globalization. In each of these
books globalization is folded into the history of postcoloniality so that the historical effects of globalization are linked inextricably with the historical condition
we call "postcolonial." Both books in their own way underscore that the history of globalization is not separate from but rather *encompasses* the history of
colonization, decolonization, and postcolonialism. Moreover, both deal with a

range of issues—identity and its relationship to ethnicity and culture, the challenges of developing a cohesive sense of social belonging among disparate populations, the effects on local communities of global economic and commodity flows, the viability of multiculturalism or cosmopolitanism for the management of difference—that are related both to the critics discussed in part 1 *and* writers normally associated with postcolonial fiction.

The God of Small Things

As I have indicated, Roy's novel, beyond the deep cynicism of its treatment of Communist rule in the Indian state of Kerala, has little to say about India as a nation-state, postcolonial or otherwise. *The God of Small Things,* rather, is about the transgression of boundaries (caste lines, "love laws," etc.), the debilitating effects of "Anglophilia," and the contemporary effects global culture and the global economy are having in Kerala. Paying scant overt attention to the political history of colonization and to the national political scene, all of this gets played out in Roy's novel within the narrow, claustrophobic confines of a family romance. The novel, Roy has insisted, is "not about history but biology and transgression."[1] Roy's title seems to bear out this claim. The God of "small things" is associated with "personal despair" and "personal turmoil," while the God of "Big Things" is associated with history and the "public turmoil of a nation" (20). For many of the characters, personal despair results from transgressing what the narrator, Rahel, calls the "love laws…laws that lay down who should be loved and how" (31). The violence her family experiences results from an uncanny confluence of events related to the transgressions of these laws, principally by Rahel's mother's love for the untouchable Velutha, her aunt's agonizing desire for a priest, Father Mulligan, and the complex web of relationships Rahel and her twin brother, Estha, have with their British cousin, Sophie Mol, and with their mother's lover, Velutha. However, the distinction between the personal and the historical gets complicated at the very outset of the novel. At the end of the first chapter, as Rahel ruminates over the cause of her family's tragedy, she is tempted to say it all began with a small thing, the arrival for a visit of their cousin Sophie, for this triggered a series of events that led to catastrophe. It turns out, however, that "to say that it all began when Sophie Mol came to Ayemenem is only one way of looking at it":

> Equally, it could be argued that it actually began thousands of years ago. Long before the Marxists came. Before the British took Malabar, before the Dutch Ascendancy, before Vasco da Gama arrived, before the Zamorin's conquest of Calicut.

Before three purple-robed Syrian bishops murdered by the Portuguese were found floating in the sea.... It could be argued that it began long before Christianity arrived in a boat and seeped into Kerala like tea from a teabag.

That it really began in the days when the Love Laws were made. The laws that lay down who should be loved, and how.

And how much. (32–33)

This other way of looking at the roots of her family's terror links the realm of small (personal) things in the novel with the realm of big (historical) things.[2] By stressing how forms of purely biological attraction have long been regulated in India by religious and political institutions, and by conjuring up the long colonial history of India as the context for emphasizing the durability of these regulations, Roy implicitly questions the very distinction between the personal and the historical her title seems founded on.[3]

Although in this passage the family's terror is traced back through the institutional and social history of religious proscriptions that long predate British colonial rule, that terror, personal and thus categorized in the novel as a "small thing," *is* linked later to the history of British colonialism and thus to "big things."[4] This is done through Roy's manipulation of a place she calls the "History House." This house, in Rahel's childhood a ruin standing in the middle of an abandoned rubber tree plantation, was once owned by an "Englishman who had 'gone native,'" a man she refers to as "Ayemenem's own Kurtz" and whom she links explicitly to the "Heart of Darkness" (51). Much later in the novel, this house, linked as it is to the history of colonialism, turns out to be the very spot where the family's personal terror comes to a head. In making the History House both the representative site of British colonial terror *and* the site of the family's personal terror, Roy explicitly links the "big things" and the "small things" in her novel and connects them to the long global history of colonialism in India.[5] However, in one of the more important plot twists, the family is "trapped outside their own history" by being "Anglophiles" (51).

Chacko [their uncle] told the twins that, though he hated to admit it, they were all Anglophiles. They were a family of Anglophiles. Pointed in the wrong direction, trapped outside their own history and unable to retrace their steps because their footprints had been swept away. He explained to them that history was like an old house at night. With all the lamps lit. And ancestors whispering inside.

"To understand history," Chacko said, "we have to go inside and listen to what they're saying. And look at the books and the pictures on the wall. And smell the smells."

"...But we can't go in," Chacko explained, "because we've been locked out. And when we look in through the windows, all we see are shadows....our minds have been invaded by a war. A war that we have won and lost.... A war that has made us adore our conquerors and despise ourselves." (51–52)

In passages like these the terror Rahel's family experiences, personal though it may be, is linked to the history of British colonization. Where early on we are invited to mark a difference between the private and the public in the distinction between the God of big things and the God of small things, Roy methodically works to undercut that distinction so that the book ends up dramatizing the extent to which the "big things," grounded in history and the nation, and the "small things" grounded in personal and familial life, are inextricably interrelated.[6] Elsewhere in the novel, Roy connects the family's alienation from its own history and identity under colonial rule to the more contemporary forces of globalization. Indeed, Roy historicizes globalization so that it not only incorporates contemporary forms and the history of British colonialism but also the successive series of invasions and migrations throughout the Indian subcontinent that run back through the Dutch, the Persians, the Muslims, the Huns (455 A.D.), Alexander the Great (326 B.C.), and the Indo-Aryans.

As noted, the novel's treatment of contemporary globalization is much more prominent than its treatment of British colonialism (a subject restricted to her treatment of the History House and Chacko's Anglophilia). Early in the book Roy makes a pointed critique of globalization in her description of Estha's walks around Ayemenem, to which he has returned in the early 1990s as an adult:

Some days he walked along the banks of the river that smelled of shit and pesticides bought with World Bank loans. Most of the fish had died. The ones that survived suffered from fin-rot and had broken out in boils.

Other days he walked down the road. Past the new, freshly baked, iced, Gulf-money houses built by nurses, masons, wire-benders and bank clerks, who worked hard and unhappily in faraway places. (14)

The material devastation brought to Ayemenem by globalization is underscored later in Roy's description of "Foreign Returnees" at Cochin airport, Indians whose exposure to the cultures and commodities of the West has profoundly alienated them from India:

And there they were, the Foreign Returnees, in wash 'n' wear suits and rainbow sunglasses. With an end to grinding poverty in their Aristocrat suitcases. With cement roofs for their thatched houses, and geysers for their parents' bathrooms.... Maxis and high heels. Puff sleeves and lipstick.

Mixy-grinders and automatic flashes for their cameras.... With love and a lick of shame that their families who had come to meet them were so...so...gawkish.

> Look at the way they dressed! Surely they had more suitable airport wear! Why did Malayalees have such awful teeth?
>
> And the airport itself! More like the local bus depot! The bird-shit on the building! Oh the spitstains on the kangaroos!
>
> Oho! Going to the dogs India is. (134)

These extended descriptions of how globalization has affected Ayemenem's waterways and those people from Kerala who have been living abroad help reinforce Roy's treatment of how British colonialism and the effects of globalization have transformed Rahel's family. Perhaps Roy's most pointed treatment in this regard comes when she describes the impact globalization has had on the life of Rahel's aunt, Baby Kochamma. Unable to overcome the love laws that kept her from Father Mulligan, Baby Kochamma transfers all her energy to the "fierce, bitter" cultivation of an ornamental garden (26). After "more than half a century of relentless, pernickety attention," however, Baby Kochamma has abandoned her garden, seduced by satellite television. Now, instead of tending her garden, "she presided over the world in her drawing room on satellite TV":

> It wasn't something that happened gradually. It happened overnight. Blondes, wars, famines, football, sex, music, coups d'état—they all arrived on the same train. They unpacked together . . . now whole wars, famines, picturesque massacres and Bill Clinton could be summoned up like servants. And so, while her ornamental garden wilted and dried, Baby Kochamma followed American NBA league games, one-day cricket and all the Grand Slam tennis tournaments. On weekdays she watched *The Bold and the Beautiful* and *Santa Barbara.* . . . She enjoyed the WWF Wrestling Mania shows, where Hulk Hogan and Mr. Perfect, whose necks were wider than their heads, wore spangled Lycra leggings and beat each other up brutally. . . . Her old fears of the Revolution and the Marxist-Leninist menace had been rekindled by new television worries about the growing numbers of desperate and dispossessed people. She viewed ethnic cleansing, famine and genocide as direct threats to her furniture. (27–29)

The worst fears of globalization's critics are telescoped into this short passage. The material world of Baby Kochamma's garden, a place linked to home and the local and the work she did with her own hands, is replaced by the electronic world of global television, a world paradoxically compelling for its being so alien, one in which American sporting events and soap operas mix so seamlessly with ghastly reports of dispossession, famine, massacres, and genocide that it seems difficult telling them all apart. They are all done up in a manner simultaneously horrifying and "picturesque." Her own localized fears have not been eased by what she sees on television. They have been *replaced* by what she sees on television. Global culture brought to her through the auspices of CNN is both menacing and self-alienating. Her addiction to television seems to mark her dispossession by global culture.[7]

The God of Small Things is in many ways a work of *postnational* fiction, since in its relentless focus on the present and the personal it pays relatively little attention to the details of British colonization and the status of India as a postcolonial nation-state. If we were to define postcolonial literature narrowly in terms of its overt engagement with the idea of the nation and the practical political challenges of constructing a viable nation-state, Roy's novel would seem only marginally a work of postcolonial fiction. Moreover, given its preoccupation with examining the effects of globalization on the characters, the novel's postnational orientation suggests it belongs to a newer category of post—postcolonial fiction. However, we have seen that the novel itself tends to undermine any useful historical distinction we might want to make between the postcolonial condition and globalization, since in her text Roy demonstrates that the postcolonial condition is itself produced as part of the history of globalization, which is in turn connected to the forces of colonization running from the Mughal Empire through the British Raj.[8] This is why the novel requires a reading sensitive both to its critique of globalization *and* the extent to which that critique relates to Roy's examination of the contemporary condition of postcoloniality. Contrary to During's concerns, such a reading does not "reconcile" globalization and the postcolonial condition in a way that scripts a happy ending for colonialism. Rather, it underscores the way in which the novel itself structures a dialectical relationship between colonialism, postcolonialism, and globalization. Roy's dual focus on the economic and cultural violence of colonialism and globalization links it to During's critical postcolonialism and Gikandi's narrative of crisis for globalization. The novel cannot be read as being *either* about postcolonialism or globalization. It is simultaneously about both because they are historically implicated with each other.

Red Earth and Pouring Rain

Roy's treatment of globalization focuses on the kind of "catastrophic" effects Said attributes to globalization, and its approach to Anglophilia tends to reinforce the skepticism of Loomba and others about the so-called liberating effects of "hybridity or multiculturalism."[9] Chandra's novel takes a decidedly different approach. *Red Earth and Pouring Rain* is less interested in isolating the contemporary effects of globalization and dismissing them as catastrophic than it is in insisting (as we have seen Appiah do) on the utter banality of cross-cultural conquest and the forms of hybridization it has facilitated. In the epic sweep of

Indian history conjured up in his novel there is no "India" that can plausibly be said to predate the kind of multicultural "mish-mash" Loomba insists is a contemporary product of the Western media. Moreover, in Chandra's hands globalization is not a purely Western phenomenon but, rather, gets connected to knowledge and technological developments rooted in the East. In his historical India "newcomers and the old ones collided and metamorphosed into a thing wholly new and unutterably old," creating a world of "great harmony" that "bursts into being as differentiation," a paradoxical world in which harmony "is visible only by becoming non-unity," where "diversity, every part of it, is sacred, because it is one" (111–12). This world is the complex historical product of Indo-Aryan migration into the Indus Valley and the development and codification of Hinduism and the caste system (1600–1000 BC), the evolution of tribes into city-states, the evolving division along color lines between Aryans and Dravidians (1000–450 BC), the conquest of parts of India by Alexander the Great (327 BC), the founding of the Maurya dynasty and the routing of the Greeks and rise of Rajput power in the north (320–184 BC), the arrival of Muslim armies from the north in 712, successive raids between 712–1525 by Turks, Afghans, and Persians that culminated in the establishment of the Mughal Empire, and, finally, the arrival in India of the British and the solidification of their domination with the collapse in 1857 of the Sepoy Rebellion. Chandra's India, in effect, rehearses the long historical view of globalization that Amartya Sen endorses, a view that locates its origins as much in the East as in the West.

Chandra's narrative moves back and forth between historical sections that focus on the rise to power of the British in India in the decades leading up to the Sepoy rebellion and sections set in the early 1990s in California that focus on a young Indian student named Abhay and the impact globalization has had on his sense of cultural identity (a narrative device Kiran Desai also employs in *The Inheritance of Loss*). This structure has the effect of linking Abhay's diasporic experiences in the contemporary age of globalization with the history of British colonization and the effects *it* has on the identity of the book's other central character, Sanjay Parasher. Abhay and Sanjay share the role of narrator in *Red Earth and Pouring Rain,* and by the end of the novel their disparate experiences with colonization and the West become the vehicle for Chandra's exploration of how the long history of globalization covering virtually the entire history of India, perpetually conjures new, hybrid identities.[10]

This is sustained with particular force in Sanjay's story. His mother becomes pregnant by eating a mysterious laddoo (a kind of doughnut) that has been produced, touched, and otherwise handled by a mongrel group including Indian mystics and British soldiers of fortune. Although he eventually helps lead the forces that rebel against the British in 1857, Sanjay's mystical paternity keeps him fascinated with the English, and in particular with their language and poetry. By the end of the novel, Sanjay has come to accept Englishness as part of his mixed identity, one that is grounded in the long history of racial and ethnic intermixing Chandra is at pains to chronicle in the novel. This acceptance is at odds with the plight of other characters Sanjay is close to, particularly his friend Chotta, who asks him:

> Do you know who we are? ... there is a new species on this earth. It is not this or that, it belongs not here or there, it is nothing. In the beginning, when we were born, Sanjay, we were just what we were, the sons of our mothers and fathers, but now we are something else.... [A] new animal: chi-chi, half-and-half, black and white. Do you know what this means, black-and-white? ... We are this new thing that nobody wants, Sanjay. (455–56)

Chotta struggles under an old principle of order linked to clear and distinct divisions, what Chandra characterizes earlier in the novel as the "most fundamental of definitive statements" about the world: "I and you, us and them, what I am and what I am not, white and black" (111). Indeed, this principle of fixed and immutable divisions is the one that begins to be displaced by the idea that "there is a unity ... of this and not this, and this great harmony, this oneness, this Brahman, bursts into being as differentiation ... visible only by becoming non-unity" (112). This might be simply dismissed as Chandra's send-up of mystical doublespeak if not for the fact that the whole force of his novel is focused on Sanjay's difficult acceptance of his hybrid identity. At the end of the novel, in London, Sanjay explains to a British detective that he is not the British subject named "Jones" he had earlier passed himself off as but Sanjay Parasher:

> "Not Jones?"
> "My name is Parasher."
> "You're not English?"
> "I am. But I am Indian."
> "How can you be English if you're an Indian?"
> "It is precisely because I'm an Indian that I'm English." (505)

Sanjay's insistence on being English *and* Indian suggests how far we are from the Anglophilia that plagued Chacko and his family in *The God of Small Things.* Indeed, the love laws Roy's characters suffer from are flouted in *Red Earth and Pouring Rain.* Sanjay's best friend, Sikander, who is like a brother to him, is the child of a Scottish father and Indian mother, and sexual relations between Indians and Anglos in the book are nearly routine. As youngsters, Chotta and Sanjay follow a friend's father to a house of prostitution. When the children are found out by the woman the father has had sex with, she tells them:

> They all come here, Brahmins and Rajputs and Company men. Here, touch-this-and-don't-touch-that and untouchability and your caste and my people and I-can't-eat-your-food is all forgotten; this is the place that the saints sang about, little men. Here, anybody can touch anybody else, nothing happens. (210)

This scene puts the world of division between castes and untouchables, and between Indian and British, in a context in which miscegenation and the production of hybrid subjectivities and cultural practices is the norm. Beneath the violent surface of caste, ethnic, religious, and cultural difference is a world of transgression and syncretism that preoccupies virtually all of the characters in Chandra's novel, Indian and Anglo. What we have come to call hybridity is not so much celebrated in the novel as simply taken as a given. Moreover, Chandra openly mocks the position of superiority based on cultural difference and purity most often ascribed in the novel to the British.[11] In this way, Chandra's novel takes a position on subjectivity very close to Appadurai's, for Sanjay uses his imagination to cobble together a series of identities rooted in the kinds of cross-cultural exchange Appadurai sees as central to the processes of globalization. Moreover, culture in this novel is born of just the kind of contamination we saw Appiah insist was the norm.

Like Roy, Chandra draws a clear connection between the histories of colonization and decolonization, the postcolonial condition and contemporary forms of globalization. He does this through his treatment of Abhay, whose life is permeated by the pull of Western culture through his experiences with film, advertising, literature, and most important of all, an old Sears catalogue:

> You know when I got obsessed with America? ... From somewhere or other there showed up in our house a nineteen-sixty-seven Sears catalog...[I] started to go through it page by page. I started with the men's wear, with all the blond, blue-eyed guys wearing checkered shirts tapering to their bodies. Then the men's underwear, then the women's dresses, then the women's underwear, then the whole family groups, the mothers and daughters wearing the same dress and same bell-shaped hair, then the garden tools ... amazing and unbelievable, drivable grass cutters.... But best of all, at the back, saved for last, whole working and usable and immaculate swimming pools! Swimming pools you could order though the mail ... so that your pretty daughters, your crewcutted sons, your bloody stunning wife could paddle and float gently under the best sun in this best of all worlds. I mean it felt as if the top of my seven-year-old head had come off, that I had seen heaven, no not that exactly, but that this, this in front of me was what life must be. (361–62)

Chandra conjures up in this passage both the flow of commodities and the bland, homogeneous Western "lifestyle" most often associated with globalization. But where for Baby Kochamma in *The God of Small Things* the flood of Western products through her television has an anaesthetizing effect, for Abhay the effect is electrifying. Confronting the abundance of American commodities and the eerie symmetry of American families as portrayed by Sears is for Abhay the beginning of a journey taking him away from the grip of British colonialism into a complex and challenging encounter with the forces of globalization. Sanjay's nineteenth-century fascination with Englishness has its late twentieth-century correlation in Abhay's fascination with America, and the shift neatly marks the transition from India's experience with colonization to its experience with globalization. When Abhay later becomes a film student at Pomona College it sets the stage for his own coming to terms with an identity profoundly marked by Westernization and globalization. Like Sanjay, Abhay's subjectivity and his experience with culture reflect the worlds theorized by Appadurai and Appiah, worlds in which neither identities nor cultural forms and practices are fixed or indigenous but are the result of complex, fluid, and often unpredictable forms of contact, appropriation, and contamination related to the long history of globalization.[12]

Both Roy's novel and Chandra's, then, draw links between colonization, the postcolonial condition, and globalization in ways that suggest we ought not to view them as separate and distinct historical periods and processes. In *The God of Small Things* Baby Kochamma's anesthetization by global television is an extension of the colonizing effects of Chacko's Anglophilia, a fate that links her to other victims of the global economy in the novel such as the Kathakali dancers.[13] Likewise, in *Red Earth and Pouring Rain* Chandra plots his complicated novel to draw an important line running from Sanjay's fascination with the colonial British to Abhay's fascination with the cultural products of a global economy.[14] Chandra's tendency to treat transcultural contact in a way that makes its complex processes part of the normal scheme of historical development, his stress on Sanjay's acceptance of his bicultural identity, and his focus on Abhay's attempt to absorb Western culture in a way that allows for its integration with his own Indian identity all mark a contrast with Roy's blanket criticism of globalization. Where Roy tends to underscore the negative effects of globalization and hybridity that Said and Loomba focus on (and so can be linked to Gikandi's narrative of globalization as failed and atrophying), Chandra historicizes globalization and is interested, like Appadurai and Appiah, in the transformative possibilities of the global imaginary (in ways that link *his* novel to the more positive narrative about globalization Gikandi wants to question). His approach to dramatizing globalization also reflects Sen's insistence that globalization has a long history marked as much by developments in the East that predate the rise of European modernity as by economic and cultural forms developed in the West.

Moth Smoke

If Roy and Chandra dramatize how contemporary fiction dealing with globalization is inextricably connected to the long histories of colonization, decolonization, and postcolonialism, what are we to do with Hamid's insistence that he belongs to a post–postcolonial generation of writers? Here is how Hamid formulates his position:

> I certainly think there is a post-post-colonial generation. I'm sure a lot of voices you're seeing coming out now are people who never had a colonial experience. We don't place a burden of guilt on someone who's no longer there. So it's like, what are we doing with where we come from, and how can we address issues here. It's our fault if things aren't going well. That's a very different stance than a lot of what's come before. Also, people are writing about the subcontinent with eyes that are not meant to be seeing for someone who doesn't live there, people who are not exoticizing where they come from. I try not to mention the minaret, because when I'm in Lahore, I don't notice it. The basic humanity is not different from place to place.[15]

This last line is key, the idea that under the processes of globalization "the basic humanity is not different from place to place," and I return to this proposition in chapter 8. But for now I want to explore how *Moth Smoke* is structured around a problematical distinction between the historical experiences of colonialism and globalization. For, while Hamid's novel stands out from much contemporary fiction about the processes of globalization in its particular focus on the *economic* effects of globalization, his novel ends up obfuscating the relationship between these forces and those Pakistan experienced under British colonial rule.

Contemporary global fiction in English tends to embody the same tension between culturalist and materialist approaches to globalization we observed among the critics discussed in part 1. Hamid's sustained focus on the effects of economic globalization distinguishes his novel from many South Asian English-language novels popular with readers and academics in the West. While the novels of writers such as Arundhati Roy, Vikram Chandra, Bharati Mukherjee, Salman Rushdie, Ardashir Vakil, Kiran Desai, Jhumpa Lahiri, and Manil Suri deal tangentially with economic change, these writers are primarily interested in the nature of cultural production and identity in an increasingly hybridized postcolonial world. Some of these texts are set in South Asia and deal explicitly with colonial and postcolonial history. In *The God of Small Things,* as we have seen, Roy writes about the myriad cultural dislocations visited on characters like Baby Kochamma in the wake of British colonialism and the acceleration of globalization, and she develops a sustained examination of Anglophilia as a cultural phenomenon in India.[16] We also saw that Chandra's *Red Earth and Pouring Rain* offers an exhaustive analysis of the cultural effects on India of the collapse of the Mughal Empire and the rise of the British Raj.[17] Other writers of South Asian descent working in the West, however, like Mukherjee and Lahiri, have written principally about diasporic experience, about the cultural dislocations that accompany migration, immigration, or exile outside South Asia.[18] Many of their stories are either set in the United States or depict (as does Suri's *The Death of Vishnu*) an India profoundly disrupted at the cultural level by colonization. Economic change and material conditions connected to colonization and postcolonization play a role in each of these texts, but the emphasis in most of them is on the cultural effects of British colonialism as they continue to manifest themselves under postcolonialism. Recalling the debates about culturalist and economic approaches to globalization, we could argue that most of these texts are primarily culturalist in their orientation and that what distinguishes *Moth Smoke* is its attention to the symbiotic relationship between economic and cultural globalization.[19]

Hamid's interest in the contemporary effects of economic globalization led him to produce a materialist analysis roughly congruent with the kind we earlier say Miyoshi and Harootunian endorse. However, that analysis is connected to the idea that, as a set of economic processes, globalization is a contemporary phenomenon, that it represents a rupture between colonialism and globalization, hence his idea that he belongs to a post–postcolonial generation. In decoupling colonialism and postcolonialism from globalization, Hamid tends, like Appadurai, to see globalization as a radical contemporary break from the past, even the recent past of Pakistan's postcolonial experience. *Moth Smoke,* which unfolds during a few months in the spring of 1998, focuses on a group of thoroughly Westernized young men and women from financially well-off families whose members hold MBAs from U.S. universities. The protagonist, Darashikoh (Daru) Shezad, has clung to the fringes of this group by virtue of the financial support of his best friend's father. Too poor to study abroad, he earned his MBA in Lahore and, at the outset of the novel, is working as a midlevel functionary in a local bank. His best friend, Aurangzeb ("Ozi"), is the son of a well-off, corrupt money-launderer with an important position in the government (184) and has just returned with his new wife, Mumtaz, from studying in New York. While Daru works at his bank for modest pay, Ozi is following in his father's footsteps, creating "little shell companies, and open dollar accounts on sunny islands, far,

far away" from Lahore (185). The main contrast at the outset of the novel is between Daru's struggle to work through the system and Ozi's belief that corruption is so widespread that prosperity can only come *through* corruption.[20] Ozi muses at one point that "people are robbing the country blind, and if the choice is between being held up at gunpoint or holding the gun, only a madman would choose to hand over his wallet rather than fill it with someone else's cash" (184). "What's the alternative," he asks?

> [T]he roads are falling apart, so you need a Pajero or a Land Cruiser. The phone lines are erratic, so you need a mobile. The colleges are overrun with fundos who have no interest in getting an education, so you have to go abroad. And that's ten lakhs a year, mind you. Thanks to electricity theft there will always be shortages, so you have to have a generator. The police are corrupt and ineffective, so you need private security guards. It goes on and on. People are pulling their pieces out of the pie, and the pie is getting smaller, so if you love your family, you'd better take your piece now, while there's still some left. That's what I'm doing. If anyone isn't doing it, it's because they're locked out of the kitchen. (184–85)

Ozi has the luxury of his father's wealth and the access to global commodities it provides, while Daru, in effect, is "locked out of the kitchen" because his family is poor. Daru's position at the beginning of the novel is precarious. He quickly loses his bank position when he mishandles an important client who is inquiring about his deposit of thirty thousand dollars. The novel chronicles Daru's slide into poverty, drug dealing, burglary, and his illicit affair with Ozi's wife (who writes newspaper articles under the pseudonym Zulfikar Manto, and eventually tries to gather evidence to exonerate Daru from a false charge engineered by Ozi).[21] By the end of the novel Ozi has discovered the affair (which is already over) and sets Daru up to be arrested for the hit-and-run death of a young boy Ozi seems actually to have killed. The novel is framed by references to Daru's trial, and throughout the narrative Daru's first-person story is countered by testimony from others, including Ozi, Mumtaz, and Daru's partner in crime, Murad Badshah. By the end the reader's sympathies are clearly with Daru and Mumtaz, but the whole narrative is calibrated to call into question the truthfulness of all the characters.[22]

The novel's particular preoccupation with the financial and economic aspects of globalization is evident from even a cursory reading, what with its references to banking, financial sectors, economic corruption, research on global capitalism, discussion of the Grameen Bank model, the economic impact of the nuclear arms race between Pakistan and India, and class differences exacerbated by the uneven flow of global capital and commodities. While the novel focuses the reader's

attention on the link between economic corruption and cultural change in Lahore, Hamid, as the quote at the outset of this essay suggests, does not connect
this corruption to Pakistan's colonial and postcolonial history. Indeed, if readers
are tempted to draw such a connection, Hamid is quick to discourage it by creating a historical context for the novel that circumvents any link between the British Raj, its aftermath, and the events chronicled in *Moth Smoke*. This happens
at the very outset of the novel (and is reinforced in its conclusion) when Hamid
draws a connection between the characters and the sons of one of the last Mughal emperors, Shah Jahan (1628–58). South Asian readers will be immediately
familiar with this story, which creates a quasi-allegorical structure for the novel.
Ill and worried about the future of his empire, Shah Jahan asks a Sufi saint to
reveal which of his sons will rule when he dies. The two principal possible heirs
are Aurangzeb and Dara Shikoh. The Sufi saint reveals that it will be Aurangzeb. This revelation accords with the historical record, for Aurangzeb, a staunch
and intolerant Islamist, imprisoned his father, took over the empire, declared a
fatwa against his brother, and eventually had him imprisoned and killed. Aurangzeb's rule was despotic and ruinous, effectively ending the Mughal Empire.
The struggle between Ozi (Aurangzeb) and Daru (Dara Shikoh) in the novel is
set up to loosely mirror the historical struggle between the intolerant Islamist son
(Aurangzeb) and the more sympathetic secular, pantheist son (Dara Shikoh).

   This kind of historical contextualization downplays the relationship between
British colonialism and the plight of the characters in the novel, something that is
reinforced by its complete inattention to the British occupation of South Asia and
the economic, cultural, and political effects of the British Raj. It also has the effect
of drawing an implicit link between conditions at the end of the Mughal Empire
and conditions related to globalization, in the sense that Hardt and Negri link it
to "Empire." Their concept of Empire "is characterized fundamentally by a lack
of boundaries: Empire's rule has no limits. First and foremost…the concept of
Empire posits a regime that effectively encompasses the spatial totality, or really
[*sic*] that rules over the entire 'civilized' world" (xiv). Hardt and Negri's concept
of Empire, linked explicitly as it is to postimperial "processes of globalization"
(xv), helps to explain why Hamid would create a link between his characters and
the end of a former empire that predates the imperial British Raj. Asked why he
chose to connect his contemporary narrative to the end of the Mughal Empire
rather than to British colonialism, Hamid explained he wanted to "bypass the colonial experience."[23] Why? We need to recall that Hamid sees himself as part of a
"post–postcolonial generation," as someone who has "never had a colonial experience." Colonialism does not get the blame in *Moth Smoke* because Hamid sees
his characters, as he sees himself, in "post–postcolonial" terms. This is why *Moth
Smoke* draws our attention away from the aftereffects of British colonialism and

toward the new regime of globalization, and why this new regime is linked to empire in a way that connects back to the end of the Mughal Empire. In effect, Hamid's post–postcolonial age is the age of globalization, and, while his politics certainly have little in common with Hardt and Negri's, he tends to see global-ization as a kind of "Empire" in the sense they define it.

Hamid's desire to bypass colonialism implies a clean historical break between the eras of colonialism and postcolonialism (in this respect the novel eschews al-together the historicism of Chandra's *Red Earth and Pouring Rain*). The so-called post–postcolonial moment becomes identified with globalization defined as a thoroughly contemporary phenomenon that, like the novel itself, seems to have begun well after colonialism. As I argued throughout part 1, this is an extremely problematical position. With regard to the relationship between colonialism and postcolonialism, there is a real problem with the prefix "post" in postcolonial. "Post," Ania Loomba notes, "implies an 'aftermath' in two senses—temporal, as in coming after, and ideological, as in supplanting" (7). However, "if the inequi-ties of colonial rule have not been erased, it is perhaps premature to proclaim the demise of colonialism," for a "country may be both postcolonial (in the sense of being formally independent) and neo-colonial (in the sense of remaining eco-nomically and/or culturally dependent) at the same time" (7). From this point of view, it makes little sense for Hamid to suggest that he and his generation have "never had a colonial experience." Born well after independence (1971), Hamid is certainly right in observing that he grew up in a Pakistan where the British were no longer present as a governing force, and that in this sense he has never had a "colonial experience." But this ignores Loomba's point that colonialism always persists past independence in profound and sometimes very subtle ways, in the concrete forms of institutions (educational, cultural, political), ideologies, cultural practices, and in the less concrete but very real psychological forces that flow from subjugation. It is one thing to want to want to stop blaming the British for Pakistan's contemporary problems, but it is another thing to suggest there is no connection between British colonialism and the world Hamid and his genera-tion have grown up in.

If there is in fact a significant connection between Hamid's post–postcolonial generation and the legacy of colonialism, these two eras, as I have argued, are also connected to the history of globalization in ways Hamid seems to ignore. *Moth Smoke,* as I have pointed out, stands out from many recent South Asian novels written in English because it focuses sustained attention on the economic forces of globalization, but it fails to draw a link between economic globalization and the histories of colonialism and postcolonialism. As we have already seen, critics like Miyoshi, Harootunian, and others argue globalization is not simply a postcolonial phenomenon but rather an *extension* of colonialism. Miyoshi insists, for example, that "the so-called globalized economy [is an] outgrowth, or continuation, of colonialism" (247), that globalization represents the hegemony of Western capitalism and thus has to be understood as a new phase of colonial domination.[24]

From this point of view, it is difficult to see how the global system at the center of *Moth Smoke* could mark the kind of clean break from the colonial system Hamid suggests it does. Rather, it clearly seems connected in the ways Loomba and Miyoshi suggest to the linked operations of colonialism and Western capitalism. When Hamid invokes the Mughal Empire at the outset of the novel it is in order to "bypass colonialism," but the Mughal Empire *was* a colonialist empire, one connected to the long history of globalization that Robertson and Sen outline. The history of colonialism in South Asia did not begin with the British Raj but has a much longer history, one that includes Persian and Islamic invasions from the north, suggesting that the forces of globalization were at work on the continent long before global capitalism and the Internet came along (a history we saw dramatized in *Red Earth and Pouring Rain* and which is congruent with Abu-Lughod's study of a pre-European world system in the East). While *Moth Smoke* marks an important departure because it focuses attention on the forces of *economic* globalization and international finance, it remains problematic for its failure to draw a link between colonialism in South Asia, Western capitalism, and contemporary forms of globalization.[25]

In order to assess the significance of this blind spot in the novel we need to take a closer look at how it treats globalization, at its exploration of international finance and class divisions, and how it presents its characters as generic inhabitants of an international city that could be located almost anywhere—New York, London, Berlin, or Tokyo. In this sense *Moth Smoke* engages the whole question of whether or not globalization is a homogenizing phenomenon. Hamid's comment that "humanity is not different from place to place" seems unintentionally calculated to underscore the increasing homogeneity of urban experience in cities like Lahore, where American capital and culture have taken hold. Virtually all of the characters (including Daru, whose schooling was paid for by Ozi's father) in *Moth Smoke* have either been educated in the United States or at elite Westernized prep schools in Lahore, so that their experience gets characterized as nearly indistinguishable from the lives of students in Boston or Los Angeles. When the novel's main character, Daru, reminisces about cruising with his best friend, Ozi, he describes his experience in terms that would be thoroughly familiar to many American teenagers:

I remember speeding around the city with Ozi in his '82 Corolla, feet sweating sockless in battered boat shoes, following cute girls up and down the Boulevard, memorizing their number plates and avoiding cops because neither of us had a license. Hair chopped in senior school crew cuts. Eyes pot-red behind his wayfarers and my aviators. Stickers of universities I would never attend on the back windshield. Poondi, in the days of cheap petrol and skipping class and heavy-metal cassettes recorded with too much bass and even more treble. We had some good times, Ozi and I, before he left. (25)

This passage is calculated to evoke the homogeneity of urban youth culture in the age of globalization. Save for the reference to *poondi,* a local term for flirtation, it could be describing teenage boys cruising the boulevards of any major American town or city. Hamid's Lahore is thoroughly westernized and bourgeois. Parties in his novel are attended mostly by Lahore's "ultra rich young jet set" (77) and feature sushi flown in from Karachi, talk about multinational import-export deals, wine, scotch, and characters on cell phones who want to "do lunch" (78). Much of this behavior is patently self-conscious, an effort by people who have lived in the West to create the illusion they are all still there. When a drunken young woman shouts that they should all go swimming in the pool, a chant breaks out: "Forget that you're Over Here! Pretend that you're Over There," and the narrator interjects that *"the utopian vision of Over There or Amreeka promises escape from the almost unbearable drudgery of the tribe's struggle to subsist"* (79, italics in original). Here mimicking Western culture in general and American culture in particular seems linked to the desire for more substantial forms of economic liberation.

The "unbearable drudgery" of this "struggle to subsist" gets dramatized in class conflict exacerbated by economic globalization that pervades the novel and is at the core of the central conflict between Daru and Ozi. (Ozi has the prestige of an MBA from a U.S. university and can draw on his father's wealth, while Daru has neither.) Daru, for example, begins the novel working for a large bank and loses his job because he mishandles a transnational financial deal. We learn from Daru's former economics professor that though he was "a bit of a seat-of-the-pants economist" who liked to "assert rather than prove" Daru "could have done some good work" and earned a PhD (36–37). The socially progressive nature of his research ("small loans to low income groups, guaranteed by the community. The Grameen Bank model and variations.[26] Explaining low default rates, analyzing claims of paternalism, social critiques, that sort of thing" [36]) suggests his bank job represents a real compromise between his ambitions and principles. Once he loses his job, Daru's tumble into poverty and crime (he begins to peddle dope and, in a pivotal scene, participates with a friend in the robbery of a trendy boutique) is connected less to his own abilities than to the fact that Lahore has a glut of foreign MBAs and that "the banking sector" is in very bad shape (53). Here the kind of perpetual movement under globalization Appadurai links to migration exacerbates class division, for it allows those like Ozi who are well-off enough to travel to the United States for their education and to return with advanced degrees to displace those who, like Daru, are unable to do so.

The class conflict marking Daru's relationships with Ozi and Daru's servant, Manucci, is part of a wider set of economic and social divisions brought on by the uneven infusion of Western capital in Lahore. In the novel's most witty analysis of these divisions, Dr. Julius Superb, Daru's former economics professor, develops a commentary on class divisions in Lahore connected to the moneyed elite's use of air-conditioning:

> There are two social classes in Pakistan.... The first group large and sweaty, contains those referred to as the masses. The second group is much smaller, but its members exercise vastly greater control over their immediate environment and are collectively termed the elite. The distinction between members of these two groups is made on the basis of control of an important resource: air-conditioning. You see, the elite have managed to re-create for themselves the living standards of say, Sweden, without leaving the dusty plains of the subcontinent. They're a mixed lot—Punjabs and Pathans, Sindhis and Baluchis, smugglers, mullahs, soldiers, industrialists—united by their residence in an artificially cooled world. They wake up in air-conditioned houses, drive air-conditioned cars to air-conditioned offices, grab lunch in air-conditioned restaurants (rights of admission reserved), and at the end of the day go home to their air-conditioned lounges to relax in front of their wide-screen TVs. (102–3)

Access to air-conditioning measures the degree to which "elites" are plugged into a global economy characterized by the kind of class division and cultural homogenization we have been reviewing. But while this wealth creates class division, it is also characterized by access to sameness; the elite's air is conditioned to be the same no matter where they go, and they consume the same scotch, sushi, and SUVs as everyone else. Money buys comfort, distance from the masses working at the margins of the global economy, and the prestige that comes from triumphing over local conditions. After Daru loses his job, his months of unemployment lead to his ultimate crisis in class identity: his servant abandons him and his air-conditioning is shut off because he can't pay his electricity bill. Daru's fall from the lower rungs of the international banking sector in Lahore to the margins of its criminal economy highlights the new class structure in Lahore and connects it to the whims of an emergent global economy.

Professor Superb's analysis of the structure of social classes in Lahore appears morally neutral. It lacks, for example, the kind of critique we find in the ruminations of Murad Badshaw, a friend of Daru's who runs a rickshaw service in

Lahore but supplements his income by robbing shops and boutiques. Badshaw's take on the disparities between social classes, unlike Professor Superb's, is calculated to justify his own moral intervention, as self-serving as it turns out to be. He explains to Daru:

> You see, it is my passionately held belief that the right to possess property is at best a contingent one. When disparities become too great, a superior right, that to life, outweighs the right to property. Ergo, the very poor have the right to steal from the very rich. Indeed, I would go so far as to say that the poor have a duty to do so, for history has shown that the inaction of the working classes perpetuates their subjugation. (64)

Badshaw uses this reasoning to justify a variety of criminal activities, from organizing the robbery of taxi cabs threatening the viability of his rickshaw business to robbing a boutique with Daru (because "high-end, high-fashion exclusive boutiques" have "symbolism: they represent the soft underbelly of the upper crust, the ultimate hypocrisy in a country with flour shortages" [213–14]). "Inaction," it seems, would guarantee his continued subjugation. Daru's tumble down the social ladder marks his shift from the world of Professor Superb to the world of Murad Badshaw, from a world of social and economic privilege fueled by a newly emergent global economy to a world in which the disparity between his former and present social class has become so great and his ability to act to change it so limited, that he is driven to petty drug dealing and robbery. He can't steal conditioned air, but he can steal the means to produce it. In the end, whatever Daru's critique of class politics may be, it is probably closer to the concrete and pragmatic one Badshaw lays out than the more abstract and intellectualized one Professor Superb works out.

Ozi, meanwhile, has his own rationale for negotiating the class differences exacerbated by globalization, one that is the upper-class flip side of Badshah's self-interested pragmatism. He insists that in a country where the infrastructure is collapsing and "people are pulling their pieces out of the pie" any way they can, you have to "take your piece now, while there's still some left" (184–85). Ozi figures he "can't change the system," so people like his father "create lots of little shell companies, and open dollar accounts on sunny islands, far, far away," taking advantage of the complex global flows of international cash they have access to (185). Ozi insists that his father's money-laundering activities are par for the course in a world where the rich make money in sordid ways. He asks:

> What about the guys who give out the Nobel Prize. What are they? They're money launderers. They take the fortunes made out of dynamite, out of blowing

people into bits, and make the family name of Nobel noble. The Rhodes Scholarship folks? They do the same thing: dry-clean our memories of one of the great white colonialists. . . . And what about the bankers of the world? . . . Where did all that money come from? How much of it was dirty once, how much came from killing union leaders and making slaves pick cotton and invading countries that wanted control over their natural resources? (187)

Ozi's perspective is as self-serving as Murad Badshah's. Both men interpret the radical unevenness of economic globalization as a license to steal, and Ozi is as critical of the ruling classes as Murad is. The difference is that he is in a position to play ruling-class games for his own benefit, whereas Murad has no choice but to rob from the rich through the point of a gun.

The whole of the novel is organized around dramatizing these contrasting responses to globalization. The more Daru struggles to find a way back into the system, the more he is ground down by it. Murad has been marginalized by the global economy but thrives on it through extortion and burglary; the more wealth it produces in Lahore, the more there is for him to "expropriate." Ozi thrives on forms of illicit trade related to global flows of capital, and he is arguably the most corrupt figure in the novel. Hamid's poorer characters seem trapped in a world where the local economy is a dead end, but where the opportunities offered by the global economy are both profoundly uneven and deeply tied to corruption. The wealthier ones, like Ozi, make money from the global economy, but in ways that contribute to the poverty of the middle and lower classes. In his social criticism, Hamid is torn between seeing globalization as a potentially productive force and one that is simply grinding down his own country. His novel dramatizes the latter view, so that taken together, his writings present a profoundly ambivalent view of globalization.[27]

This ambivalence, as we have seen, is shared by many critics writing about globalization. Appadurai, for example, writes that he is "deeply ambivalent" about globalization (9). He recognizes the radically uneven economic development it fosters, yet much more than Miyoshi he resists the idea that globalization is a homogenizing force (as it appears to be in *Moth Smoke*) and remains optimistic about its potential to actually liberate people from forms of domination. Appadurai insists, we will recall, that "there is growing evidence that the consumption of the mass media throughout the world often provokes resistance, irony, selectivity, and in general, *agency*. . . . T-shirts, billboards, and graffiti as well as rap music, street dancing, and slum housing all show that the images of the media are quickly moved into local repertoires of irony, anger, humor, and resistance" (7).[28] However, this view is hardly presented in *Moth Smoke*, where there is little if any resistance to westernization, little of the "selectivity" and "irony" Appadurai sees as characteristic of the work of the imagination in forging postnational hybrid identities. Frederic Jameson, in "Notes on Globalization as a Philosophical Issue" (1998) is also torn between conflicting views of globalization. If (like Appadurai) "you insist on the cultural contents" of "new communicational form," he writes, "I think you will slowly emerge into a postmodern celebration of difference and differentiation: suddenly cultures around the world are placed in tolerant contact with each other in a kind of immense cultural pluralism which it would be very difficult not to welcome" (56–57). If, however (like Miyoshi), "your thoughts turn economic, and the concept of globalization becomes colored by those codes and meanings, I think you will find the concept darkening and growing more opaque" (57). For Jameson, globalization becomes an "ambiguous ideological concept" with "alternating contents" through which "we may now provisionally explore a few paths" (58). Hamid's divided view of globalization, then, need not be simply dismissed as hypocritical. Rather, it reflects debates about globalization and the ambivalence of its critics.

Hamid is, to be sure, interested in the cultural disruptions globalization causes, but his own experience in international finance leads him in very productive ways toward a novelistic analysis of the uneven effects of economic globalization. However, in his attempt in this novel to sever the "post–postcolonial" condition from the long history of Western colonization, he oversimplifies the historical context of that condition. Hamid's decision to link his story to the last years of the Mughal Empire extends the history of colonialism backward from the British occupation in South Asia so as to underscore colonialism's origins in a time that long predates the establishment of the British Raj. However, the value of that historical link gets undercut by Hamid's refusal to see contemporary globalization as an extension of Western colonialism, for the story *Moth Smoke* so adeptly chronicles cannot stand apart from the history of colonization in South Asia.

I think Hamid's ambivalence about globalization, in the end, reflects the fact that colonialism and globalization have a dialectical relationship, that their two histories cannot be untangled from each other. The three novels I have been discussing here dramatize this dialectical relationship, attention to which ought to inform the study of transnational literatures and cultures. They also underscore the difficulty of treating categories like the local and the global, the personal and the historical, and the cultural and the economic as if they reflected strict and unproblematical distinctions. Roy's novel, in particular, with its contrast between the gods of big and small things, also suggests the difficulty of creating a totalizing historical view that also takes account of the local, the particular, and the personal. Taken together, these three novels suggest we cannot discuss postcolonial literature in isolation from the phenomenon of globalization and, conversely, that it is impossible to study globalization without dealing with the complex history of colonialism and postcolonialism. From this point of view, a transnational approach to literary studies informed by globalization theory should not be seen as a threat to postcolonial studies but as a widening of its historical scope and a deepening of the relationship between what it encompasses and the larger world of historical change and transformation. Nor should it be thought incapable of taking a critical position toward both. As we have seen in this discussion of the three novels by Roy, Chandra, and Hamid, the discourses of postcolonialism and globalization can be employed together in forging a contemporary approach to the study of transnational literatures and cultures that attends both to the negative effects of globalization and hybridization that Said, Loomba, Roy, and Hamid call attention to *and* the more positive and potentially liberating ones Sen, Appadurai, Appiah, and Chandra highlight. We ought not to approach these problems in either/or terms, but recognize that the contradiction between these two approaches reflects the contradictory effects of globalization itself.

As the grip of Eurocentrism continues to give way in literary and cultural studies, and as we continue to develop approaches to the study of literature in a transnational context, as Said warns, we ought to avoid approaches reflecting a fragmented range of "particularistic" or "identity-based" choices under the umbrella of "a globalized, postmodern consciousness from which...the gravity of history has been excised." However, I have been arguing that we ought to connect transnational literary studies to the phenomenon of globalization precisely because it *does* focus on the gravity of history. If we analyze historically forms of personal and cultural hybridity as they have developed in the context of economic, military, religious, and cultural globalization, we can avoid recycling the banal academic version of multiculturalism Said and Loomba rightly point out would be unrecognizable in the real world of ethnic conflicts. In order to underscore how such a project would unfold I turn in the next chapter to a discussion of Kiran Desai's Man Booker Prize–winning novel, *The Inheritance of Loss,* with its focus on what Said calls the "gravity of history" and "real world ethnic conflict."

Globalization and Nationalism in Kiran Desai's *The Inheritance of Loss*

Contemporary globalization is characterized, not by the withering away of the nation-state in the face of homogenizing, westernizing, or cosmopolitan tendencies, but by the *simultaneous* acceleration of globalization and nationalism. This suggests we are living in a paradoxical (but not unprecedented) historical moment in which, on the one hand, migration, the media, and global capitalism are producing subjects whose identities and cultural interests are increasingly appropriated and adapted from a shared westernized pool of images, fashions, foods, and music, and, on the other hand, older historical forces related to long-standing territorial, ethnic, and religious disputes continue to fuel nationalist aspirations and identities, resulting in a dizzying production of new states and nations. At the same time that globalization seems to be fostering new cosmopolitanisms, both celebratory and critical, the forces of nationalism, often fueled by critical reactions against both the forces of globalization and cosmopolitanism, are at work dividing up local territories into ever more discrete and carefully defined fragments (sometimes based on a divisive form of the kind of culturalism we saw Appadurai analyze earlier). Indeed, as I write, nationalism seems alive and well on a number of continents.[1]

This simultaneous late twentieth-century proliferation of old nationalist aspirations and economic and cultural globalization is a central subject in Kiran Desai's novel *The Inheritance of Loss* (2006), in which both the gravity of history and the real world of ethnic conflict stand at the center of her engagement with the historical effects of globalization. Historical conflicts that might seem to belong to an earlier era of colonialism emerge in Desai's novel as one of the central effects of globalization. This linked relationship between the history of ethnic/nationalist conflicts and the forces of globalization is inscribed in the narrative structure of her book. The New York portions of *The Inheritance of Loss* explore the contemporary effects of globalization on a diasporic group of migrant workers in a metropole that could be almost anywhere, while the alternating chapters set in Kalimpong analyze the persistent effects of colonialism and long-simmering, very local ethnic conflicts in northeast India. In both narratives ethnic conflicts and the gravity of history shape the experiences of a disparate range of characters, a well-off Anglophile judge; his young granddaughter, Sai; their impoverished cook; the cook's son, Biju, who is an illegal immigrant struggling with others like himself to carve out a living in New York; and a group of young men of Nepalese descent who are active in the Gorkhaland National Liberation Front (GNLF) in Darjeeling. (The novel is set in 1985–86.) In Desai's book ardent forms of nationalism with deep historical roots exist side by side with economic globalization, belying the simple, overly schematic idea that the latter is replacing the former. Here, as in the other novels I have been discussing, distinctions between "local" and "global" tend to collapse, economic and cultural forms of globalization intersect, and personal lives are shaped by historical forces in the most complex of ways.

As I have suggested, the novel's narrative structure is designed to sustain an analysis of this phenomenon as the story moves back and forth between the lives of South Asian and African immigrants working in the kitchens of Manhattan and the simultaneous nationalist uprising of Nepalese in northeastern India. On its surface, the novel seems to be telling two very different stories, one rooted in the contemporary economic and cultural politics of globalization, the other in an older, fading history of ancient territorial disputes, ethnic rivalries, and nationalist aspirations. Read more carefully, however, it becomes clear that its two narratives are linked in a way that underscores a continuity between the stories they each tell, emphasizing the extent to which the relationship between migration, identity, and belonging under the forces of globalization mirror long-standing problems created by territorial, cultural, and personal disputes about identity among national groups. Desai's narrative about contemporary globalization unfolds in New York and focuses on Biju, a nineteen-year-old man from

Kalimpong who has entered the United States with a tourist visa in 1983 and is now living and working illegally in New York. Biju's story can be linked to Hamid's *Moth Smoke* in the sense that Desai is preoccupied with the effects of contemporary globalization on postcolonial populations in a metropolitan context. But Desai's narrative does not focus on upper-class, educated characters in a South Asian city such as Lahore but on poor illegal immigrants living in New York who belong to a vast illegal global underclass struggling with cultural displacement, poverty, and racial discrimination. Desai complicates the kind of approach to the effects of globalization we get in a novel like Hamid's (or Roy's) by shifting the location of her analysis from a postcolonized city in the East to a Western metropolitan location (something we will see again in the London of Zadie Smith's *White Teeth*). The characters in the New York portion of Desai's narrative are people with precious little time for celebrating their diversity or experiencing the liberatory possibilities of hybridity or multiculturalism. Moreover, *The Inheritance of Loss* is only tangentially interested in the relationship between globalization and the cultural politics of cosmopolitanism Roy and Chandra explore. (Those who might be construed as cosmopolitans in Kalimpong do not fare very well when the Nepalese population begins to agitate for political autonomy.) Instead, the novel focuses our attention on the decidedly uneven economic and cultural effects of globalization in the metropolitan West, on its tendency to both create and exploit a kind of tribal underclass of transnational diasporic workers whose experiences call attention to a set of class-related issues we saw explored in *Moth Smoke*. In doing so, Desai develops an analysis of the relationship between economic and cultural forms of globalization that engages many of the issues debated in part 1 and which emphasizes the debilitating effects of economic globalization on underclasses and stakes out a position that implicitly questions the generally happy, upbeat, liberatory take on globalization found in Appadurai. Instead, her novel features the role that class and economic inequities play in globalization. At a deeper structural level, the stories set in New York City and Kalimpong mirror one another in a way that allows Desai to draw connections between the struggle with nationalism taking place in India and the struggle with globalization in the United States.

When we are introduced to Biju he is like a "fugitive on the run" with "no papers," working with other illegal global migrants in a seemingly endless series of ethnic restaurants in New York with names like "Ali Baba's Fried Chicken" (3) and "Le Colonial" (20):

> Above, the restaurant was French, but below in the kitchen it was Mexican and Indian. And, when a Paki was hired, it was Mexican, Indian, Pakistani.... On top, rich colonial, and down below, poor native. Colombian, Tunisian,

Ecuadorian, Gambian.... There was a whole world in the basement kitchens of New York. (20–21)

Desai's upstairs-downstairs stress on economic and class divisions between patrons and workers recalls Hamid's focus on class and underscores the uneven economic effects of globalization. Her focus on national divisions among the undocumented kitchen employees Biju works with points to the difficulties of having to negotiate a complicated set of relationships based on unfamiliarity with one another's cultural worlds and old historical antagonisms carried over from their homelands. The workers, of course, bring their ethnic conflicts with them when they migrate. Biju, who is Hindu, loses a job because he fights with another worker who is a Muslim from Pakistan, and later he has to come to terms with old prejudices about Africans as he begins to make friends with a man from Zanzibar.

Biju's problems are both economic and cultural. As an illegal Indian immigrant he is doomed to low-wage jobs in a succession of restaurants. (That they are all "ethnic" restaurants underscores the transnational character of New York under the ever-accelerating effects of global migration.) He lives in impoverished conditions (at one point in the very basement kitchen where he works)[2] and is continually being harassed about how he smells or looks. The economic challenges he faces are complicated by cultural ones. For example, as a Hindu he is continually troubled by having to serve beef to his customers. He struggles to distinguish between the holy cows of his Hindu upbringing and the unholy cows his customers consume, but his religious beliefs are too close to the core of his identity to be overcome: "One should not give up one's religion, the principles of one's parents and their parents before them.... You had to live according to something. You had to find your dignity ... those who could see a difference between a holy cow and an unholy cow would win. Those who couldn't see it would lose" (136). Unwilling to make such a compromise, he settles on a job at a vegetarian restaurant called "The Gandhi Café."

Desai's New York City is a sea of global migrants like Biju, diasporic "tribes" (96) hustling subsistence wages in kitchens beneath the city's visible wealth. In these sections of the book the emphasis is on how what Said has called "real world history" and the actuality of "ethnic conflict" travel with the migrants to the cultural world of New York, complicating their ability to do the kind of liberatory work of the imagination Appadurai sees as central to the experience of globalization. One of the first things Biju learns after arriving in New York is that he belongs to a global South Asian diaspora with a long history, and this knowledge upsets everything he knows about his own identity. Confused about where his coworkers come from and about the fact that no matter where they come from they seem to be familiar with migrant Indians, Biju's identity breaks loose from Kalimpong and becomes connected with a global diaspora of other Indians whose experiences he is beginning to share. The more disconnected he becomes from his past, the more connected he feels both to this global diaspora of Indians and to other tribes of migrant workers from disparate parts of the globe. These men are like those who have come seeking out his Zanzibaran friend Saeed Saeed, whose "mother was dispensing his phone number and address freely to half of Stone Town [the village in Zanzibar he comes from]," men who "arrived at the airport with one dollar in their pocket and his phone number" (95–96). Far from finding these new connections liberating, Biju finds them confusing. They circumscribe rather than expand the possibilities for imagining a new subjectivity free from old ethnic divisions.

When Biju finds himself drawn to Saeed Saeed he must come face-to-face with a prejudice against dark-skinned people ("he remembered what they said about black people back home...in their own country they live like monkeys" [76]), which is connected to the old animosity he feels toward Pakistanis. In a key scene Biju struggles to develop a logic to justify friendship with Saeed Saeed (who is Muslim) in spite of the prejudice he feels toward him:

> Saeed was kind and he was not Paki. Therefore he was OK?
> The cow was not an Indian cow; therefore it was not holy?
> Therefore he liked Muslims and hated only Pakis?
> Therefore he like Saeed, but hated the general lot of Muslims?
> Therefore he liked Muslims and Pakis and India should see it was all wrong and
>   hand over Kashmir?
> No, no, how could that be and—(76)

Here his earlier struggles with his Pakistani coworker get folded into his conflicted feelings about Saeed Saeed, and in a way that makes clear his experiences in the United States are challenging the very logic of beliefs he thought lay near the core of his being. "The habit of hate had accompanied Biju," Desai observes, "and he found that he possessed an awe of white people, who arguably had done India great harm, and a lack of generosity regarding almost everyone else, who had never done a single harmful thing to India" (77).

Beyond her interest in how these old ethnic conflicts continue to haunt these characters in New York, Desai is also interested in exploring class differences among the immigrants she writes about. While Biju and his fellow workers struggle to come to terms with the dramatic economic inequities they face in New York and with the cultural prejudices they have brought with them, the more successful immigrants upstairs, who own one of the restaurants where Biju works, take a jaundiced view of their workers' plight and the plight of those who remain in their employees' homelands. Odessa and Baz, the immigrant owners of a French restaurant called "Brigitte's," are reading the international news section of the *New York Times,* and the collective impact of what they find there is "overwhelming" (133):

> Former slaves and natives. Eskimos and Hiroshima people, Amazonian Indians and Chiapas Indians and Chilean Indians and American Indians and Indian Indians. Australian aborigines, Guatemalans and Colombians and Brazilians and Argentineans, Nigerians, Burmese, Angolans…Senegalese, Maldivians, Sri Lankans, Malaysians…Laotians, Zaireans coming at you screaming colonialism, screaming slavery, screaming mining companies screaming banana companies oil companies screaming CIA spy among the missionaries screaming it was Kissinger who killed their father and why don't they forgive third-world debt…Agent Orange; dirty dealings by Xerox. World Bank, UN, IMF, everything run by white people. Every day in the papers another thing! (133–34)

Odessa draws from this litany of complaints what she calls a "rule of nature" (134), that people, wherever they are, will become overwhelmed with settling historical scores if they become preoccupied with unearthing and settling injustice from the past. "Imagine if we were sitting around saying, 'So-and-so-score years ago, Neanderthals came out of the woods, attacked my family with a big dinosaur bone, and now you give back'" (134). Baz is proud of what he calls the "cosmopolitan style" Odessa exhibits, and while this style is superficially linked to her looks—Baz "loved the sight of her in her little wire-rimmed glasses"—Desai also wants the reader to see a link between Odessa's cosmopolitanism and the style of her politics. Her cosmopolitanism is characterized by her belief she has risen above the fray of politics and history. To be cosmopolitan for Odessa is to transcend the political effects of colonialism and globalization by identifying with the triumph of the powerful. She insists that "Nestle and Xerox were fine upstanding companies, the backbone of the economy, and Kissinger was at least a patriot. The United States was a young country built on the finest principles, and how could it possibly owe so many bills? Business was business. Your bread might as well be left unbuttered were the butter to be spread so thin. The fittest one wins and gets the butter" (134).

Odessa's complaint marks a moment in the novel, as I have suggested, where the two stories Desai is telling begin to clearly intersect, for while Biju is busy in New York trying to get a foothold in Odessa's cosmopolitan world, the political situation in his native Kalimpong is being roiled by just the kind of score settling she finds so vulgar. Desai's northeastern Indian narrative focuses on the rise of the Gorkhaland National Liberation Front, a group of Nepalese Indians agitating for political and cultural autonomy in Kalimpong. Their political struggle seems to fall squarely within the law of nature Odessa has drawn up, based as it is on the Nepalese assertion of a long history of domination and oppression by the Bengali majority in northeastern India. The question of how far back this oppression goes, based as it is on competing historical understandings of indigenity, origins, and territorial rights complicated by a complex web of ancient patterns of migration and border crossings, makes the political struggle in Kalimpong a kind of microcosm for the global political struggles Odessa finds so offensive. What is particularly important about Desai's interweaving of these two stories is how she historicizes the relationship between the troubles in Kalimpong, which are grounded in centuries of migration, colonization, and struggle over territory, and those in New York, which are driven by the utterly contemporary forces of economic globalization and the opportunities and displacements it fosters. By the time we finish *The Inheritance of Loss* these two stories and the historical epochs they encompass have utterly fused in a way that stresses the long historical continuities linking the various epochs of an ever-accelerating globalization. As the novel's title suggests, we also end up with a very bleak picture both of nationalism in northeastern India and globalization in New York.[3]

Desai's Kalimpong narrative focuses on four characters, one of whom is Biju's father, a cook employed by a retired judge named Jemubhai. The other two characters are Sai, the judge's orphaned granddaughter, and Gyan, a young man employed as Sai's mathematics tutor who later becomes her boyfriend. Each of these characters has a literal or figurative relationship with Biju that Desai uses to draw connections between her two narratives and the stories of cultural displacement they tell. Throughout the novel the reader moves back and forth between Sai's point of view and Biju's in a way that sets up a complex dialogue between the two characters' experiences. Her grandfather, retired as a judge with the Indian Civil Service, is an alienated and bitter Anglophile whose experiences in England are made to resonate with Biju's in the United States. And, finally, Gyan, Sai's tutor and boyfriend, serves in a number of ways as a foil for Biju. Whereas Biju has left Kalimpong and its political world for a life in the West, Gyan, who is Biju's age, has stayed in Kalimpong where he becomes increasingly involved in the GNLF. The link between each of these stories is the old literary motif of the journey, but updated to focus on a critical topic for globalization studies—*mobility*. This focus on mobility is launched with the story of Biju's journey to the United States, which Desai then connects to the judge's earlier journey by sea from India to Oxford to study law. In linking these two stories the judge's Englishness, born of colonialism, is connected to the pressure to westernize under globalization that Biju experiences in New York; the focus

on mobility features the kinds of crises related to personal and cultural identity that come with the increasing mobility of populations as globalization accelerates. Moreover, the literal and figurative borders they both cross form the
backdrop for Desai's exploration of the porous borders and mobile populations
(Nepalese, Bengali, Tibetan, Bhutanese) that constitute the territory now known
as Darjeeling. All of these connecting devices serve to underscore the historical
continuities between migration, colonialism, and globalization in the lives of her
disparate characters and their various locations.

The novel's preoccupation with the shifting borders between territories, cultures, and classes that characterize this location is signaled early in the book.
Kalimpong, we are told, is a place "where India blurred into Bhutan and Sikkim" (9), a place on a "messy map" in which a "great amount of warring, betraying, bartering had occurred; between Nepal, England, Tibet, India, Sikkim,
Bhutan; Darjeeling stolen from here, Kalimpong plucked from there—despite,
ah, despite the mist charging down like a dragon, dissolving, undoing, making
ridiculous the drawing of borders" (9).[4] Kalimpong is near the center of a complex network of trade routes linking what are now the West Bengali districts
of Sikkim and Darjeeling with Bhutan, Nepal, and Tibet. Desai is careful to
weave an analysis of the long histories of migration, displacement, and territorial
disputes in the region into her narrative about the 1986 GNLF uprising, so that
contemporary disputes about origins, belonging, identity, and nationality get historicized backward as well as forward into the moment of globalization Biju is
struggling with in New York.

These contemporary disputes are featured in a way that emphasizes the paradoxical nature of historical claims to original status in the region. The novel is
located in a fluid border zone of contested space not unlike the ones in the discussion of border studies in part 1 (the U.S. Southwest, Kashmir, and Ireland). For
Lola, who, along with her sister, Noni, is a friend of Sai, "this state-making [is]
the biggest mistake that fool Nehru made. Under his rules any group of idiots
can stand up demanding a new state and get it, too.... It all started with Sikkim.
The Neps played such a dirty trick and began to get grand ideas—now they
think they can do the same thing again" (128). Her sister, Noni, takes a more
complicated historical view of the situation: "But you have to take it from their
point of view.... First the Neps were thrown out of Assam and then Meghalaya,
then there's the king of Bhutan growling against" them (128). Lola responds
that this is simply a case of "illegal immigration," but Noni reminds her that the
Nepalese have rights in Darjeeling because "they've been here, most of them,
several generations" (128). But since when, interjects Lola, "did Darjeeling and
Kalimpong belong to Nepal? Darjeeling, in fact, was annexed from Sikkim and
Kalimpong from Bhutan.... It's an issue of a porous border is what. You can't tell

one from the other, Indian Nepali from Nepali Nepali" (129). To which her sister replies, "Very unskilled at drawing borders, those bloody Brits" (129). Desai's interest here, of course, is not in cutting through the historical fog of claims and counterclaims in order to construct an accurate account of territorial ownership and national identity. She wants, rather, to emphasize the obscurity and murkiness of all historical and territorial claims in the region. The histories of migration, displacement, conquest, colonization, decolonization, and state making here are so complicated as to render useless claims to priority and authenticity. There are no originary borders here that existed prior to the claims and counterclaims Desai enumerates in this exchange. In this sense, the whole enterprise of separating the migrant and the indigenous founders is futile, and there is no firm conceptual ground for staking originary claims to a particular national identity or territorial border. Identities and borders in the novel are the constant product of historical forces outside of which no one can stake a claim to anything.

Passages like this are obviously meant to complicate local political disputes about the status of the Nepalese in Kalimpong by linking them to contemporary ways of theorizing territoriality and identity. In a sense Desai is taking a loosely deconstructive approach to both, or at least a postfoundational one, in which neither national territories nor identities can be grounded in some a priori, originary space standing outside of the historical and social forces that constructed them in the first place. Borders and identities here are the product of perpetual and ceaseless forces of syncretization. But such exchanges as the one between Lola and Noni are also calibrated to link Biju's contemporary experience in New York under globalization to the long history of state making and identity formation under conquest and colonization in northeastern India. When Lola remarks that the Nepalese in Darjeeling are "illegal immigrants," for example, Desai draws a clear link between the politics of migration in northeastern India, which stretch deep into the past, and the politics of migration Biju is experiencing under the contemporary regime of globalization. His problems as a migrant, and the challenges they pose to his ethnic and national identities, become a contemporary extension of the historical persistence of these same challenges in Darjeeling.

This dual stress on migration is connected to Desai's interest in mobility. The key figures in this regard are Jemubhai (the judge); his granddaughter, Sai; and their cook's son, Biju. In each of these cases their literal journeys are linked to westernization, so that the experience of westernization becomes itself a kind of journey. Personal and cultural identity becomes mobile, fractured, challenged, open to change, but change linked as much to fear as to liberation. This is most explicitly the case with Jemubhai, who leaves India as a young student to voyage by sea to England in 1939 where he is to study law. Importantly, Jemubhai's story is told through his own memories, which are triggered by the arrival of his orphaned granddaughter, Sai, who has just journeyed north from a convent where she lived while her parents resided in the Soviet Union. (Her father was an astronaut in the Soviet space program, but he and his wife have died in a traffic accident.) The judge responds to his granddaughter's arrival by "thinking of his own journeys, of his own arrivals and departures, from places far in his past" (35). Her journey serves as a trigger for the recollection of his own journey, one that is connected to his Anglophilia and that belongs to a past he has long and systematically repressed. Much later in the novel he realizes that "Sai, it had turned out, was more his kin than he had thought imaginable. There was something familiar about her; she had the same accent and manners. She was a westernized Indian brought up by English nuns, an estranged Indian living in India. The journey he had started so long ago had continued in his descendents" (210). The judge's immersion in Englishness during his student years turns him into an Anglophile, a young man his landlady takes to calling "James" (39) and who internalizes a loathing for the otherness the English project onto him ("girls held their noses and giggled, 'Phew, he stinks of curry!'" [39]) and so "grew stranger to himself than he was to those around him" until "eventually he felt barely human at all" (40). Jemubhai returns to India having succeeded to a judgeship, but with a powder puff to whiten his face, eating habits and tastes that are thoroughly British, and a sense of alienation and self-loathing that ruins his marriage and leaves him perpetually detached from himself, "a foreigner in his own country" (29).[5]

The long and sad history of Jemubhai's westernization casts a shadow over our reading of Biju's experiences in New York. Desai sets up a clear set of parallels between the judge's experiences in the West and Biju's, and their two stories are in turn linked to the tense identity politics in Kalimpong, for one of the central points of tension there is between the Ghorka nationalists and upper-class Anglicized Indians like the judge, the widowed sisters Noni and Lola, and various other characters. This tension is part of the larger set of ethnic and religious divisions in the area (Nepali/Indian/Tibetan/Hindi/Muslim), and as Sai grows into a young woman she finds herself inexorably caught up in them. At the same time that her journey from the convent to Kalimpong, and from an Indian to a Western identity, links her to her grandfather, it also links her to Biju, and becomes the point of departure for her own traumatic immersion in the long political history of colonialism and globalization in Kalimpong. This happens most dramatically through her relationship with Gyan, her mathematics tutor. Sai knows nothing about Gyan or his family when they first meet, but as their relationship becomes more intimate they both become aware of the cultural and political differences separating them. With this awareness, the story of Sai and Gyan's romantic relationship begins to parallel the earlier, embittered one between her grandfather

Jemubhai and his wife Nimi, and Desai uses these parallel stories to explore the complex relationship between personal lives and political history.

Desai has Sai and her tutor fall in love at precisely the moment when GNLF demands for statehood begin to develop into an insurgency:

> They played the game of courtship, reaching, retreating, teasing, fleeing—how delicious the pretense to objective study, miraculous how it could eat up the hours....Gyan was twenty and Sai sixteen, and at the beginning they had not paid very much attention to the events on the hillside, the new posters in the market referring to old discontents, the slogans scratched and painted on the side of government offices and shops. "We are stateless," they read. "It is better to die than live as slaves." "We are constitutionally tortured. Return our land from Bengal"..."Gorkhaland for Gorkhas. We are the liberation army."...Quite suddenly, everyone was using the word *insurgency*. (125–26)

Their innocence as lovers becomes progressively undermined by the political divisions spawning the insurgency, for it turns out that Gyan's family is impoverished and of Nepalese descent, so that Sai's upper-class westernized habits and status come to represent just the forms of domination the insurgency insists have been oppressing families like Gyan's for centuries. Desai takes great care to link the fate of their love affair to the politics of the insurgency and the long history it is connected to.

As is typical in Desai's novel, the political and cultural differences that separate Sai and Gyan are first indicated by how they eat their food. (Food is culturally coded in the novel; what and how one eats regularly carries symbolic import among the characters.)[6] The first indication that there will be trouble between them occurs when they are eating at a restaurant (a setting which, of course, links their own cultural problems to the ones Biju encounters while working in restaurants in New York).

> *Gyan and Sai's romance* was flourishing and the political trouble continued to remain in the background for them...but during the time they ate together at Gompu's, Gyan had used his hands without a thought and Sai ate with the only implement on the table—a tablespoon, rolling up her rote on the side and nudging the food onto the spoon with it. Noticing this difference, they had become embarrassed and put the observation aside. (140)

They pass over this moment of embarrassment, but it will come back to haunt their relationship. Directly after this scene, we learn about Gyan's past and discover that his family had left Nepal in the nineteenth century for work in the colonial tea plantations of Darjeeling (141). Later, his great-grandfather is recruited into the British army. He "swore allegiance to the Crown, and off he went, the beginning of over a hundred years of family commitment to the wars of the English" (142). It isn't long before Gyan begins to connect his own family history to the narrative of oppression being promulgated by the GNLF, and to see Sai as the enemy. In a key chapter Desai has set at the exact middle of her novel, Gyan happens upon a demonstration by members of the GNLF, and, seeing how the history of domination they recount seems to explain his family's poverty, he is converted to their cause. Watching the demonstration, "Gyan remembered the stirring stories of when citizens had risen up in their millions, and demanded that the British leave" (158), and he begins to see the link being drawn between the oppression of India by the British and of Nepalese by Bengalis in Darjeeling. "Fired by alcohol," Gyan "finally submitted to the compelling pull of history and found his pulse leaping to something that he felt entirely authentic. He told the story of his great grandfather" to the other demonstrators, emphasizing how little they had gained from their association with the British (160). Desai writes that at this point it suddenly became clear to Gyan "why he had no money and no real job had come his way, why he couldn't fly to college in America, why he was ashamed to let anyone see his home," and why he "felt a moment of shame remembering his tea parties with Sai on the veranda, the cheese toast, queen cakes from the bake, and even worse, the small warm space they inhabited together, the nursery talk" (160–61).

This is a key moment in the novel, one in which personal experience becomes transformed when it is read through the lens of history. Gyan's submission to "the compelling pull of history" represents a moment in which the confusing, disparate, even ancient circumstance of his family get quickly refocused through the seeming logic of historical explanation. This is underscored in the scene where he watches the marchers, at first not sure whether to join in or not as he shifts between, on the one hand, the "ancient and usual scene" of the marketplace, and, on the other, the "making of history" (157). "As he floated through the market," Desai writes, Gyan "had a feeling of history being wrought, its wheels churning under him.... But then he was pulled out of the feeling, by the ancient and usual scene, the worried shopkeepers watching from their monsoon-stained grottos. Then he shouted along with the crowd...an affirmation he'd never felt before, and he was pulled back into the making of history" (157).[7]

Once he's committed himself to the goals of GNLF insurgency Gyan's relationship with Sai begins to deteriorate, because her westernized ways come to represent the very enemy he is now bent on destroying. At their first meeting after the march, Gyan erupts in anger at Sai's intention to celebrate Christmas. "I am not interested in Christmas," he shouts. "Why do you celebrate Christmas? You're Hindus and you don't celebrate Id or Guru Nanak's birthday or even Durga Puja or Dussehra or Tibetan New Year.... You are like slaves, that's what you are, running after the West, embarrassing yourself. It's because of people like you we never get anywhere" (163). Like his earlier embarrassment at seeing her eat with a spoon while he ate with his hands, Gyan sees her celebration of Christmas as a violation of cultural authenticity (as a Hindu she should be celebrating only Hindu holidays) and complicity with Western oppression ("Don't you know, these people you copy like a copycat, THEY DON'T WANT YOU!!!!" [164]). Gyan has come to view the personal through the lens of the historical, and everything has taken on a new significance (a process Biju is also undergoing in New York). In an echo of Roy's novel, the gods of small things and big things have become one. Gyan's experience is calibrated to underscore how the personal is always political, that what may seem like everyday behaviors and innocent beliefs are in fact part of a complex web of historical forces connected to the border crossings Desai has emphasized earlier in the book. As in Roy's novel, the line between small and big things, between personal experience and historical events, is a porous one.

The more frustrated Gyan becomes with his own identity, and the more he becomes a victim of the conflict between his Nepalese identity and his attraction to the westernized Sai, the more he takes out his frustration on Sai. The historical, class, and economic divisions tied to the political world of Kalimpong that are driving a wedge between Sai and Gyan come to a head near the end of the novel when Sai finds her way to Gyan's family home and is shocked by the poverty she finds there.

> There were houses like this everywhere, of course, common to those who had struggled to the far edge of the middle class—just to the edge, only just, holding on desperately—but were at every moment being undone, the house slipping back, not into the picturesque poverty that tourists liked to photograph but into something truly dismal—modernity proffered in its meanest form, brand-new one day, in ruin the next. The house didn't match Gyan's talk, his English, his looks, his clothes, or his schooling...she felt distaste, then, for herself. How had she been linked to this enterprise, without her knowledge or consent? (255–56)

She is shocked by the gulf between Gyan's modernity and the pedestrian nature of his local rural poverty, but more telling is the distaste she has for herself as she lashes out at her connection to Gyan's Nepali identity and his family's poverty. A little later Desai underscores the extent to which their relationship is the casualty of historical and political forces largely beyond their control, when Sai tells him, in an echo of Roy's novel, "you hate me...for big reasons, that have nothing to do with me" (260). The "big reasons," here, are of course the historical forces Roy associates with the god of big things, which are ever at work undoing relationships supposedly overseen by the god of small things. Later, when Gyan has retreated from political activism at the insistence of his mother, he thinks to himself that "he didn't want to fight. The trouble was that he'd tried to be part of the larger questions, tried to become part of politics and history. Happiness had a smaller location" (272), but of course Desai's point, like Roy's, is that politics, history, and the kind of happiness Gyan wants to associate with smaller locations are inseparable. Sai realizes this by the end of the novel when the narrator says of her: "Never again could she think there was but one narrative and that this narrative belonged only to herself, that she might create her own happiness and live safely within it" (322–23).

On the one hand, Sai's unsympathetic view of Gyan and the larger Nepalese community is insensitive, betraying her naiveté about the region's political history, but, on the other hand, Gyan's increasing hostility to Sai suggests the extent to which he is willing to unthinkingly tie her to a colonial history she doe not feel connected to. Surely this is all intentional on Desai's part, an attempt to dramatize the damage brought to the region by centuries of complicated political and social struggle. Gyan and Sai have a shared history they have little control over and which pits them against each other in Kalimpong's political landscape. What Gyan sees as Sai's orientation toward the West is a cosmopolitanism that connects her to the sisters Lola and Noni, who have innocently taken sides in a political struggle they are hardly aware of by adopting Western ways and modeling a kind of cosmopolitanism more pronounced than the young Sai's and more akin to the judge's. Once the politics of the GNLF insurgency takes hold, they are suddenly marked as cultural—and therefore political—enemies by the poorer local Nepalese population. "*It didn't come from nothing*" (241), Lola observes, as the insurgents begin to take over her property and people in town treat the sisters with increasing disdain. It came "from an old feeling of anger that couldn't be divorced from Kalimpong":

> It was in the eyes that waited, attached themselves to you as you approached.... These people could name them, recognize them—the few rich—but Lola and Noni could barely distinguish between the individuals making up the crowd of poor.... It was natural they would incite envy...every now and then, somebody suffered the rotten luck of being in the exact wrong place at the exact wrong time when it all caught up—and generations worth of trouble settled on them. Just when Lola had thought it would continue, a hundred years like the one past—Trollope, BBC, a burst of hilarity at Christmas—all of a sudden, all that they had claimed innocent, fun, funny, not really to matter, was proven wrong. (241–42)

In Lola and Noni deep historical and political divisions related to the long history of migration, settlement, displacement, and colonization in northeastern

India merge with the unthinking cosmopolitanism of their interest in Trollope, the BBC, Christmas, and Western food. Things they didn't think mattered suddenly did matter.

> It *did* matter, buying tinned ham roll in a rice and dal country; it *did* matter to live in a big house and sit beside a heater in the evening...it *did* matter to fly to London and return with chocolates filled with kirsch...the wealth that seemed to protect them like a blanket was the very thing that left them exposed....Lola and Noni...were the unlucky ones who wouldn't slip through, who would pay the debt that should be shared with others over many generations" (242).

Here common sense divisions between the cultural and the political that the sisters are hardly aware of fall away; their interest in Trollope, London, and tinned ham end up being political interests central to historical struggle and agents of their own demise when nationalism in Kalimpong heats up. Their interest in modernity and the West breeds a kind of cosmopolitanism linked to the forces of globalization like the ones Biju struggles with in New York, but which here come into conflict with local identities and nationalist aspirations.

The fact that Lola and Noni would have to "pay the debt that should be shared with others over many generations" points to a central issue in the novel, one we discussed earlier when we observed Odessa, owner of "Brigitte's," the French Bistro where Biju briefly works, complaining that the contemporary descendents of "former slaves and natives" (11) keep trying to fight ancient battles they should just let go of. Desai draws a clear link between this sentiment (Odessa, we will recall, insists it is a "rule of nature" [134]) and the way history works in northeastern India. For example, after Gyan has given his allegiance to the GNLF insurgency the men he has told his story to

> sat unbedding their rage, learning, as everyone does in this country, at one time or another, that old hatreds are endlessly retrievable. And when they had disinterred it, they found the hate pure, purer than it could ever have been before, because the grief of the past was gone. Just the fury remained, distilled, liberating. It was theirs by birthright, it could take them so high, it was a drug. (161)

The hatred Lola and Noni suffer as cosmopolitans in Kalimpong is connected to this cycle of "endlessly retrievable" injustices that need to be righted. This idea gets repeated by a variety of characters in Desai's novel. While it is first introduced by Odessa, it is later echoed by Sai, who, reading a particularly odious passage about racial discrimination by the British in India, feels "a rush of anger" that "surprised her" (199). She concludes that "it was unwise to read old books; the fury they ignited wasn't old; it was new.... But the child shouldn't be blamed for a father's crime, she tried to reason with herself.... But should the child therefore also enjoy the father's illicit gain?" (199). Later in the novel, the judge, frustrated in his job, muses that "India was too messy for justice...every-one handed their guilt along so as to augment yours: old guilt, new guilt, any passed-on guilt whatever" (264). And, later, as people begin to die in the GNLF insurgency, the narrator elevates this idea to the very principle whereby history operates: "This was how history moved, the slow build, the quick burn, and in an incoherence, the leaping both backward and forward, swallowing the young into old hate" (276). We saw this principle at work in Biju's New York, where his anger at a Pakistani coworker and unease around the African, Saeed Saeed, haunt him.

In Desai's Kalimpong, then, there is little that is "post" about the postcolonial generation Sai, Gyan, and the GNLF activists belong to, and in this way the novel endorses Loomba's caution about invoking the term, for colonialism lives on in a myriad of ways in "postcolonial" India. The oppressive operations of colonialism continue to work in Jemubhai's psyche in dramatic and debilitating ways, while Lola and Noni's lives, not to mention those of Sai and the cook, are largely determined by the continuing and persistent legacy of various colonial-isms. This makes the novel decidedly bleak (a fact indicated by Desai's choice of title, for it is loss each character inherits). For example, the debilitating effects of the judge's repression of his own Indian identity in the cultivation of a West-ern cosmopolitanism (which he shares with the sisters, Lola and Noni) fuels his steady collapse in the final sections of the novel. Desai's is a very bleak version both of contemporary nationalism and of the long historical effects of globaliza-tion, one that is at odds with some of the more upbeat assessments we reviewed earlier. It is difficult to see how a productive version of Appiah's cosmopolitan-ism could emerge in the world Desai has created, for example, nor is it very easy to see how the kind of liberatory agency Appadurai envisions for the work of the imagination under globalization can operate for either the characters in Kalim-pong or those, like Biju, in New York.

The novel is much less interested in exploring the liberatory possibilities of cultural hybridity than in confronting its readers with the stark economic and social realities of a global underclass of migratory workers, and in this sense it develops a critique of the uneven economic effects of globalization like the one we saw in Hamid's novel. Even those immigrants who seem to have "made it," like Harish-Harry, the owner of the Gandhi Café, can be seen struggling with many of the same problems as their counterparts who have stayed behind in places like Kalimpong. Harish-Harry's westernized identity, for example, is as divided against itself as the judge's: "The two names, Biju was learning, indi-cated a deep rift that he hadn't suspected when he first walked in and found him.... [Harish-Harry] tried to keep on the right side of power, tried to be loyal to so many things that he himself couldn't tell which one of his selves was the authentic, if any" (147–48). The identity Harish-Harry forges for himself under the forces of globalization parallels the one the judge creates under colonialism. In trying to keep "on the right side of power" both men end up with inauthentic selves (though we ought to acknowledge the novel begs the question of what an *authentic* self would be). Certainly cross-cultural experience for both men does not work in positive ways to create what Appadurai would like to see as liberated postnational identities happily cut loose from tradition in a world offering new postmodern forms of subjectivity. Biju insists this problem is rampant even with the younger, more trendy "*'half 'n' half'* crowd, the Indian students coming in with American friends, one accent one side of the mouth, another the other side; muddling it up, wobbling then, downgrading sometimes all the way to Hindi to show one another" (148). Biju becomes increasingly dismayed by these problems, increasingly concerned not only about how he is doing financially, but about who he is and what he is becoming, concerned that he is doomed to the same kind of divided identity he observes in others.

In the end, Biju decides to return to Kalimpong, partly because he has become aware of the increasing violence associated with the GNLF insurgency and so worries about his father's safety, but also because he has become disillusioned about his possibilities in New York:

> Year by year, his life wasn't amounting to anything at all; in a space that should have included family, friends, he was the only one displacing the air. And yet, another part of him had expanded: his self-consciousness, his self-pity—oh the tediousness of it.... Shouldn't he return to a life where he might slice his own importance, to where he might relinquish this overrated control over his own destiny.... And if he continued on here? What would happen? Would he, like Harish-Harry, man-ufacture a fake version of himself ... ? (268)

It is significant that Desai's New York narrative about globalization, so preoc-cupied as it is with the complex circulation of populations, cultural behaviors, and identities, ends in a return, one that specifically rejects what Biju sees as "the overrated control over his own destiny" that sits close to the center of so many upbeat narratives about globalization. As critical as her novel is of claims to au-thenticity, tradition, and originary belonging, Desai does not want to let go here of some notion of an authentic self connected to historical traditions that is more valuable than fake subjectivities manufactured under the auspices of coloniza-tion and globalization. Or, at least, she wants to insist that the tension between these two versions of subjectivity remains real, and that there is a clear continuity between how this tension surfaced under colonialism (exemplified in Jemubhai's narrative) and under globalization (emphasized in Biju's).

There are, of course, no "authentic" identities in the novel to offset the "fake" ones Desai confronts us with, none who float free of the cultural forces Desai evokes in passages like those quoted here. None of them predate forms of migration and the cultural mobility that facilitate the kind of contamination Appiah invokes in *Cosmopolitanism*. The ancient migrations Desai invokes in her treatment of Kalimpong, and the more recent ones taken by Jemubhai, Biju, and Sai, merge in her novel into a fluid tapestry of transformation and remaking that suggests it is impossible to step outside history to find a location or an identity that is "authentic" in the sense of its existing free of and prior to such a history. Indeed, all of the "identity" problems Appiah and Appadurai have grappled with are dramatized with striking breadth in Desai's novel. While she explores the historical and cultural circumstances that make the cosmopolitan ethics Appiah advocates so daunting, she also dramatizes how identities cannot be easily reduced to a single ethnic or national one, that all of us embody multiple, sometimes contradictory sites from which we, and those around us, can work to construct what we like to call our "identities."

When Biju finally makes it back to Kalimpong he is systematically robbed and literally stripped of all his belongings by GNLF insurgents. He has absolutely nothing left from his life in New York. When Desai's parallel stories finally meet up, we find that whatever Biju has lost in the United States is compounded by the losses he suffers at the hands of the GNLF, who "appropriate" his luggage, the goods he has purchased for his father, and the very clothes he is wearing. The hopelessness of this conclusion is underscored by the fact that at the very moment Biju is staggering in the dark mists back to the home his father shares with the judge and his granddaughter, Sai sits inside deciding she must leave Kalimpong. "She thought of all the *National Geographics* and books she had read. Of the judge's journey, of the cook's journey, of Biju's. Of the globe twirling on its axis. And she felt a glimmer of strength. Of resolve. She must leave" (323). (The phrase "She must leave" appears in the original hardback edition, was mistakenly dropped from the first paperback edition, and was then restored in subsequent printings.) This seems to her like a moment of strength and hope, but she is unaware that at that very moment Biju is limping half-naked toward her door. The end of his journey, not to mention the terror behind her grandfather's, hardly bodes well for the one she is now tempted to take. The very avenue of escape she has decided to take seems already to have failed Biju. This scene, emerging as it does in the last pages of the novel, takes us back to its opening. There, too, Sai sits with a *National Geographic* magazine on her lap, an emblem of escape in what will turn out to be a sea of trouble. In that opening scene, we will recall, everything around her is rendered insubstantial by fog and mists, and the borders and boundaries between things seem illusory. In the end, the border between Sai's hope and the reality of Biju's experience seem to merge. Biju is reconciled with his father in the conclusion—a happy moment for both—but the meaning of his experiences abroad do not seem to have anything to offer Sai, or the other characters in the book. Both nationalism and globalization are marked in the novel by *loss*. Moreover, nationalism is figured not as something that came before globalization but as its inheritance, and they tend to get presented in the bleakest of terms. Both sets of forces have conspired to produce the dead-end that Sai, Gyan, and Biju encounter together at the end of the novel.

7

The Cultural Politics of Development in Zakes Mda's *The Heart of Redness*

In this chapter I want to return to controversies about the relationship between culture and identity I explored in part 1, particularly to the question of how modernization and development can threaten cultural traditions deeply connected to personal, social, and national identity. Recalling Pratt's work on contact zones and Appiah's stress on how cultures are never pure but develop and thrive on intercultural contact facilitated by voluntary travel, forced migration, and trade, we know that this is not a new process. The forces of modernization and globalization have accelerated a basic phenomenon that actually has a long history. The specific nature of this history, along with debates about the particular relationship between tradition and change under modernization, are examined in a detailed way in Zakes Mda's 2000 novel, *The Heart of Redness,* a book that explores the cultural politics of identity and economic development in postapartheid South Africa.[1] Mda's novel moves fluidly between the eras of nineteenth-century colonial domination and late twentieth-century economic development in order to stress continuities between colonialism and globalization (discussed in chapters 2 and 3). In doing so, Mda's novel deepens, and makes more concrete, our understanding of the troubled relationship between economic development and cultural preservation.

Like Desai's *The Inheritance of Loss,* Mda's novel shifts back and forth between two stories, one set in the mid-nineteenth century and the other in the
late twentieth century. The central protagonist is a well-educated, cosmopolitan
man named Camagu who fled South Africa during the apartheid years and has
returned to his homeland in 1994 after thirty years of self-imposed exile in the
United States, with the hope of making a new life in a seemingly liberated South
Africa. Unable to find a suitable job in Johannesburg and increasingly cynical
about the state of democracy in South Africa, Camagu comes under the spell of
a young woman, whom he tracks to the remote Xhosa village of Qolorha-by-Sea
on the Indian Ocean. Camagu's story parallels and intersects with a story set in
the same Xhosa village 150 years earlier during the time of the so-called cattle-
killing movement, which was inspired by the teenage prophetess Nongqawuse.[2]
The villagers Camagu finds there are still divided between the descendents of
those who believed in Nongqawuse's prophecy (the Believers) and those who did
not (the Unbelievers). The Believers still blame the Unbelievers for the failure of
the mid-nineteenth-century cattle-killing movement, while the Unbelievers view
the Believers as backward traditionalists who have kept the village from embracing modernity for almost 150 years. The Believers are associated with rural life,
cultural preservation, darkness, tradition, and the past, while the Unbelievers are
associated with urbanization, development, "civilization," and modernization.

Camagu's earlier engagement in Johannesburg with arguments about tradition, democracy, change, and modernization intersect with similar debates rag-
ing in the village. These debates have their source in arguments about a proposal
to create a resort and casino on village land. In this way, Mda sets up a historical
parallel between the 1840s cattle-killing movement as a response to English colonialism and the modern village's resistance to proposals for a resort as a response
to the new forces of globalization. Mda's extended analysis of the cultural and
economic politics of development in the village of Qolorha is linked in the early
sections of the novel to Camagu's frustration with the urban political realities of
postapartheid Johannesburg. He has come back to vote in the elections of 1994,
"in his mid forties, a stranger in his own country" (29).[3] Originally planning to
stay in South Africa only long enough to register his vote, Camagu gets "swept
up by the euphoria of the time" and decides to "stay and contribute to the development of his country" (29). As he begins to look for work, Camagu encounters
resentment from those who stayed in South Africa to fight against apartheid,
and he becomes frustrated with how they have become firmly entrenched as the
new ruling class. "Who is he?" they ask. "We didn't see him when we were dancing the freedom dance" (29). In his defense Camagu cites his experience with a
host of international agencies helping to manage globalization, but he finds that

he cannot penetrate the resentment others feel toward him for having left the country thirty years ago.

Mda uses Camagu's profound sense of displacement and his struggle to come to terms with his identity in a new South Africa to construct an extended meditation on the relationship between the personal and the political. The division Camagu feels between his African identity and his cosmopolitan experience in the West gets played out both in urban Johannesburg and rural Qolorha-by-Sea, enabling Mda to explore the contemporary effects of modernization and globalization in both settings. Moreover, as the story moves back and forth between the Xhosa struggle against colonialism in the mid-nineteenth-century and its struggles with late-twentieth-century economic and cultural modernization, Mda is able to explore the continuities between these two historical periods. In the novel, the disruptive forces of economic and cultural domination, threats to tradition and opportunities for development that complicate Xhosa identity and their relationship to the land unfold under colonialism and accelerate under globalization.

Structured in this way around the cosmopolitan Camagu's journey into rural Africa and his encounter with arguments about colonialism and the "primitive," *The Heart of Redness* performs a kind of rewriting of Conrad's *The Heart of Darkness,* a text that regularly haunts postcolonial fiction in complex ways. (It is worth remembering, for example, that Roy's *The God of Small Things* explicitly evokes Conrad.) Camagu's voyage into "the heart of redness" (redness here refers to a "red ochre that women smear on their bodies and with which they also dye their isikhakha skirts" [71]) recalls Marlow's journey upriver from "civilization" into the heart of darkness, and his confrontation with the effects of colonialism creates a subtle but unmistakable connection to Conrad's novel. However, Mda's narrative is calculated to perform a kind of ritual reversal of the terms of the earlier one, for while in Conrad's text "darkness" marks the world of the jungle as backward, barbaric, and "primitive," Mda's redness is linked to a lush and edenic place of great beauty, a kind of countercivilization that is safe, for a time, from the ravages of modernity. While the Unbelievers of Qolorha see "redness" in negative terms as a symbol of the tribe's backwardness, the Believers, along with Camagu, come to see it as a sign of authentic culture and a valuable set of traditions. Where Conrad's novel embodies a critique of colonialism and yet traffics in all of the racist stereotypes that informed it, Mda's novel develops a sustained social, cultural, and economic critique of colonialism and its effects; engages in a complex dialogue about cultural and racial xenophobia; and leaves Camagu, unlike Marlow, deep in the heart of redness, where he eventually decides to make a life for himself.

The resentment Camagu experiences from others about his having left South Africa instead of staying to fight against apartheid (referred to throughout the novel as "doing the freedom dance") erupts early in the novel as he searches for work:[4]

> That was when Camagu realized the importance of the dance. He had tried to explain about his skills in the area of development communication, how he had worked for international agencies, how as an international expert he had done consulting work for UNESCO in Paris and for the Food and Agricultural Organization in Rome, and how the International Telecommunication Union had often sought his advice on matters of international broadcasting. The interviewers were impressed. They commended his achievements. He had done his oppressed people proud in foreign lands. And now, the freedom dance? Alas! His steps faltered. (29)

On the one hand, Camagu has the kind of international experience South Africa needs as it emerges from apartheid and seeks to join the international economic community, but on the other, he did not stay to help liberate his country, and he is accused of not being "familiar" with "South Africa and its problems" (30). "Gradually losing his enthusiasm for this new democratic society," (30) Camagu discovers "the corporate world did not want qualified blacks" (30). Instead, "they preferred the inexperienced ones who were only too happy to be placed in some glass affirmative-action office where they were displayed as paragons of empowerment. No one cared if they ever got to grips with their jobs or not. All the better for the old guard if they did not. That safeguarded the old guard's position" (30). Feeling locked out of any meaningful position with the new government, Camagu spends the next four years teaching part time at a trade school in Johannesburg, discovering the resentment among South Africans who fought apartheid on the front lines toward exiles like himself who were seeking important positions in the new South Africa. "We were the ones who bore the brunt of the bullets," he overhears one man say. "We threw stones and danced the freedom dance . . . while they were having a good time overseas we were dying here. We were the cannon fodder for those who are eating softly now" (32). Camagu wants "to serve his country on merit" but comes to believe that "he did not qualify for any important position because he was not a member of the Aristocrats of the Revolution, an exclusive club that is composed of the ruling elites, their families, and close friends. Some of them were indeed leaders of the freedom struggle, while others had used their status and wealth to snake their way into the very heart of the organization" (32–33).

In this section of the novel Mda foregrounds tensions in the postapartheid political culture between a kind of revolutionary idealism and the pragmatic, practical needs of nation building, especially in the economic and social sectors Camagu is familiar with. These tensions are at once local and specific to South Africa in the postapartheid period and familiar from the other novels I have been discussing. This is particularly the case in terms of how Mda links these contemporary divisions to earlier ones under colonialism, drawing the kind of historical connection between the forces of colonialism and globalization at work in nearly all of the novels looked at here. The division between authentic and inauthentic identities, for example, between those who stayed in South Africa and did the "freedom dance" and those who fled to the West, gets linked to similar divisions shaping responses to colonialism in the nineteenth century. To the extent the cattle-killing movement called for by Nongqawuse's prophecy constituted resistance to colonialism, the mid-nineteenth-century split between the Believers and the Unbelievers is structurally similar to the late twentieth-century one Camagu gets caught up in, a split between those who believed in "the freedom dance" and those who embraced modernity and the West.

Mda makes this link explicit as Camagu, disillusioned with the political culture of the new South Africa, leaves Johannesburg for Qolorha-by-Sea.[5] Here he is quickly introduced to the division in the village between the Believers and the Unbelievers, one that ends up mirroring the divisions he experienced in Johannesburg. In Qolorha, Camagu's cosmopolitanism, born of his thirty years' exile in the West, is tested by his immersion in Xhosa culture and its rootedness to the land. The narrative structure of the novel is calibrated to underscore the historical link between the periods of colonialism and an accelerating late-twentieth-century globalization, as Camagu's experiences in Johannesburg and among the villagers of Qolorha are narrated in sections of the novel that alternate with historical sections (set in 1856–7) about the plight of the Xhosa under colonialism, Nongqawuse's prophecy, and the divisions erupting around the cattle-killing movement.[6] These alternating sections of the novel are linked, in turn, to the village's contemporary struggle over development, a struggle that mirrors both the contemporary ones in Johannesburg and earlier historical ones under colonialism.

Mda's treatment of the nineteenth-century cattle-killing movement is central to his larger narrative. The movement, which lasted for fifteen months during 1856–7, proved crucial to Britain's final subjugation of the Xhosa and was connected to a series of frontier wars that took place between 1779 and 1878, as British policy aimed systematically to contain the Xhosa and appropriate their lands.[7] Nongqawuse prophesied after a vision that if the Xhosa killed all of their cattle (which had been suffering from an epidemic of lung sickness) the ancient Xhosa chiefs would return and help drive the British off their land.[8] Most historians now believe that Nongqawuse's prophecy was instigated by her uncle,

Mhlakaza, a shaman. Nongqawuse's prophecy was embraced by the Xhosa chief, Sarili, who directed the tribe to carry out the extermination of all their cattle, an act that turned out to have horrific results. Not only did thousands of Xhosa starve to death as a result of the cattle killing, but the British, under the direction of Sir George Grey, governor of the Cape Colony, saw it as an act of rebellion against British rule. Consequently, he used the movement as a pretext for subjugating the Xhosa, appropriating their land, and distributing it to whites and to tribes hostile to the Xhosa. Nongqawuse was eventually captured and imprisoned on Robben Island. Thus, the cattle-killing movement backfired, resulting not in the expulsion of the British from the Cape but in the consolidation of their dominance over the Xhosa.

As Mda presents it, the division between Believers and Unbelievers has persisted to the present day, something that is evident to Camagu as soon as he arrives at Qolorha.⁹ The Unbelievers, he finds, are "somber people" who "do not believe even in those things that can bring happiness to their lives. They spend most of their time moaning about past injustices and bleeding for the world that would have been had the folly of belief not seized the nation a century and a half ago" (3). The current leader of the Unbelievers is Bhonco, who has "resurrected the cult" of unbelief and insists that his "relatives subscribe to it" (6). It does not "matter to him that people have long forgotten the conflicts of generations ago. He holds to them dearly, for they have shaped his present, and the present of the nation" (6). The irony here, of course, is that Bhonco *believes* in unbelief to the point that it constitutes a kind of faith for his group that paralyzes them in the present. "Unbelieving," Mda writes, had been "elevated to the heights of a religion" (5), a point that is not lost on Camagu. Both sides blame each other for their current plight. While the Unbelievers blame the Believers for backing the cattle-killing movement and plunging their people into subjugation, the Believers blame the Unbelievers for failing to follow Nongqawuse, dooming her prophecy. According to Bhonco, the Believers instigated the demise of the Xhosa: "That Believer started it. Doesn't he know? It is because his ancestors forced the amaXhosa people to kill their cattle. That is why we are suffering like this" (45). Zim, a descendent of the Believers, responds, "tell the Unbeliever that it is because his ancestors refused to slaughter the cattle even when prophetesses like Nongqawuse…instructed them to do so. That is why life is so difficult" (45–46).

Both the earlier cattle-killing movement and the reticence of Believers in the late twentieth century to embrace development are presented as forms of resistance to cultural and economic colonization. While those who supported the cattle-killing movement were thought to be in rebellion against the British, those who did not support it are seen as complicit with colonial occupation. For example, Twin-Twin, a leader of the mid-nineteenth-century Unbelievers, felt his "unbelief was sinking him deeper into collaboration with the conquerors of his people. Although he was strong enough to resist conversion, some of his fellow Unbelievers were becoming Christians. And when they did, they sang praises of the queen of the conquerors" (133).[10] Likewise, in the twentieth century, those Unbelievers who support the development of a casino are positioned as complicit with the colonizing forces of economic and cultural globalization. The proposed casino is to be built by a large hotel company at the mouth of the Gxarha River, adjacent to the lagoon where Nongqawuse had her vision (66). The movement against this development is based both on a belief that sacred land will be desecrated *and* that the casino will disrupt the economy of the village. Resistance to the casino is being spearheaded by Zim, "a Believer to the core of his soul" (67). He has been joined by a white trader named John Dalton, who wants to defend the cultural integrity of the Xhosa and develop an ecotourism business featuring the cultural history of the Xhosa. Staking out a counterposition, the Unbelievers supporting development of the casino believe they "are moving forward with the times" (67). The Unbelievers insist they "stand for civilization" and that the Believers "want us to remain in our wildness. To remain red all of our lives! To stay in the darkness of redness" (67).[11]

While the narrative point of view shifts methodically back and forth between the Believers and the Unbelievers, eventually Camagu's struggle to find a middle ground between the two begins to dominate the novel. Camagu is searching for a pragmatic solution that will transcend the ideological debates between Believers and Unbelievers. Of course this search becomes inextricably connected to his own personal search for identity and belonging in a new, postapartheid South Africa, a link Mda uses to underscore the relationship between the personal and the political. "Camagu," Mda writes, "with all his learning, cannot make up his mind.... He has tried to observe the patterns of believing and unbelieving at this village, to try to make sense of them" (91–92). On the one hand, as Bhonco insists to Camagu, "the Unbelievers stand for progress" (92). "We want developers to come and build the gambling city," which Bhonco insists will "bring money to this community. That will bring modernity to our lives, and will rid us of our redness" (92). However, Zim (the leader of the Believers) insists that such "progress" will destroy the land of the their ancestors and obliterate their culture: "Those so-called tourists! They come here to steal our lizards and our birds...our aloes and our cycads and our usundu palms and our *ikhamanga* wild banana trees" (94). Camagu eventually sides with those who are against development of a casino on Xhosa land (117), joining forces with Dalton in his proposal to develop cultural tourism in the area.[12]

Mda uses Camagu's struggle to find a pragmatic middle ground between modernity and tradition to explore the larger clash between indigenous cultures and development as it has unfolded in an arch from colonialism through the contemporary era of globalization, all calibrated to present a balanced exploration of both sides. Mda is interested in Camagu's search for identity and his engagement with the politics of cultural belonging in the novel, but he is also deeply engaged in exploring economic issues related to development, modernization, and globalization. (Many of the organizations Camagu has worked with in the past are those that Stiglitz links to the institutional structures of globalization in *Globalization and Its Discontents*.)

In the end, Dalton manages to get the entire area declared a national heritage site (269). This seems a palatable alternative to the casino but raises a number of important questions. Dalton's project, in seeking to preserve and respect Nongqawuse's story, seems committed to preserving indigenous traditions and practices. However, Mda is careful to connect such preservation of "native" practices to colonial domination. At the height of the cattle-killing movement, we are told, Sir George Grey "commissioned an exhaustive research of native laws and customs in support of [his] system of managerial rule." "When you know their customs you will be a much more effective magistrate over the natives" (206), he tells John Dalton's grandfather. Grey adds that during his posting in New Zealand he "built an important collection of the languages, customs, and religions of the natives...because they are destined to disappear along with the savages who hold them" (206). Grey's project, laid out to John Dalton's grandfather in the middle of the nineteenth century, is clearly linked to the younger Dalton's late twentieth century vision of a cultural-heritage theme park. The contemporary project will be a "cultural village owned and operated by the villagers."

> He already had two formidable women in NoManage and NoVangeli who are experienced in entertaining tourists by displaying cultural performances and practices of the amaXhosa. This is a proven kind of business. Tourists like visiting such cultural villages to see how the people live. Women will wear traditional isiXosa costumes as their forebears used to wear. They will grind millet and polish the floors with cow dung. There will be displays of clay pots and other earthenware items. Tourists will flock to watch young maidens dance and young men engage in stick fights. (247)

With his review of Grey's nineteenth-century colonizing interest in the cataloguing and preserving of indigenous traditions and practices coming just a few pages before this description of Dalton's twentieth-century project, the reader is positioned to see a symmetrical relationship between the two. This relationship gets underscored by Camagu's critical reaction to Dalton's plan. Initially sympathetic to cultural tourism as an alternative to the casino, Camagu balks at what he perceives to be the *inauthenticity* of Dalton's cultural theme park, pointing out various ways in which the performances Dalton envisions will distort ama-Xhosa life. "That's dishonest," Camagu insists, "it is just a museum that pretends that is how real people live. Real people in today's South Africa don't lead the life that is seen in cultural villages" (247). Camagu's protests develop into a full-blown intellectual argument against the exploitation and commodification of indigenous peoples:

> It is an attempt to preserve folk ways…to reinvent culture. When you excavate a buried precolonial identity of these people…a precolonial authenticity that is lost…are you suggesting that they currently have no culture…that they live in a cultural vacuum?…I am interested in the culture of the amaXhosa as they live it today, not yesterday. The amaXhosa people are not a museum piece. Like all cultures, their culture is dynamic. (248)

Camagu's position here recalls debates about the politics of culture under globalization we reviewed in part 1. It is, in fact, very close to the one Appiah takes in *Cosmopolitanism* when he argues that all cultures are fluid and changing ("dynamic," to use Camagu's word), and that it is wrong to insist on freezing their traditions and practices for the sake of cultural tourism.[13] Like Appiah, Camagu rejects the whole idea that cultures are pure and unchanging or suffer contamination in their contact with others, insisting that all cultures develop in the context of contact with other cultures. From this point of view, it is striking the degree to which Camagu's cosmopolitanism aligns with Appiah's. It is tested during his time in Johannesburg, where it makes him suspect among South Africans who stayed to fight against apartheid, and again in Qolorha, where he is torn between supporting development, on the one hand, and traditional Xhosa beliefs and practices, on the other. From the point of view Camagu finally works out, Dalton's project, however well meaning it might be, must be seen as oppressive and exploitative. (All of this recalls Roy's exploration of the impact of cultural tourism on the Kathakali dancers in Kerala.) Moreover, Camagu's critique of cultural tourism raises a complex set of questions regarding culture, identity, preservation, and economic development. His concern regarding Dalton's approach to cultural tourism is that it presents a freeze-frame caricature of local cultures and identities (the diorama approach to cultural preservation seen in part 1) that can actually undermine forms of development that contribute to the modernization of both infrastructures and institutions. Camagu's interest, ideally, is in finding a way to both respect and nurture cultural beliefs and practices that does not prohibit needed forms of economic modernization and development.

These are vexing challenges that, again, recall Appiah's discussion of culture, homogenization, and diversity. It is easy to view development and modernization along the lines represented by the proposed casino in Qolorha as a form of cultural imperialism, but here we should recall Appiah's qualms about making such claims. The charge of "cultural imperialism," he points out, is usually made by "cultural preservationists" who, he insists, misconstrue the very nature of culture (107): "In broad strokes, their underlying picture is this. There is a world system of capitalism. It has a center in a set of multinational corporations. Some of these are in the media business. The products they sell around the world promote the interests of capitalism in general. They encourage consumption not just of films, television, and magazines but of the other non-media products of multinational capitalism" (108). From this point of view, the outside interests behind the casino are complicit with cultural imperialism. Resistance to this kind of imperialism involves protecting and preserving the authenticity and autonomy of local cultures and traditional practices, something that seems at the center of Dalton's proposed cultural heritage park. However, like Camagu, who insists that identity is not buried in some "precolonial identity" or "authenticity" to be excavated but is fluid and changing and informed by contemporary beliefs and practices, Appiah finds this approach "deeply condescending" (111) because the idea of "cultural purity" it is based on is "an oxymoron" and because "people in each place" ought to "make their own uses even of the most famous global commodities" (113). Mda complicates all of these issues in the same way Appiah does. Both the essay and the novel invoke and then question the ethical position in favor of cultural preservation because it is based on a theoretically and historically unsound understanding of what culture is and how it works. At the same time, the authors are against an idealized conception of cultural preservation imposed from outside because it undercuts the economic autonomy of local cultures. Camagu's attempt to work out a position that both respects and supports tradition without undermining positive economic development constitutes a kind of fictional dramatic enactment of the issues Appiah treats in philosophical and theoretical terms. It stages a simultaneous critique of both the cultural-preservationist and the cultural-imperialist positions, searching for some kind of middle ground between them.

When it comes to the question of identity, Camagu articulates a position much like the one I have been endorsing in this book, one that values, respects, and seeks to foster a living connection to cultural traditions without reifying them into some kind of absolute, fixed, or transcendental category to be marked off absolutely from modernity and change. Camagu's argument here is close to the one we saw Appadurai make, in which identity is rooted historically in a set of beliefs and practices but is also a constant "work of the imagination" in which contemporary practices are appropriated, transformed, and incorporated into traditional ones. Seeking to meld a kind of late twentieth-century cosmopolitanism with a commitment to protecting local cultural practices, Camagu struggles with many of the same issues we have seen characters in the other novels discussed here—Abhay in *Red Earth and Pouring Rain* and Sai in *The Inheritance of Loss* come particularly to mind.[14]

In the end, John Dalton thwarts development by the casino operators by having the government declare Qolorha-by-Sea a "national heritage" site (269). The arguments between Believers and Unbelievers in Qolorha-by-Sea, in effect, get displaced by the argument between Dalton, a descendant of British colonial administrators, and Camagu, a well-educated cosmopolitan returnee from the West. From Camagu's point of view, Dalton's cultural heritage village makes the villagers subservient to him and replicates a kind of colonial paternalism. "Your people love you," he tells Dalton, "because you do things for them.... You are thinking like the businessman you are...you want a piece of the action" (248). The cooperative he is trying to foster, on the other hand, puts the villagers to work for themselves producing and selling traditional products. "I am talking of self-reliance," he insists, "where people do things for themselves.... I do not want a piece of any action. This project will be fully owned by the villagers themselves and will be run by a committee elected by them in the true manner of cooperative societies" (248). The novel ends with Dalton's cultural heritage park and the cooperative business Camagu creates both thriving. However, Bhonco, leader of the Unbelievers, is particularly displeased with the way things have turned out, since he associates anything that preserves cultural traditions with the Believers: "To Bhonco, all these things represent defeat. The Believers have won. He has nothing more to lose. And it is all John Dalton's fault. He brought that despicable Camagu to this village. They both stood with the Believers against the Unbelievers. As a result...the village itself lost a glittering gambling paradise that would have changed life for everyone. Instead it got a rustic holiday camp that lacks the glamour of the gambling city" (273). While both Dalton and Camagu believe their two projects have protected the indigenous culture and ecology of the Xhosa, we have already seen that as outsiders they are linked quite specifically by Mda to a kind of colonialist paternalism, so neither vision emerges at the end of the novel as a completely satisfying example of progressive change. And, while Bhonco laments the loss of jobs and material progress and modernization the casino development would have brought to Qolorha, Mda is hardly endorsing his position over against Dalton's and Camagu's. Instead, he has staged a kind of dramatic debate between belief in tradition and the so-called primitive, on the one hand, and a form of unbelief associated with development and modernization, on the other. The novel is calibrated, as we have seen, to present a balanced articulation and interrogation of both sides, an interrogation sustained by a narrative structure that moves temporally between the past and the present and ideologically between the positions of Believers and Unbelievers. Mda clearly identifies with Camagu and the position he takes, but there is plenty of aesthetic distance between himself and his character, and Mda is at pains to present the range of ideological positions he foregrounds in the book, staging a set of debates that intersect with many of the issues discussed here in part 1.

Mda interweaves his treatment of largely sociological content—his exploration of economic, cultural, and ideological issues—with Camagu's own personal struggle with his identity and his effort to discover where he belongs in the tensions between urban and village life in postapartheid South Africa. This interweaving is foregrounded in the novel's elaborate (if somewhat schematic) romance plot, a plot that emphasizes the crucial role that women play in the villagers' contemporary struggle with development and modernization. Camagu finds his way to Qolorha-by-Sea in search of a beautiful woman named Noma-Russia he briefly met in Johannesburg, and once he arrives, he gets caught up in romantic relationships with two other women. One, Xoliswa, embodies the position of the Unbelievers, while the other, Qukezwa, is a leading figure among the Believers. As the novel shifts between the past and the present and the positions taken by Believers and Unbelievers, it also shifts methodically between Camagu's infatuation with each of these women, complicating the ideological divide between the two camps with Camagu's romanticism and his own erotic desires, while underscoring the key role gender has played among the Xhosa since the time of the prophetess Nongqawuse.

Camagu encounters NomaRussia when he wanders into a Johannesburg wake for a young man from Qolorha who, according to the man delivering his eulogy, has suffered and died from the "wickedness of the city":

> This brother was gifted.... His hands could create wonders. His fingers were nimble, and could mold enchanted worlds. Yet this city swallowed him, and spewed him out a shriveled corpse. This ungrateful city decided that he could survive only if he created ugly things that distorted life as we knew it. He refused, for he was attached to beautiful things. He wasted away as a result, until he was a bag of bones. (27–28)

This passage foreshadows the novel's later exploration of the idea that traditional cultural forms and practices have a kind of indigenous, organic integrity ruined by forms of modernization that have "distorted life" as the villagers knew it. However, Camagu is less interested in the eulogy than in NomaRussia, who is singing "Nearer My God to Thee." Mda writes that "Camagu's eyes cannot leave her alone. Her beauty is not in harmony with this wake. It does not speak of death. It shouts only of life. Of the secret joys that she harbors" (25). Beyond the "lust" he feels is something deeper, for "she is more like a spirit that can comfort him and heal his pain. A mothering spirit" (28). In a brief conversation he has with NomaRussia she tells him she is from Qolorha, which she emphasizes is the birthplace of the prophetess Nongqawuse (35).

Camagu eventually heads by car to Qolorha in search of NomaRussia, partly because he is haunted by her beauty, but more importantly because she has become associated in his mind with his own "searing longing for an imagined blissfulness of his youth....he remembers the fruit trees" and "can see dimly through the mist of decades all the lush plants that grew in his grandfather's garden" (59). In his dissatisfaction with Johannesburg and his frustrating struggle with its modern, insular, and seemingly elitist economic and political system, his romantic yearning for an alternative world becomes embodied in NomaRussia and Qolorha. This becomes clear in a dream reverie he recounts soon after meeting her:

> In his dream he was the river, and NomaRussia was its water. Crystal clear. Flowing on him. Sliding smoothly on his body. Until she flowed into the ocean. He ran after her, shouting that she should flow back. Flow back up the river. Upstream....When he failed to catch her, he tried to catch the dream itself, to arrest it, so that it could be with him forever (60).

The setting and imagery here clearly link NomaRussia with Nongqawuse and her ocean-side lagoon, and, though he is never able to find her, his search leads him to Qolorha and to the two women who embody the terms of the village's debates about modernization, Xoliswa and Qukezwa.

Xoliswa is Bhonco's daughter and the village schoolteacher; she is a kind of "celebrity" in Qolorha because she has "a B.A. in education from the University of Fort Hare, and a certificate in teaching English as a second language from some college in America" (4–5). She embraces a kind of cosmopolitan worldliness that makes her anathema to the village's Believers because of her flaunting that she has "been to America...across the oceans" (12). To her, America is "a fairy-tale country, with beautiful people. People like Dolly Parton and Eddie Murphy. It is a vast country that is highly technological," and she registers wonder at everything from its monuments to its cities and subway systems, exclaiming that "it is the best country in the world. I hope to go back one day" (64–65). Throughout the novel she endorses modernization and development and scorns tradition. As Camagu becomes increasingly infatuated with traditional life in the village, for example, she taunts him about it: "You are an educated man,

Camagu, all the way from America. How do you expect simple peasants to give up their superstitions and join the modern world when they see educated people like you clinging to them?" (150). "Most people" in the village, she insists, "want to see development happening. They want clean water. They want health delivery services," and they see the Believers and Unbelievers fighting with each other as "clowns who are holding desperately to the quarrels of the past. But the whole thing frustrates development" (116). Eventually, as Camagu's cooperative and Dalton's cultural heritage park become operational, she decides to leave the village altogether, declaring "it is high time I live in more civilized places" (226).

Camagu is infatuated with Xoliswa, his erotic attraction to her linked in part to her beauty but, more important, to the articulate arguments she makes about development. At the same time, he falls under the spell of the equally attractive and mysterious Qukezwa, who is just as articulate on behalf of the Believers' commitment to Nongqawuse, tradition, and ridding the village of developers. Mda uses Camagu's romantic infatuation with these two women to underscore the power they exert in an otherwise patriarchal world, as a device to foreground the positions for and against development they take, and to emphasize the role Camagu's romantic idealism plays in a debate that seems, on the surface, purely ideological. Qukezwa is the daughter of Zim, leader of the Believers and, at nineteen, is the same age as Nongqawuse when she delivered her prophecy (39). Initially taken by her wisecracking and her "acerbic tongue" ("get her on your side, he tells himself" for "she can be a deadly enemy" [101]), Camagu finds her arguments against the casino (which he initially supports), increasingly compelling. She rejects the idea that villagers will have the qualifications to work in the casino, and Camagu is "taken aback both by her fervor and her reasoning" (103). She seems right that "the gambling city may not be the boon the Unbelievers think it will be," and if development comes "at the expense of the freedom to enjoy the sea and its bountiful harvests and the woods and the birds and the monkeys...then those few jobs are not really worth it" (103).

Initially put off by Qukezwa's flippant dismissal of the attractions of development, Camagu becomes increasingly enchanted by her arguments, which are presented in a way calculated to contrast with Xoliswa's educated discourse about modernity. Camagu, Mda writes, "is grudgingly developing some admiration for the scatterbrained girl with a Standard Eight education who works as a cleaner at Vulindela Trading Store" (103). His attraction of Qukezwa soon gets linked to the prophetess Nongqawuse, and turns erotic when she leads him down into Nongqawuse's valley, a kind of edenic, primitive, and seductive place meant to contrast with Xoliswa's world of urban modernity:

They walk silently among tall grasses that are used for thatching houses. Then they get to the rocks that are covered with mosses of various colors. Camagu is fascinated by the yellows, the browns, the greens, and the reds that have turned the rocks into works of abstract art. Down below he can see a hut of rough thatch and twigs. It looks like the nest of a lazy bird. Outside, naked *abakhwetha* initiates are sitting in the sun, nursing their newly circumcised penises. The white ochre that covers their bodies makes them look like ghosts. (104)

The rhythms of this world contrast pointedly with that of the village, torn as it is by arguments between Believers and Unbelievers. It is a kind of paradise associated with Nongqawuse's world, but one beginning to suffer the ravages of modernization. As she guides Camagu through the valley, Qukezwa reveals her intricate knowledge of the ecology of the valley, which is meant to counterbalance the modern education Xoliswa has.[15] As he listens to her, Camagu observes, "You know a lot about birds and plants," and Qukezwa responds, "I live with them" (103). When Camagu observes banana plants growing in the valley, she corrects him: "It's not really a banana tree. It is called ikhamanga. White people call it wild banana. But it bears only the banana flower, never the fruit. Birds enjoy its nectar and its seeds" (105).

Qukezwa's deep knowledge of the ecological world of the valley is linked to her reverence for its mythic and cultural history. Indeed, the two are fused in her mind. She explains to Camagu that during Nongqawuse's time

> visions appeared in the water. Nongqawuse herself stood here. Across the river the valley was full of ikhamanga. There were reeds too. They are no longer there.... And a few aloes. Aloes used to cover the whole area. Mist often covers this whole ridge. It was like that too in the days of Nongqawuse. We stood here and saw the wonders. The whole ridge was covered with people who came to see the wonders. Many things have changed. The reeds are gone. What remains now is that bush over there where Nongqawuse and Nombanda first met the Strangers. (105)

Environmental degradation here both registers the destructive nature of colonization and development and the extent to which tradition and belief are linked to the integrity of the land. Qukezwa's is a vision of life in Qolorha calculated in every way to be diametrically opposed to Xoliswa's, and the fickle Camagu, torn between the arguments of the Believers and Unbelievers, becomes torn between his desire for Xoliswa and his desire for Qukezwa. At the end of Qukezwa's soliloquy about the valley

> Camagu is seized by a bout of madness. He fights hard against the urge to hold this girl, tightly, and kiss her all over. It is different from the urge he once had: to hold and protect Xoliswa Ximiya. This woman does not need protecting. He does. He is breathing heavily as if he has just climbed a mountain, and his palms are sweating.

Every part of his body has become a stranger to him. He convinces himself that this
is temporary insanity: he is merely mesmerized by the romance of the place and the
girl's passion for the prophets. (103)

By weaving together the novel's overt interest in ideological and sociological debates about tradition, modernization, development, indigenity, and identity with
an exploration of the historical relationships between colonialism and globalization, and by embedding both themes in a romance plot involving two women
who represent the novel's competing positions about modernity, Mda complicates the cultural and economic politics he is exploring with attention to the so-
called irrational forces of romance and the erotic. It is tempting to see Xoliswa
embodying rationality and Qukezwa some kind of mythic or poetic knowledge,
except that Qukezwa's knowledge of history and the environment is every bit
as rational as Xoliswa's. If, in the end, Camagu sides with Qukezwa, vowing to
marry her, it is because she embodies—literally, for his attraction to her body
is key here—a kind of synthesis of the poetic and the rational, of history and
the present in an ecological vision whose integrity and balance trump anything
Xoliswa or Dalton have come up with.

There are gains and losses in Mda's incorporation of this romance plot in a
novel principally interested in sociological and ideological issues. The role these
women play in the novel successfully foregrounds gender as a key topic, and
these women have real agency in Qolorha. Having Camagu fall in love with
both Xoliswa and Qukezwa gives Mda the opportunity to explore how political
and cultural debates are often inflected, not only by gender, but by relationships
both romantic and erotic. Indeed, it is hard to think of a novel among those I
treat in part 2 that does not deal in a fundamental way with the relationship
between sex and politics, something that is particularly the case in the two novels
I discuss in chapters 8 and 9, Zadie Smith's *White Teeth* and Junot Díaz's *The
Brief Wondrous Life of Oscar Wao*. Qukezwa's commitment to, and knowledge of,
the land around Qolorha and, in particular, Nongqawuse's valley, underscores
the value and integrity of the local over and against the forces of colonization
and globalization, and her ecological understanding of the land makes environmental issues central to the novel. However, Mda ends up, particularly with
Qukezwa, trafficking in fairly stereotypical (and thus, patriarchal) associations
of women with the land, nurturance, the emotions, and irrationality. Seen in this
light, Qukezwa's triumph over Xoliswa is the triumph of a woman with very
traditional maternal associations over a modern, educated one, something that
is problematical in a novel about coming to terms with complex twenty-first-
century problems. Nevertheless, Mda's romance plot gives him a way to explore
gendered responses to modernization and globalization, and creates the context

for giving women a sustained voice across the novel's political spectrum. While their agency is at times both enabled and circumscribed by Camagu's erotic desire, they nevertheless have a collective force in debates about the Xhosa tribe's future that we do not see in novels like Roy's, Hamid's, or Desai's, where women are more often than not only the victims of change.

Multiculturalism and Identity in Zadie Smith's *White Teeth*

Mobility, which is central to the production of heterogeneous cultural identities under globalization, takes disparate shapes in the novels I have discussed so far. Under forms of colonization like those covered in the historical sections of *Red Earth and Pouring Rain* it is driven by violent displacement, the mobility of those on the move fleeing subjugation or struggling against it. In *The God of Small Things* and *The Inheritance of Loss* relatively privileged postcolonial subjects like Chacko and Jemubhai journey to England and back, bringing with them perverse forms of Anglophilia that feed their own self-hatred and their loathing of others. In *Moth Smoke* Ozi and others like him with enough wealth travel to the United States for elite educations and then return to reproduce the culture of the West in the privileged sanctuaries of their compounds in Lahore. The more impoverished, like Biju and the other global migrants he works with in Desai's novel, scrape together enough money to travel to New York City where they try to gain a foothold in basement kitchens, only to be buried by poverty and exploitation; or they return, like Biju, without anything to show for their journey. In Mda's *The Heart of Redness,* as we have seen, Camagu returns to South Africa after an exile of thirty years in the United States, and then he journeys from urban Johannesburg to rural Qolorha-by-Sea. These relatively contemporary forms of mobility intersect with more ancient ones conjured up in *Red Earth and Pouring Rain* and *The Inheritance of Loss,* where individuals and cultures have for centuries traveled across porous borders and through disparate locations, creating an intersecting web of hybrid identities and syncretic cultural forms. Both novels dramatize how what Appiah calls contamination is central to the production of personal and cultural identities, especially in regions with historically porous borders.

Together these novels weave a composite vision of the intersecting histories of overtly violent colonization under imperialism and more benign displacement and exploitation under contemporary economic globalization. The experience of displacement and cultural colonization in the historical sections of Chandra's novel resonates with the history of displacement and cultural colonization both in Mda's South Africa and Desai's West Bengal State, and those experiences are linked in turn to the contemporary journeys of Abhay to California, Biju to New York City, and Camagu to Qolorha. In fiction like this the eras of colonization, decolonization, postcoloniality, and globalization flow together, complicating the idea that globalization can be approached simply as a contemporary phenomenon. Each historical period contributes to an accelerating and inexorable rush toward the fracturing and reformation of locations, borders, identities, cultures, and processes that can crush or liberate. In all of the novels we have discussed so far, most of these changes take place in postcolonial nations. Abhay studies in California, Biju works in New York City, while Chacko, Rahel, Ozi and his wife Mumtaz, Jemubhai, and Camagu all study or work abroad. But they return, and their stories are about home, about the disruptive effects of mobility on life in formerly colonized areas of the world.

Smith's novel, however, takes a decidedly different approach, for *White Teeth* (2000) is set in contemporary turn-of-the-century London and is interested in exploring the effects of mobility tied to accelerating globalization on the Western metropole. The other novels tend to reinforce the overly schematic structure of much early work on globalization, based as it is on the distinction between core and periphery. South Asia, Africa, the Caribbean, and the other locations referenced in these novels lie on the margins of power, which flows in a unidirectional way from industrialized, urbanized westernized centers. In setting her novel in London, Smith does not simply shift our attention from the periphery to the core. She actually works to disrupt or deconstruct this central binary. In *White Teeth* the imperial machinery of colonization has gone into reverse. The mobility of the colonizer has become the mobility of the colonized, and it is used to retrace the journey of those who conquered their ancestors. The descendents of those dislocated by colonial conquest have relocated to the very center of colonial power, and it is Englishness, not indigenity, that is at stake.

By exploring the twin effects of colonialism and globalization on the Western metropole, *White Teeth* deals with all of the issues related to personal and cultural identity treated by the novelists and critics we have already discussed. However, it is unique in explicitly foregrounding multiculturalism and fundamentalism as the two main cultural responses to difference in the West, and this is my focus of analysis. Smith is particularly interested in how the discourse of multiculturalism has emerged in the metropolitan West as a way to manage the kind of diversity produced by colonization and globalization. British "multiculturalism" is worth distinguishing from its counterpart in the United States or Canada.[1] Unlike in the United States or Canada, multiculturalism in Britain is fundamentally a product of colonization and decolonization. Multicultural London is a hybrid child of these forces, the result of a complex historical gestation rooted in the colonization of South Asia, Africa, and the Caribbean; the disruptive transformation of indigenous, slave, and Anglo identities; the construction of new postcolonial identities in the wake of independence; and, finally, of migrations from formerly colonized countries to the urban colonial metropolis.[2] *White Teeth* is interested in the construction of postcolonial subjectivities among its South Asian and Caribbean characters in the colonizing metropolis, but it is also interested in how all of the complex forces it explores have remade Englishness, not just the Englishness of its Anglo characters (principally, Archie Jones's family and the Chalfens), but the Englishness of its South Asian and Caribbean characters as well. As such, Smith's novel transcends (or synthesizes) the categories of "British" or "postcolonial" fiction. It surely draws from these two traditions, but it has its roots in the hybrid mix of Asian and Caribbean cultural forms that have emerged in London and elsewhere since the late 1980s. Smith's post–postcolonial orientation has to be located in the cultural politics of the last two decades of the twentieth century, when her novel takes place.[3]

Smith's turn-of-the-century multicultural London is nicely captured in a June 2000 *New York Times* article by Yasmin Alibhai-Brown:[4]

> This emerging London is sharp and cosmopolitan. It is where many of the young love Fun-Da-Mental, a multiracial group of musicians led by the devout Muslim Aki Navaz, who merges rap with Sufi and hip-hop music. Or Asian Dub Foundation, with young British Bangladeshis mixing hard lyrics with yielding, soft harmonies. Both of these pop groups are aggressively demanding of their right to this city. Their songs are raw and real; they rail against racism, exclusion and all inherited categories and celebrate instead the essential hybridity of their own lives. As does the phenomenally successful Jazzie B of Soul II Soul. He says that his inspiration is his complex British identity, which includes"back home," in his case the Caribbean, but also his upbringing in London, where he lived intimately and easily with Greeks, Asians, Jews, Muslims, Catholics and Rastafarians.

If this London is "cosmopolitan," it is clearly in sync with the kind of critical cosmopolitanism Walter Mignolo advocates. Alibhai-Brown rightly sees this new multicultural cosmopolitanism as the inevitable legacy of British imperialism in South Asia and the Caribbean, but she makes a distinction between what she identifies as Britain's insatiable colonialist appetite for the exotic that led explorers like Sir Francis Drake to return with "all manner of foreign booty, spices and recipes for cooking peacocks" and a newly emergent group of cosmopolitan and culturally mixed "ethnic minorities" who have transformed British culture in a way that is "beginning to redefine the very essence of what it means to be a Londoner." As Stuart Hall puts it in Alibhai-Brown's article:

> For the first time being black and Asian is a way of being British. It is also sexy, and cool—all things that the Puritan English culture has both reviled and desired. In London especially, young blacks and Asians have turned marginality into a creative life force. They have styled their way into British culture—which is not hard because it was very unstylish. They have made it their own.

The sources of this transformation are historical, demographic, and political. Post–World War II London has long had a demographic mix of postcolonial populations, but until the period Smith explores, conventional notions of "Englishness" insured these populations remained marginal to British culture. But the post-Thatcher era, presided over in London by its progressive mayor, Ken Livingstone, coincided with and helped foster the emergence of literature, music, and film produced by a new generation of post–postcolonial artists plugged into the increasingly global flow of transnational artistic idioms that have transformed both Englishness and its cultural products. This led in literature to the production of texts by writers like Hanif Kureishi, Meera Syal, Monica Ali, Hari Kunzru, and Zadie Smith, all of whom explore the complex roots of contemporary multicultural identities, as well as films and television shows exploring immigrant experience and the development of complex musical idioms like bhangra that collapse distinctions between "Eastern" and "Western" music (Talvin Singh, Fun-Da-Mental, Asian Dub Foundation, Nitin Sawhney, and M.I.A.). This is the cosmopolitan, multicultural world out of which Smith's novel emerges, a world that distinguishes it from the traditionally postcolonial settings of the other novels we have looked at. It is in this sense that *White Teeth,* more than any of these other texts, is the product of all the forces, both historical and contemporary, of what we now call globalization.

The complexity and sophistication of Smith's novel stems in part from its sustained engagement with the effects of globalization and the discourse of multiculturalism, but it is also rooted in its historical sweep (from the British slave

trade in the Caribbean and the 1857 Sepoy Rebellion in India through World
War II, the assassination of Indira Gandhi, the fall of the Berlin Wall, the fatwa
against Salman Rushdie, and controversies about stem cell research) and its focus
on two generations of three different families. This makes the novel busy, if not
audacious. It casts a wide net in every way: historical, philosophical, sociological,
and political. But no other contemporary novel reflecting on the long histories of
colonialism, postcolonialism, and globalization gets at the core of what is going
on in the contemporary globalized metropole in the last decades of the twentieth
century more than does *White Teeth*.

Added to this complexity is Smith's desire to trace the complicated intersection of family, place, race, and identity in the lives of her characters in a way that
simultaneously explores the historical roots and the contemporary permutations
of that intersection, and to do all this while trying to sustain both a philosophical
discourse about identity and a social analysis of the clash between multiculturalism and all types of fundamentalism in the West. *White Teeth* deals with identity
by fusing a curious reliance on dental symbolism[5] with Paul Gilroy's idea that
Englishness is grounded broadly in a black Atlantic experience in which that
identity is a product both of roots *and* routes. Historical inquiry in the novel is
repeatedly and punningly referred to as a "root canal"[6] in ways that recall Paul
Gilroy's insistence that "marked by its European origins, modern black political
culture has always been more interested in the relationship of identity to roots
and rootedness than in seeing identity as a process of movements and mediation
that is more appropriately approached via the homonym routes" (19).[7] Smith's
novel is rooted in a set of mobile, paradoxical locations, the metropolitan postcolonial space of London, South Asia, and Gilroy's black Atlantic. She draws in
particular on Gilroy's formulation in her treatment of the Bowden family, Jamaican immigrants of African descent who have settled in London. She explores
the roots/routes of their identity through four generations of women: Ambrose
Bowden, a slave (who is impregnated by a white man); her daughter, Hortense,
who migrates to Britain; Hortense's daughter Clara; and finally, Clara's daughter, Irie. Irie's struggle to come to terms with the complex historical sources of
her Englishness in contemporary London eventually leads her to recognize how
her personal history is embedded in the political history of the black Atlantic
migrations. At the same time, however, Smith expands Gilroy's general formulation about the intersection of roots and routes in the construction of Englishness
to include a Bengali family, the Iqbals, linking Gilroy's black Atlantic to the
spaces inhabited by members of the South Asian diaspora. Samad Iqbal joins
the British army to fight in World War II and in 1972 migrates with his wife Alsana to London, where they raise identical twin boys, Magid and Millat. Gilroy's
insistence that identity is a complex product of roots and routes is dramatized

quite systematically in Smith's treatment of the Iqbals, a family struggling to come to terms with the disruptive effects of migration, modernization, and secularization on conflicting models of identity held by Samad, Alsana, and their young sons. The Bowden and Iqbal families in *White Teeth* become enmeshed in the lives of two Anglo families, the Joneses and the Chalfens. Samad Iqbal becomes acquainted with Archie Jones when they serve together in World War II, and they subsequently become close friends after the Iqbals move to London. At the same time and as the novel opens, Archie Jones meets and marries Clara Bowden. Their daughter, Irie, becomes close friends with the Iqbal twins, who later become involved with the white upper-middle-class family of Marcus and Joyce Chalfen through their friendship with their son, Joshua. Structuring her story across generations and through the intersecting lives of families from disparate parts of Britain's former empire, Smith puts in play a set of relationships carefully calibrated to explore how the histories of colonialism and globalization have rerouted and disrupted genealogical and cultural roots both for her immigrant *and* her Anglo characters. In this way Smith historicizes the politics of contemporary British multiculturalism by linking them to the histories of colonialism and globalization, but also to a variety of contending responses to the new cultural demographics of cosmopolitan London, which run the gamut from the reactionary racial politics of Enoch Powell to the often saccharine celebrations of diversity by liberal multiculturalists like Joyce Chalfen and the teacher Poppy Burt-Jones, and finally and most forcefully, to forms of religious and scientific fundamentalism associated with a variety of the novel's characters.

Samad at War

Although the plot of *White Teeth* is loosely organized around Archie Jones, it is Samad Iqbal who initially carries the weight of Smith's complicated analysis of how history and genealogy have produced a conflict between multiculturalism and fundamentalism in turn-of-the-century London. Samad's paradoxical experiences as a Bengali Muslim fighting to defend the British crown in World War II, his agonized responses to the forces of assimilation in London, and his struggle to reconnect his twin sons with a Bengali identity, culture, and religious perspective that he believes the West has corrupted are all central to Smith's larger ambitions in the novel. Samad is particularly important because through him Smith focuses on a set of transitional forces shaping contemporary globalization, and in a way that historicizes their processes. Moreover, by juxtaposing the Iqbals' experiences with those of the Jamaican Bowdens, Smith underscores the globalized nature of empire's structures and effects. For all of their differences, the

Iqbals and the Bowdens suffer through the same kind of historical experiences, and in contemporary London their children confront many of the same challenges: how to imaginatively construct English identities that are both rooted in—and routed through—the complex histories of their families and the nations that produced them.

Smith presents World War II as a kind of liminal point for the forces at work in her story. The war marks for Samad the transition between a history marked by colonialism and a postcolonial future inaugurated by independence and partition. It consolidates the acceleration of political, economic, and cultural globalization that is at once linked to the long history of colonialism that has shaped Samad's identity *and* structures the terms through which his new westernized identity will be imagined. When we first meet Samad on the Russian front we find him bitterly ambivalent about his predicament. On the one hand, he insists on underscoring his Bengali identity and in setting the historical record straight about his roots, but, on the other, he speaks with disparagement about his Indian identity and seems reconciled to being "stuck" in the "British machine" as a "British subject" (73). He reacts angrily, for example, when Mackintosh, one of his fellow soldiers, insists on calling him "Sultan," but a few pages later he emphasizes the stature of his Indian identity by insisting he is the great-grandson of Mangal Pande, the man who fired the first shot in what became the 1857 Sepoy Rebellion against the British.[8] Given his association with Pande, Samad resents the low-level, obscure assignment he has been given, a result of his being wounded in the hand earlier in the war while fighting with an Indian regiment in Italy's Po Valley. At this point, he begins to reveal a deep resentment toward India and the Bengali identity he had earlier sought to clarify and defend.

Samad's sense of anguish about his identity, caught as he is between a "British machine" responsible for the colonization of his Bengali identity and his thankless treatment by India, a "place for fools," comes to a head in a drunken attempt at suicide (an act repeated years later by Archie in the scene that opens the novel). Samad is at war with himself, and this war manifests itself here as a frustrating struggle with displacement. On the one hand, "he saw where he was–at the farewell party for the end of Europe—and he *longed* for the East" (94), yet, on the other, he sees little chance of a future in either the East or the West:

> What am I going to do, after this war is over, this war that is already over—what am I going to do? Go back to Bengal? Or to Delhi? Who would have such an Englishman there? To England? Who would have such an Indian? They promise us independence in exchange for the men we were. But it is a devilish deal. What should I do? Stay here? Go elsewhere? (95)

This chapter (5) sets up the terms of Samad's predicament. The narrative of Samad at war becomes a narrative of Samad at war with *himself,* and the divisions he experiences on the Russian front persist and deepen as he tries to assimilate to life in London after settling there in 1973 with his wife Alsana.[9] Samad's psychic displacements wreak havoc with his identity and are mirrored by the routes of his geographic migrations as he moves from Bengal to Italy, the Russian front, back to Bengal, and, finally, to London. In the chapters following the story of Samad's experiences on the Russian front, Smith shifts her attention back to London. It is 1984, Samad and Alsana are raising twin sons, Magid and Millat, and the terms of Samad's earlier ruminations about his identity have reshaped themselves around both a struggle with the abstract forces of purity and corruption, on the one hand, and his increasing frustration with how westernized his sons are becoming, on the other. This shift is significant in a couple of ways. It marks Smith's interest in how identities develop through families and genealogies via the forms of displacement Samad agonized over on the Russian front, and it foregrounds her commitment to exploring some of the philosophical conceptions we invoke when we talk about the roots of identity. In London Samad does not worry about the conflicted nature of his own identity until he becomes aware of how his sons are turning into thoroughly westernized subjects, and he blames his own sins for their condition:

> And the sins of the Eastern father shall be visited upon the Western sons.... Because immigrants have always been particularly prone to repetition—it's something to do with that experience of moving from West to East or East to West or from island to island. Even when you arrive, you're still going back and forth; your children are going round and round. There's no proper term for it—*original sin* seems too harsh; maybe *original trauma* would be better. A trauma is something one repeats and repeats, after all, and this is the tragedy of the Iqbals—that they can't help but reenact the dash they once made from one land to another, from one faith to another, from one brown mother country into the pale, freckled arms of an imperial sovereign. (135–36)

In Samad's view, his sons' westernization is a penalty for the renunciation of his own Bengali identity, an act that has worked its way into the very roots of their identities. Confronted with how his sons are turning out (Millat models himself on the character played by Ray Liotta in Martin Scorsese's film *Goodfellas,* while Magid wants to be called Mark Smith), Samad begins to see the accidents of migration and cross-cultural experience in terms of sin and corruption: "I have been corrupted by England, I see that now—my children, my wife, they too have been corrupted" (120). Having abandoned both Bengali traditions and his Muslim faith, Samad views that abandonment as a sin and a corruption being visited on his sons. They have "no respect for tradition," he blurts out to Archie. "People call it assimilation when it is nothing but corruption. Corruption!" (159).[10]

His impurity is rooted in his self-division. Samad thinks of himself as a "foreign man in a foreign land caught between borders" (148), a "split" person: "Half of me wishes to sit quietly with my legs crossed, letting the things that are beyond my control wash over me. But the other half wants to fight the holy war. Jihad!" (150). He does not think he can save himself from the corrosive forces of Western assimilation, but he thinks he can save his sons, or rather, he decides to deal with his own guilt by first displacing it onto his sons, and then saving them. "What is done is done," he tells Archie. "I am hell-bound, I see that now. So I must concentrate on saving my sons" (158). In this Samad sees no middle ground. His sons will either continue to become English or be forced to reconnect with their father's Bengal roots.[11] Smith makes it clear that there is something "sinister" about Samad's line of thinking:

> If religion is the opiate of the people, tradition is an even more sinister analgesic, simply because it rarely appears sinister. If religion is a tight band, a throbbing vein, and a needle, tradition is a far homelier concoction. . . . To Samad . . . tradition was culture, and culture led to roots, and these were good, these were untainted principles. That didn't mean he could live by them, abide by them, or grow in the manner they demanded, but roots were roots and roots were good. . . . Roots were what saved, the ropes one throws out to rescue drowning men, to Save Their Souls. (161)

Here both "tradition" and "roots" are "sinister" analgesics because they are connected to a fundamentalist discourse about "untainted principles." In Smith's view, Samad's mistake is seeing "tradition" as something pure, fixed, and unchanging. He draws, that is, a clear binary distinction between tradition and change.

Samad settles on the radical idea of sending his sons back to Bangladesh. However, since he cannot afford to send them both back, he flips a coin to choose between them.[12] As a result of the secret coin toss Magid is sent back to Bangladesh, while Millat remains with his parents in London. Heavy-handed as this plot twist is, it becomes the point of departure for Smith's humorous interrogation of Samad's theories about roots, tradition, assimilation, and corruption, for it turns out that the longer Magid remains in Bangladesh the more westernized he becomes, while Millat, remaining in the West, moves progressively from unfocused teenage alienation to an embrace of Islam and its critique of Western modernity. Samad's intervention effectively works in reverse; his flip of the coin backfires. Magid's letters home chronicle an educational experience in which he insists that a backward South Asia needs to become more like Britain. Attracted to the law, Magid writes home that "it had long been my intention to make the Asian countries sensible places, where order prevailed.... But many of us are uneducated, many of us do not understand the world. We must be more like the English.... They do not listen to history unless it is telling them what they wish to hear" (239–40). Magid becomes increasingly attracted to Western rationality over the course of the novel, rejecting Islam and the larger Bengal culture Samad had hoped would reroute his identity. While Magid spends his time in Bangladesh adopting a British identity, Millat tries on a series of identities inspired by Western popular culture. He becomes increasingly wedded to a swaggering identity informed by films about mafiosi like *Goodfellas* and *The Godfather*. However, this identity becomes fused in an uneasy way with another that is informed by the multicultural mix of South Asian and Caribbean teens he hangs out with, a group that eventually takes the hybrid name, "Raggastani" and which leads him, inexorably, to the Islam Magid rejects in Bangladesh:[13]

> It was a new breed, just recently joining the ranks of the other street crews. Becks, B-boys, Nation Brothers, Raggas, and Pakis; manifesting itself as a kind of cultural mongrel of the last three categories. Raggastanis spoke a strange mix of Jamaican patois, Bengali, Gujarati, and English. Their ethos, their manifesto, if it could be called that, was equally a hybrid thing: Allah *featured,* but more as a collective big brother than a supreme being...kung fu and the works of Bruce Lee were also central to the philosophy; added to this was a smattering of Black Power...but mainly their mission was to put the Invincible back in Indian, the Bad-aaass back in Bengali, and the P-Funk in Pakistani. (192)

Of course this "new breed" represents the emerging identity of a cosmopolitan, multicultural London transformed by the migration of formerly colonized populations from South Asia and the Caribbean, but more significantly, it represents a "mongrel" or contaminated cultural identity directly at odds with the kind of purity Samad associates with traditional culture. As such it is closer to Mignolo's critical cosmopolitanism than it is to traditional cosmopolitanism. Samad and the Raggastanis represent two diametrically opposed responses to the forms of difference produced by colonialism and globalization. Samad sees the kind of mongrelization Millat embraces as evidence of the essentially corrupting nature of assimilation, while Millat identifies with a range of marginal identities that have come into contact through the accident of historical forces, and he seeks to assert his own power as a subject through what Appadurai would call the imaginative work of cultural appropriation and transformation.

While we may be tempted to see the hybrid processes at work in the formation of the Raggastanis as a specifically postmodern condition fueled by globalization, Smith insists on historicizing or naturalizing them. We get a good example of this argument in the person of Samad's wife Alsana in an exchange that comes right after the passage about the Raggastanis. Samad and Alsana are arguing about the fatwa issued against Salman Rushdie's novel, *Satanic Verses,* with Samad supporting the fatwa and Alsana arguing against it. Samad sees the issue in terms of "protecting one's culture, shielding one's religion from abuse" (195). He accuses his wife of being "too busy" trying to find forms of accommodation with her Hindi friends to pay attention "to your own culture" (195):

"My *own* culture? And what is that please?"
"You're a Bengali. Act like one."
"And what is a Bengali, husband, please?"
"Get out of the way of the television and look it up."

Alsana took out BALTIC–BRAIN, number three of their twenty-four-volume-set of *Reader's Digest Encyclopedia,* and read from the relevant section:
   The vast majority of Bangladesh's inhabitants are Bengalis, who are largely descended from Indo-Aryans who began to migrate into the country from the west thousands of years ago and who mixed within Bengal with indigenous groups of various racial stocks. Ethnic minorities include the Chakma and Mogh, Mongoloid peoples who live in the Chittagong Hill Tracts District; the Santal, mainly descended from migrants from present-day India; and the Biharis, non-Bengali Muslims who migrated from India after the partition. (196)

It turns out Samad's own "Bengali" identity is no less a hybrid construction than Millat's Raggastani one, born as it is of migration and the mixing of "indigenous groups of various racial stocks" with "ethnic minorities" from a variety of locations. Both of Samad's sons complicate his reductive link between culture, tradition, and purity, Magid by returning to Bangladesh and promptly becoming Anglicized, and Millat by staying in London and adopting a hybrid identity, which, while on the surface diametrically opposite Samad's Bengali model, is in fact its mirror image.

The irony of Samad's experiment with his sons is that it is Millat, not Magid, who eventually embraces Islam (albeit in a hybrid version far from the one Samad had in mind for Magid). "The one I send home comes out a pukka Englishman, white-suited, silly wig lawyer," Samad laments, while "the one I keep here is fully paid-up green-bow-tie wearing fundamentalist terrorist" (336). Millat embraces Islam when he joins a group that Smith dubs, with tongue in cheek, KEVIN (Keepers of the Eternal and Victorious Islamic Nation). Millat is introduced to this group by a young man named Hifan, who proselytizes against drinking and sex and insists to Millat there is a cultural "war" going on in the West (244). Although Samad believes Millat has become a "fundamentalist," KEVIN is as globally hybrid an organization as the Raggastanis:

> KEVIN had been born within the black and Asian community. A radical new movement where politics and religion were two sides of the same coin. A group that took freely from Garveyism, the American Civil Rights movement, and the thought of Elijah Muhammad, yet remained within the letter of the Qur'an. (390)[14]

This hodge-podge mix complicates the idea that KEVIN is an Islamic fundamentalist group in any conventional sense, a complication underscored by Millat's struggle to accommodate himself to its teachings. KEVIN has four criteria Millat must follow: "To be ascetic in one's habits.... To remember always the glory of Muhammad.... To grasp a full intellectual understanding of KEVIN and the Qur'an.... To purge oneself of the taint of the West" (367). "In the first three areas he was doing fine" (367), writes Smith, but he had a "problem. Number four. Purging oneself of the West" (368).

Millat is burdened by what Smith calls a "split-level" subconscious (366), the division between a westernized "gangster" identity informed by American mob films like *Goodfellas* and an Islamic one he struggles to construct as a member of KEVIN. At key points, however, they merge, for he has "the seething violent anger of a gangster, a juvenile delinquent, determined to prove himself, determined to run the clan, determined to beat the rest. And if the game was God, if the game was a fight against the West...he was determined to win it" (369). Millat, of course, is at war with himself in much the same way his father was. His split-level subconscious is a product of the same contending forces, but worked out in a different turn-of-the-century cultural and political context. Where Samad's struggle unfolded within the discourses of assimilation and traditional Islam, Millat's unfolds within the very different discourses of multiculturalism and a globalized, pop postmodern form of Islam. While the comic elements in Smith's treatment of Millat and his involvement with KEVIN might suggest a dismissive attitude toward Islam and the personal struggle he is undergoing, there is plenty of evidence Smith is quite serious in her analysis of Millat's experience, and that she understands the attraction of Islam's response to secular modernity to young men like him as a key development in the contemporary history of globalization (whether that response is elaborated in "fundamentalist" terms or in the more globalized, pop culture form KEVIN represents).

It is important to see the connection between what I have been calling Samad's war with himself and the pull Islam has on Millat. Islam, however, is only one of a number of transnational sources that inform Millat's subjectivity, and they are all connected to the forces of globalization and various crises surrounding the rise of "multiculturalism" as a strategy for dealing with difference in the metropolitan West. But they are all connected historically to his father's experiences under colonialism. Samad's war with himself plays itself out in his twins; his own self-division gets mirrored both in the two routes they take (Magid to Englishness in Bangladesh, Millat to Islam in London) and in Millat's "split-level" subconscious.

Irie Jones's Root Canals

While Millat is struggling with the legacy of his father's war with himself and the need to mediate between the Western and Eastern roots/routes of his identity, Irie Jones, Archie's daughter, is on a parallel kind of journey, performing what Smith likes to call a "root canal" into her own Jamaican past. While religion and its relationship to culture and tradition are paramount for both Samad and Millat, race and class are at the center of Irie's attempt to come to terms with her own mixed identity. Like Millat's, that identity is produced by the long history of British colonialism and the more recent, accelerating forces of globalization, including the metropolitan imperative to be "multicultural." When we first meet her she is self-conscious about her race and would like nothing better than to fade into the white middle classes, to be free of the racial polarities that define her identity. She longs for a "neutral space" (426) free of race and historical struggle. Her self-consciousness about race is rooted in her relationship to her body, for "the European proportions" of her mother's "figure had skipped a generation, and she was landed instead with" her grandmother's "substantial Jamaican frame, loaded with pineapples, mangoes, and guavas" (221). Where Millat's *subconscious* is "split level," it is Irie's *body* that is divided between the two identities she has inherited. She becomes obsessed with losing weight in order to get rid of what she thinks of as her "Caribbean flesh" (222) and gets extensions to transform her kinky hair into "a full head of long, straight, reddish-black hair" (235).[15] At school she identifies her own dark body with the female figure in Shakespeare's "Dark Lady" sonnets (127 and 130). Irie wonders whether there might be a connection between her own body and the body being described in the sonnets, and she grasps at a link between the poems' discourse about blackness and beauty and her own anxieties about the beauty of *her* black body.

Irie's self-consciousness about race is paralleled by her increasing awareness of how class differences shape her identity. "Englishness," she begins to see, is defined not only in terms of whiteness but in terms of a vaguely defined middle-class status. Her preoccupation with middle-class Englishness develops when she becomes involved, along with Millat and Magid, with the family of one of their school friends, the Chalfens. Marcus Chalfen is a brilliant scientist working on stem cell research and his wife Joyce Chalfen is a successful pop horticultural writer (*The New Flower Power* and *The Inner Life of Houseplants* are two of her titles), and when Irie first meets them she realizes "she'd never been so *close* to this strange and beautiful thing, the *middle class,* and experienced the kind of embarrassment that is actually intrigue, fascination" (267). She develops a "nebulous fifteen-year-old's passion for them, overwhelming, yet with no real direction or object. She just wanted to, well, kind of, merge with them. She wanted their Englishness" (272). Irie begins to work part time for Marcus, organizing his files, and when she comes across his meticulously ordered Chalfen family tree and compares it with the chaotic disorder of the Jamaican Bowdens she becomes further seduced by what she comes to call "Chalfenism": "She *wanted* to merge with the Chalfens, to be of one flesh; separated from the chaotic, random flesh of her own family" (284).[16] The Chalfens represent a seductive mix of order, whiteness, an absence of the burden of history, and middle-class Englishness. They seem to Irie to offer a refuge from the randomness and chaos of her own family, marked as it is by the roots/routes of interracial couplings, disruptive migrations, and the pressure to fit into an assimilationist identity that ill suits them.

Irie's encounter with the Chalfens marks the beginning of her attempt to understand her own Englishness. She furthers a growing rift with her mother Clara when she abruptly leaves home and moves in with her grandmother Hortense. She toys with fleeing to the Chalfens' house, but at this point, Irie thinks, "there were no answers there, only more places to escape" (314). Irie's decision to distance herself from the Chalfens and move in with her grandmother underscores how she is being pulled in two directions, one defined by what she calls "Chalfenism," and the other by what she calls "Bowdenism" (315).[17] Of course Irie's experience repeats both Samad's and Millat's, for Smith interweaves Irie's story both with her narrative about Samad's fear that assimilation has corrupted his identity and the complex story of how Millat develops a split-level consciousness, a device that serves to underscore the link between the Iqbal and Bowden families and the deep structure of the experiences they share. In this way British, South Asian, and Caribbean roots become entangled through the routes of colonization and migration in ways that make the stories of each of these characters merge into a single palimpsest.

Irie's time in the Bowden household is dominated by her encounter with old pictures and letters from her grandmother's Jamaican past. As she slowly excavates the contours of that past, she slips, Smith writes, back into "darkness" (330). Reading through her grandmother's odd library of books about the Caribbean,[18]

Irie encounters a new past rooted in a place "Columbus called St. Jago but the Arawaks stubbornly renamed Xaymaca, the name lasting longer than they did....She laid claim to the past—her version of the past—aggressively, as if retrieving misdirected mail" (322). These books relocate her identity in a way that suddenly marginalizes the English soil of her birth. "It just seemed tiring and unnecessary all of a sudden, that struggle to force something out of the re-calcitrant English soil. Why bother, when there was now this other place?" (332). This other place, of course, is in good measure a product of her imagination, what Salman Rushdie has called an "imaginary homeland," so we ought not to romanticize it:[19] "Irie imagined her homeland. Because *homeland* is one of the magical fantasy words, like *unicorn* and *soul* and *infinity* that have now passed into the language. And the particular magic of *homeland,* its particular spell over Irie, was that it sounded like a beginning. The beginningest of beginnings" (332). The more problematic their English identities become, the more both Irie (and Samad) look to a "homeland" as a place to reground their identities. Irie's imaginary homeland is a place "where things sprang from the soil riotously and without supervision" (332). However, Irie does not end up in the novel rejecting "Englishness" and embracing her Jamaican identity (choosing, that is, between her white father's roots and her black mother's). Nor does she make a pilgrim-age of return. Instead, she yearns for a neutral space beyond the historical con-flicts about identity with which she's been so caught up. Tired of listening to the Iqbals and Joneses arguing with one another, Irie bursts out in a harangue about normal silent families who just live their lives free of the cultural and historical conflicts that seem to determine the course of *their lives:*

> What a peaceful existence. What a *joy* their lives must be. They open a door and all they've got behind it is a bathroom or a living room. Just neutral spaces. And not this endless maze of present rooms and past rooms and the things said in them years ago and everybody's old historical shit all over the place. They're not con-stantly making the same old mistakes. They're not always hearing the same old shit....And every single fucking day is not this huge battle between who they are and who they should be, what they were and what they will be. (426)

Here the novel's interest in the relationship between identity and location, how place and displacement route identity, organizes itself around the desire for a space free of historical context and struggle, a place wholly present, out-side the past, and in this sense "neutral." Irie, like Millat and Magid, is *overde-termined,* marked in London by a complicated Otherness whose parts seem at cross-purposes with one another. The challenge of reconciling those parts, forg-ing them into a single identity, comes at such a cost that Irie longs for a neutral space in which all competing historical claims on her identity are erased, where the very pressure to think about "who" she is evaporates.[20]

Neutrality, of course, is about choosing not to choose; it is about not taking sides, about the desire to find a way to avoid the pitfalls and divisiveness of identity politics. It is a strategy for dealing with difference, and Smith's book is all about exploring late twentieth-century strategies for dealing with difference. However, while Smith moves Irie to the point where she desires a neutral place more than anything else, she has already made it clear in an earlier passage that such places are illusory:

> A neutral place. The chances of finding one these days are slim...the sheer *quantity* of shit that must be wiped off the slate if we are to start again as new. Race. Land. Ownership. Faith. Theft. Blood. And more blood. And more. And not only must the *place* be neutral, but the messenger who takes you to the place, and the messenger who sends the messenger. There are no people or places like that left in North London. (378)

Race, land, ownership, faith, theft, and blood (a mixture concocted and whirled together by accelerating forms of mobility) all play major roles in the constellation of identities Irie struggles with, and Smith strongly suggests they cannot be "wiped off the slate" but must be reintegrated in a subjectivity that is not neutral or indifferent, but *different*. Samad cannot be Bengali or English in any traditional sense, nor can Millat or Magid; and Irie is not Jamaican, and her Englishness will be different than the Chalfens', her father's, *and* Samad Iqbal's. While Englishness has always been shaped by transnational forces, the combined effects of the history of colonialism and those of more contemporary forms of globalization, Smith shows, have forged new identities vastly different than older ones. In this sense Smith's is a twenty-first-century novel, with characters more closely connected to a post–postcolonial world than those in *Moth Smoke* or any of the other novels we have discussed.

Multiculturalism, Fundamentalism, and Managing Difference

These new identities are linked in the novel to a set of philosophical discourses about difference, hybridity, and multiplicity connected to a late twentieth-century interest in multiculturalism. While Smith in her own way sides with this multiculturalist discourse, she also uses satire to critique it. Indeed, there is something distinctly postliberal, even paradoxical, about Smith's novel. She clearly embraces the kind of commitment to an often transgressive hybridity we associate with writers and critics like Rushdie, Bhabha, Appadurai, and Appiah, and her novel is a product of the new postcolonial and cosmopolitan London in which Englishness is undergoing profound transformations. Yet she is critical of fatuous talk about multiculturalism and the kind of uninformed pieties it can embrace.[21] While she is careful to have Irie reject the desire for racial and cultural purity associated with her grandmother Hortense and Samad Iqbal, she creates in Irie a character whose reconnection with her Jamaican roots is serious and moving. Moreover, Smith clearly takes seriously Samad's experience of disconnection from his own Bengali culture. She is critical of the kind of religious fundamentalism associated with both Hortense Bowden (a devout Jehovah's Witness) and KEVIN, yet she writes movingly and with deep conviction about the reality of the Muslim experience with racism in London and why it leads to an embrace of this Islamic organization.[22] KEVIN's ideology, Joyce Chalfen's commitment to cultural hybridity, Samad Iqbal's romance with the purity of a Bengali identity, Poppy Burt-Jones's commitment to multiculturalism, all come off as cheesy, but underneath the social satire Smith takes seriously the philosophical, moral, and cultural claims being made by each in her or his attempt to manage diversity. In the final analysis, she comes down on the side of what, in one crucial passage, she calls "multiplicity." Here she is invoking Zeno's paradox of the motionless arrow in flight and applying it to the plight of the immigrant. "We often imagine," she writes, "that immigrants are constantly on the move, footloose, able to change course at any moment, able to employ their legendary resourcefulness at every turn...happy and willing to leave their difference at the docks and take their chances in this new place, merging with the oneness of this green and pleasant libertarian land of the free" (384). Smith links this oneness (the chimerical ideal of assimilation) to Zeno's paradox and its insistence that "multiplicity, the *Many* [is] an illusion" (384). Yet, she insists in the end that "multiplicity is no illusion. Nor is the speed with which those-in-the-simmering-melting-pot are dashing toward it.... Yeah, Zeno had an angle. He wanted the One, but the world is Many." Immigrants "will race toward the future only to find they more and more eloquently express their past, that place where they have *just been*. Because this is the other thing about immigrants ('fugees, émigrés, travelers): they cannot escape their history any more than you yourself can lose your shadow" (384–85).

Smith's embrace of multiplicity, hybridity, and syncretic cultural forms is in the novel set against a variety of pseudo-purist fundamentalisms embodied in Samad's mania about purity, Hortense Bowden's allegiance to the Jehovah's Witnesses, the Islamism of KEVIN, and the scientific theories of Marcus Chalfen. Oddly, Hortense Bowden and Marcus Chalfen share a kind of fundamentalist commitment to the idea that reality is ultimately driven and ordered by a discoverable design. For Hortense that design is divine, while for Marcus it is coded in the genetic order of things. Both of these fundamentalisms are connected to a desire to eliminate the random, a devotion to certainty and perfectibility that is of a piece with Samad's obsession with purity and that ultimately translates into a racialized resistance to difference. Hortense Bowden is quite explicit about this. When her daughter Clara announces she is going to marry Archie (who is white), Hortense disowns her:

> When Hortense Bowden, half white herself, got to hearing about Clara's marriage, she came round to the house, stood on the doorstep, said, "Understand: I and I don't speak from this moment forth," turned on her heel, and was true to her word. Hortense hadn't put all that effort into marrying black, into dragging her genes back from the brink, just so her daughter could bring yet more high-colored children into the world. (272)

Later, Hortense explains her resistance to racial mixing to Irie: "But it more de principle of de ting, you know? Black and white never come to no good. De Lord Jesus never meant us to mix it up.... When you mix it up, nuttin' good can come. It wasn't *intended*" (318). Hortense here is drawing a kind of distinction between the pure and the random, and Marcus Chalfen's scientific work is aimed squarely at eliminating the kind of randomness that she worries over (along with Samad Iqbal). His stem cell research is about to culminate in the production of what he calls a "futuremouse," a mouse whose genetic program he controls. Marcus hopes that by reengineering the mouse's "actual genome...you're no longer dealing with the *random*. You're *eliminating* the random.... You eliminate the random, you rule the world.... One could program every step in the development of an organism: reproduction, food habits, life expectancy" (282–83). It is precisely this release from the random and the accidental that makes Chalfenism initially so attractive to Irie. "She *wanted* to merge with the Chalfens," Smith writes, "to be of one flesh; separated from the chaotic, random flesh of her own family and transgenically fused with another. A unique animal. A new breed" (284). Hortense's desire to "drag her black genes back from the brink" of an interracial marriage has its mirror image in Marcus's genetic program, so that the "new breed" Irie identifies with here is one that promises protection from the kind of racial mixing Hortense abhors.

The link between Hortense's paranoia about racial mixing and Marcus Chalfen's attempt to eliminate the random is made explicit in a confrontation Chalfen has in an airport with a young South Asian woman who is reading one of his books on genetic engineering. (He does not tell her he is the author.) "A good book" he innocently asks her? (344). "Bit bloody weird. Bit of a headfuck...not so much weird, I guess, more *scary*" (344). Pressed by Chalfen to explain what is scary about it, she responds:

> They talk about leaps and bounds in the field of medicine, yada yada yada, but bottom line, if somebody knows how to eliminate"undesirable" qualities in people, do you think some government's not going to do it? I mean, what's undesirable? There's just something a little fascist about the whole deal...at points you do think: where are we going here? Millions of blonds with blue eyes? ...I mean if you're Indian like me you've got something to worry about, yeah? (346)

It is in passages like this that the schematic plan of Smith's novel gets both clarified *and* complicated. The binary distinctions between purity and corruption, design and randomness, and unity and multiplicity she regularly invokes are inextricably linked to the lives of her mixed-race characters in a way that underscores how their responses to difference are mediated through philosophical conceptions about identity. (Hortense's tendency to define her identity in religious terms and to subordinate her worldview to the kind of apocalyptic fundamentalism associated with the Jehovah's Witnesses is not unlike Samad's efforts to reorganize his identity around Islam and see the world in terms of a fundamental division between purity and corruption.) Although Hortense's religious framework seems wholly at odds with Chalfen's scientific one, they are actually linked in their commitment to a kind of fundamentalist conception of purity and perfectibility, one that, intentionally or not, marginalizes characters like Irie and Millat.

Each of these characters see the world as determined and ordered, organized along clear lines of separation in racial, moral, and cultural terms. The juxtaposition of multiculturalism with fundamentalism in *White Teeth,* as I have suggested, presents the reader with two different contemporary discourses for handling diversity and difference. On the one hand, the book's fundamentalist characters see a link between design, purity, faith, unity, and tradition, while those who embrace some version of multiculturalism side with chance, corruption, multiplicity, and innovation. In this way, a fundamentalist discourse about tradition, identity, and culture grounded in a set of fixed and essential realities gets contrasted with a counterdiscourse embracing multiplicity, hybridity, multiculturalism, and the random in a way that paradoxically views the corruption Samad fears as the *norm* (a norm thoroughly consistent with Appiah's notion of contamination).

The connection between Smith's analysis of binary oppositions, such as oneness and multiplicity, design and change, and purity and corruption, and her overriding interest in *fundamentalism* becomes explicit in the epigraphs she uses at the beginning of the novel's final section, entitled "Magid, Millat, and Marcus, 1992, 1999" (341). The first two are dictionary definitions of the words "fundamental" ("1. Of or pertaining to the basis or groundwork; going to the root of the matter. 2 Serving as the base or foundation; essential or indispensable. Also, primary, original; from which others are derived") and "fundamentalism" ("The strict maintenance of traditional orthodox religious beliefs or doctrines; *esp.* belief in the inerrancy of religious texts"). The last is a stanza from the Herman Hupfeld song "As Time Goes By," made famous in the film *Casablanca:*

> You must remember this, a kiss is still a kiss,
> A sigh is just a sigh;
> The fundamental things apply,
> As time goes by.

Smith's analysis of fundamentalisms in the novel comes to a head in her treatment of the "Islamic fundamentalism" Millat embraces when he joins KEVIN, which is, of course, linked to the kind of apocalyptic fundamentalism central to Hortense Bowden's religious devotion to the Jehovah's Witnesses. Hortense is totally consumed by her belief "in the inerrancy of religious texts," and both she and the followers of KEVIN maintain "traditional orthodox religious beliefs or doctrines" in the face of, and as an antidote to, a corrupting secular modernity. Their fundamentalism is *foundational* and *essentialist* in the sense captured by the dictionary definition of "fundamental." Samad veers toward this kind of fundamentalism in his attempt to strictly maintain a distinction between purity and corruption, but so does Marcus Chalfen, who believes he has discovered the very "basis or groundwork" of being, an "essential," "primary," and "original" genetic code that can erase multiplicity and variability. And, like Marcus, the leader of KEVIN, Ibrahim ad-Din Shukrallah, preaches the saving purity of oneness against the corrupting effects of multiplicity ("the entire world is affected by a disease known as *Kufr*—the state of rejection of the oneness of the Creator" [387]).[23] All these forms of fundamentalism are deployed in the context of Smith's analysis of a specific historical struggle with difference. It will not do, in our reading of the novel, to deal with these fundamentalisms in an abstract way. They are localized, defined, and played out in London in the last three decades of the twentieth century, a London that is paradoxically being colonized by its postcolonial subjects in a way that is becoming paradigmatic in metropolitan centers all over Europe, fueled by the interrelated histories of colonization and globalization. The discourse of liberal multiculturalism, a central topic in *White Teeth,* provides the backdrop for Smith's analysis of how cultural difference and national identity get managed in this context in the cosmopolitan West, and what I earlier called the discourse of fundamentalism looms up in the novel as the counterdiscourse to multiculturalism.

Smith is not interested in the question of whose fundamentalism is correct but in analyzing how fundamentalism functions as a discourse to manage difference in an era of increasing migration, secularization, and the proliferation of hybrid cultural forms. Nor, I believe, is she interested in simply condemning "fundamentalism" (just as she is not interested in simply condemning multiculturalism). Her sympathy with the characters who are tempted to take recourse in a fundamentalist discourse to ground their identities, particularly Irie Jones, Millat Iqbal, and Moe Hussein, but Samad and even Marcus Chalfen as well, belies such a reading. When Smith quotes the lines from "As Time Goes By," moreover, she explicitly acknowledges the sentimentality that often gets attached to the fundamental, something that is tempting to Irie for a while as she explores the roots of her own identity in Jamaica. (Another aspect of "fundamental" in the dictionary definition Smith quotes is "going to the root of the matter," which is precisely what Irie does when she researches her family's Jamaican past—indeed, all of the "root canals" in the book are connected to Smith's treatment of the fundamental.) Smith's interest is in how the various fundamentalisms she treats in the book make up a language for talking about identity, truth, morality, and difference that structures competing claims about national identity and cultural belonging at the end of a twentieth century that will give birth to the attacks of 9/11, the Madrid and London subway bombings, and the riots in France during the fall of 2005.

Smith's novel is an important literary document for our own time because it both historicizes globalization and connects its contemporary character to the eruption of reactionary forces we tend to lump together under the term "fundamentalism." The global flows of populations and cultures Smith tracks in *White Teeth* are mapped and historicized in a way that insists we see identity and culture marked by difference and hybridity all the way down and all the way back. In the historical world Smith delineates there is no going back to a time in which identities or cultures were pure and uncorrupted. In this sense she is in complete accord with Appiah's notion of contamination. Whether we consider the Bowdens with their roots in Africa and colonial Jamaica, the Iqbals with their roots in the tangled history of migration and mongrelization in Bengal, or the Chalfens and the Joneses whose "Englishness" is also a complex product of British colonialism, there are no identities or cultures in the novel that are not the product of global economic and social forces that are continually reshaping human subjectivity and the social structures that sustain it. In linking the fate of its characters to the long history of globalization Smith also complicates one of the central tenets of globalization theory, the idea that globalization is characterized by a one-way flow of cash and cultural commodities from the core to the periphery. This binary is thoroughly upended in *White Teeth*. Smith's London is postcolonial, perhaps even post–postcolonial in Hamid's sense of the term. The core has become the periphery, and it has done so in a way that reminds us there has always been a fluid relationship between the metropolis of the colonizer and the world of the colonized. The commodity and cultural flows characteristic of this relationship are circular and mutually transformative. The irony of the metropolitan world Smith explores in *White Teeth* is that colonization has come full circle and has begun to produce a counter or critical cosmopolitanism.

Transnational Masculinities in Junot Díaz's *The Brief Wondrous Life of Oscar Wao*

All the novels I have discussed so far dramatically underscore how the transnational turn in literary and cultural studies is mirrored by an explosion of writing in English that is both transnational in its locations and engaged with a range of issues related to contemporary globalization. There is, of course, a symbiotic relationship between the criticism discussed in part 1 and the fiction analyzed in part 2, for the transnational turn in literary production provides an increasing body of texts for analysis by critics interested in the contemporary intersection of literature, culture, and globalization, and the work of those critics feeds back into and informs that literature. (One good example, as noted in the last chapter, is the extent to which *White Teeth* draws on some of Gilroy's key formulations in *The Black Atlantic*.) Whether it is the question of the historical relationship between colonialism, postcolonialism, and globalization, the linked cultural and economic effects of globalization on those living under its influence both in developing nations and Western metropolitan centers like London and New York, or the impact of the long history of globalization on the construction of personal, cultural, and national identities, these issues are being explored by numerous writers working in English in disparate parts of the world.

Central to this enterprise is the transnational character of the *locations* within which these novels are set. All the novels examined here engage multiple intersecting locations and feature mobility as a central and accelerating force under globalization. Each one features (and historicizes) different forms of mobility, some determined, like Jemubhai's in *The Inheritance of Loss* and Chacko's in *The God of Small Things,* by the paradoxical opportunities and limitations facilitated by travel from colony to metropole and back, others by more complicated postcolonial circuits of migration connected to work or schooling, some legal, others illegal. Abhay in *Red Earth and Pouring Rain,* Rahel in *The God of Small Things,* Ozi and Mumtaz in *Moth Smoke,* Camagu in *The Heart of Redness,* and Biju in *The Inheritance of Loss* all come and go from their homelands, and then return in a circuit determined by the forces of accelerating globalization. The characters in *White Teeth,* on the other hand, have arrived at what used to be the very center of colonial power by migrating from former colonial locations to a London undergoing dramatic transformations that shake the very foundations of "Englishness." Identities (personal, cultural, national) in Smith's novel get worked out in the complicated intersections of disparate locations and the histories they embody. We move from location to location in these novels because they are about the production of subjectivity in a world in which, increasingly, the borders and the histories of discrete nation-states cannot contain and do not determine experience.[1]

All of these novels underscore how the structure and rhythm of migration is changing as globalization accelerates. Junot Díaz, whose *The Brief Wondrous Life of Oscar Wao,* I will be discussing in this concluding chapter, makes the distinction, in a September 2007 interview with Christopher Lydon, between a traditional one-way form of migration to the United States and a new form of migration in which individuals and families move back and forth constantly between their home and adopted countries:

> We are in a complete new world.... There are still plenty of people who come and never go back. There are still plenty of people who stay and never can leave. But there's also this other dimension...that's completely unstable, where people are back and forth all the time, and I think that is something that, as artists, as writers, that is really cool to deal with because it's new, because no one's really seen it before, a community that can kind of just jump back and forth...constantly exchanging information and experiences both from home and carrying them from home to the United States, and back, people who jump back and forth kind of like the shuttles on a loom because they're really strengthening and reinforcing connections between two places.[2]

Díaz's "back-and-forth" people extend and complicate the forms of mobility we have observed operating in each of the novels I have discussed so far. The principal characters in his novel—Belicia, Oscar, Lola, and Yunior—live their lives in the literal and virtual spaces between nations, perpetually in transit between locations. However, these spaces are not neutral ones in the sense we saw Irie long for in *White Teeth,* spaces outside of or beyond the kinds of historical conflicts and ethnic tensions that characterized her experience, and those of Magid, Millat, and the other characters in Smith's novel. Rather, they are defined by those conflicts and tensions, complicating the need to construct U.S.-based identities that grow out of the complex historical intersection of American and Dominican histories, subjectivities, and cultures.

Structuring his novel around this back-and-forth movement, Díaz melds together the narrative techniques used by both Smith and Desai. Like Smith, Díaz creates a generational structure for his narrative, one that features alternating chapters about Belicia's life in the Dominican Republic under the dictatorship of Rafael Trujillo with chapters about her children who live in New Jersey in the last two decades of the twentieth century. This device works to dramatize how Belicia's experiences in Trujillo's Dominican Republic have helped define the contemporary subjectivities of her children. The effect of this structural device is connected to a central idea underlying Smith's text, Samad's observation early in the novel that "our children will be born of our actions. Our accidents will become their destinies" (87). The same principle is at work in Díaz's novel, for Belicia's children, Oscar and Lola, are born of her actions, and Díaz ties their destinies to the accidents of her experience. This generational structure gives the novel temporal fluidity, as the reader moves back and forth between long historical chapters about Belicia that are set in the Dominican Republic (chapters 3 and 5) and those centered on her children and the narrator, Yunior, that are set in New Jersey. The effect of this shuttling back and forth is to locate the reader not in New Jersey or the Dominican Republic, but in a kind of virtual space in which the two locations intersect and combine into a single, fluid space. The Belicia chapters roughly approximate those in *White Teeth* set in historical Jamaica, so that Irie's "root canal," her exploration of the Bowdens' family history there, is mirrored in Yunior's exploring Belicia's early life in Trujillo's Dominican Republic. The historical chapters in both novels work to dramatize how the subjectivities of each of the children in them are constructed out of the historical accidents of an older generation whose experiences are rooted in other places that nevertheless impinge on the present.[3]

The generational relationships in both these novels are constructed to allow both Smith and Díaz to explore whether or not there is some kind of systematic design directing the fate of their characters (a question that, in looser form, haunts all of the novels looked at here). We saw that in *White Teeth* Smith's interest in how the historical "accidents" of one generation can affect another was counterbalanced by an interest in design (or fate), which exist in the novel as two competing principles or explanatory systems. Religious and scientific systems, embodied in Islam, the Jehovah's Witnesses, and Marcus Chalfen's scientific quest to rid the world of randomness, continually clash with Archie Jones's propensity for flipping coins and assuming events in his life just unfold by chance. This preoccupation carries over into Smith's treatment of the histories of colonization that she traces in both South Asia and the Caribbean, for a key question both Samad and Irie grapple with has to do with the extent to which their own lives have somehow been designed by the colonial roots/routes of their families' experiences.

A similar question surfaces dramatically at the very outset of Díaz's novel, which begins by introducing the idea that the "New World" suffers under a curse, what he calls a "*fukú*," one that has worked its way down from the slave trade and colonization into our own time, exercising a kind of fate over the characters in his novel:

> They say it came first from Africa, carried in the screams of the enslaved; that it was the death bane of the Tainos, uttered just as one world perished and another began...*Fukú americanus,* or more colloquially, fukú—generally a curse or a doom of some kind; specifically the Curse and the Doom of the New World. Also called the Fukú of the Admiral [Christopher Columbus] because the Admiral was both its midwife and one of its great European victims. (1)

Díaz's fukú is a curse born of conquest, colonization, and slavery—a curse on the New World brought from the old, visited on its agents as well as its victims, on indigenous peoples, slaves, admirals, plantation owners, and slave traders alike. Rafael Trujillo, Yunior insists, became "its hypeman," but "no one knows whether Trujillo was the Curse's servant or its master, its agent or its principal" (2–3). This historical, hemispheric fukú persists into the present and shapes the lives of Díaz's characters: "The fukú ain't just ancient history, a ghost story from the past, with no power to scare. In my parents' day the fukú was real as shit, something your everyday person could believe in" (2). This fukú is both a curse and a story, and it affects the shape of the book, for Yunior, the novel's narrator, experiences the fukú as a kind of *narrative.* "Whether I believe in what many have described as the Great American Doom is not really the point," he insists, for if "you live as long as I did in the heart of fukú country, you hear these kinds of tales all the time" (5). You tell them, too, for Yunior wraps up this opening section of the novel by linking the narrative we are about to read to fukú tales: "As I'm sure you've guessed by now, I have a fukú story too...one that's got its

fingers around my throat" (6). Yunior envisions his narrative as a kind of counterspell (what he calls a "*zafa*"), one with the potential to undo the power of a
curse: "Even now, as I write these words, I wonder if this book ain't a zafa of
sorts. My very own counterspell" (7).

Díaz's fukú is a New World curse, but in its broadest outlines it is a trope
shadowing all of the novels I have been discussing, for each of them in their own
way seeks to weave a counterspell against the set of historical forces linked to the
curse or doom the characters measure their lives against. In this sense fukú puts
a name on a constellation of historical processes shaping the lives of displaced,
mobile, transplanted, rerouted people. It emphasizes the shaping power the histories of colonization, decolonization, and postcolonialism have in our own time,
especially when we see them as part of the long historical process we now call
globalization. In this sense it embodies the transnational turn in English. In both
its locations and its subject matter *The Brief Wondrous Life of Oscar Wao* conjures
up the kind of world we saw Doris Sommer call attention to in chapter 1 of this
book, a world in which cultures and literatures and the forms we use to study
them have awakened from a romantic enchantment with singular languages and
nations and in which "home means not a here but a there, somewhere else,"
a world in which "strangeness is the norm" (3).

Díaz's novel, mirroring Sommer's formulation, traffics in multiple languages
(English, Spanish, Dominican slang) and hybrid forms of national belonging
("American," Dominican, diasporic). It is haunted by a strangeness born of historical forces and contemporary paradoxes that seriously question the very notion of "somewhere else," since everywhere and everything from the past seems
present to its characters. Identity, citizenship, and cultural belonging in late
twentieth-century New Jersey are multiply determined and historically vexed
in ways that, as we have seen throughout this book, are increasingly the norm.
The American kids in his novel share a hemispheric identity rooted in the global
history of conquest, colonization, slavery, dictatorship, exile, and the ceaseless
back-and-forth rhythm of travel between the Antilles and the United States that
characterizes new forms of mobility under globalization. However, while they
are "American" kids, their conditions are linked inextricably to those of the characters we have encountered in the other novels. In what follows I want to explore
how Díaz connects these disparate histories and locations in a way that links his
novel to the other texts discussed in earlier chapters, broadening the geographical scope of their fictional worlds, yet underscoring how, at a deeper structural
level, Díaz's black Atlantic text shares a number of affinities with those worlds.

While Díaz's novel embraces a range of locations (Spain, Africa, the West Indies, and the United States) that specifically evoke Gilroy's black Atlantic and
are thus connected with the historical world Smith conjures up in *White Teeth,*
it is centered, like her novel, on the lives of young people growing up in the

metropolitan West. Smith's London has its corollary in Díaz's Paterson, New Jersey. Like Irie, Magid, and Millat, who struggle to cobble together a new kind of Englishness in a London defined by the competing discourses of multiculturalism, cosmopolitanism, and fundamentalism, Díaz's younger characters Oscar, Lola, and Yunior have to reconcile the heritage of their parents' Dominican identities with the pressures of being American in twenty-first-century Paterson. Their stories are linked by Díaz's interest in how competing models of masculinity, femininity, and sexuality in his novel are both shaped by and feed into the wielding of social power, power that is ultimately historicized in the novel in ways that connect it to the wielding of destructive forms of political power in the Americas. This is a topic that has received scant treatment by the critics I discussed in part 1. While we saw them pay general attention to the relationship between the personal and the political, none of them have looked closely in the way Díaz does at how colonizing and dominative forms of political power are informed by particular models of masculinity keyed to a brutalizing sexuality. The following discussion of *The Brief Wondrous Life of Oscar Wao* is meant to begin to fill this gap.[4]

Gender and sexuality are woven into the book through Díaz's overarching interest in storytelling.[5] In this respect the narrator, Yunior, becomes a key figure, nearly as important as Oscar. Both characters explore their masculinity and their sexuality through writing, and Díaz uses both their stories to underscore how their emerging identities as Americans are shaped by historical forces that collapse the personal into the political, and vice versa. In this way, the whole question of national identity (as with "Englishness" in both Gilroy's book and Smith's novel) has to be negotiated not within the narrow boundaries of the nation but between intersecting transnational spaces and histories. For this reason we cannot separate the novel's historical inquiry into the long histories of conquest, colonization, slavery, dictatorship, and exile in the Americas from its interest in the emergence of new American identities at the end of the twentieth century and the beginning of the twenty-first.

These links are written into the narrative structure of the book. While the first two chapters are about Oscar and his sister, Lola, and cover the period 1975–85, their lives are contextualized by the novel's opening seven-page section on the fukú, and the chapters that follow contain a strategic set of historical footnotes about Trujillo's regime that serve in particular to connect the pressures on Oscar as a young Dominican man to models of masculinity rooted in Trujillo's world. Oscar's problem is featured at the very beginning of chapter 1 and then immediately linked by a historical footnote to the Dominican world of his mother:

> Our hero was not one of those Dominican cats everybody's always going on about—he wasn't no home-run hitter or a fly bachatero, not a playboy with a million hots on his jack.

And except for one period early in his life, dude never had much luck with the females (how *very* un-Dominican of him).

He was seven then.

In those blessed days of his youth, Oscar was something of a Casanova. One of those preschool loverboys who was always trying to kiss the girls, always coming up behind them during a merengue and giving them the pelvic pump.... You should have seen him, his mother sighed, in her Last Days. He was our little Profirio Rubirosa. (11–12)

The reference to Rubirosa is the occasion for a long historical footnote (a device Díaz uses in the introductory section on the fukú and throughout the novel) emphasizing both Rubirosa's murderous work for Trujillo (he was married for a time to one of his daughters) and his status as an international playboy. "Rubirosa," Díaz writes, was a "tall, debonair prettyboy...the quintessential jet-setting car-racing polo-obsessed playboy," a man who models the kind of Dominican sexuality Díaz features throughout the book and that Oscar is never able to live up to. This seemingly off-hand anecdote at the beginning of the book is crucial, for it both announces the problem that plagues Oscar and connects his life to the world of Trujillo's dictatorship and, through that connection, to the larger New World fukú with which he begins the book.

Oscar's inability to live up to what seems at the outset of the book to be a thoroughly trite form of Latin machismo is used to weave a complex transnational meditation on the relationship between masculinity, voice, storytelling, and performance, one in which the wielding of power depends on a performance that masks vulnerability, short-circuiting the capacity for intimacy and leading to forms of brutality that flow out of Trujillo's world into Oscar, Lola, and Yunior's America. The historical footnote is central not so much because it tells us who Profirio Rubirosa is but because it calls attention to and *historicizes* the ultimate fukú or curse plaguing Oscar, the pressure to perform a model of masculinity that Díaz traces back through the narrator, Yunior, then a series of lovers his mother had in the Dominican Republic, and finally, to Trujillo himself. Social and political power are viewed here through a transnational lens and linked to the performance of a brutal and hypersexualized masculinity in the novel, first through the footnote connecting the young Oscar with the pretty playboy, Rubirosa, and then later, in chapters that recount Yunior's failed attempt to get Oscar to conform to this model of masculinity, one that plagues Yunior's own life.

While these historical footnotes are crucial, the novel does not really take off until another set of footnotes begin to link the outsize, cartoonish sexuality of the Dominican gangsters in the book to the world of science fiction, genre literature, and computer role-playing games that Oscar is obsessed with. The link between the novel's interest in genre literature and Dominican history, a link that will eventually hook up with the novel's dominant interest in masculinity and sexuality, begins to become clear in a long footnote (21–22) elaborating Oscar's "outsized love of genre" literature. While Díaz draws some clear connections late in the novel between Trujillo's theatricalized sexuality, the exercise of his power, and some of the superheroes Oscar follows, here Oscar's status as a "reader/fanboy" serves to underscore the "nerdliness" (the term Diaz uses to describe Oscar's nerdiness) that isolates him from both the girls he wants to pursue and the boys who emulate the sexuality he seems to lack. Díaz writes:

> What is clear is that being a reader/fanboy (for lack of a better term) helped him get through the rough days of his youth, but it also made him stick out in the mean streets of Paterson even more than he already did. Victimized by the other boys—punches and pushes and wedges and broken glasses and brand-new books from Scholastic, at a cost of fifty cents each, torn in half before his very eyes.... You really want to know what being an X-Man feels like? Just be a smart bookish boy of color in a contemporary U.S. ghetto. (22)

In passages like these Oscar's "nerdliness" sets him apart from the other boys and marks his alienation from his Dominican identity. However, Díaz writes that Oscar's interest in genre literature may in fact be *connected* to his "being Antillean":

> Where this outsized love of genre jumped off from no one quite seems to know. It might have been a consequence of his being Antillean (who more sci-fi than us?) or of living in the DR for the first couple of years of his life and then abruptly wrenchingly relocating to New Jersey—a single green card shifting not only worlds (from Third to First) but centuries (from almost no TV or electricity to plenty of both). After a transition like that I'm guessing only the most extreme scenarios could have satisfied.... Or was it something deeper, something ancestral?
>   Who can say?

While the novel relentlessly explores Oscar's fascination with genre in a way that links his identity to a thoroughly contemporary set of Western cultural forms (see, in particular, chapters 4, 6, and 7), here Díaz links this fascination to his Antillean world and, more specifically, to his experience of dislocation, the disjunction between his Dominican and American experiences. Thus, while his pursuit of genre serves to alienate him from other Dominican boys and make him unattractive to girls, Díaz connects it at a deeper level to his Dominican identity and to the diasporic condition he shares with his mother.

This connection between his interest in genre and its association with forms of disjunction Díaz associates with the diasporic condition gets underscored later in the novel as its complex web of allusions to characters and scenes from Tolkien books, Marvel comics, and a host of other genre forms get increasingly associated with Trujillo and the Dominican world from which his mother came, associations that come increasingly to call attention to links between the cartoonish theatricality of the Trujillo regime, Trujillo's reliance on narrative performance to govern, and connections between Trujillo's outsize sexuality and some of the superheroes who populate the books and comics Oscar reads.

Díaz has been quite outspoken both about the novel's engagement with models of masculinity and about the seriousness of his treatment of genre literature. When I interviewed him in March 2008, I spoke with him about the importance of Oscar's engagement with genre literature.[6] In his response to a question about how he weaves together the personal and the political, he insisted that "for the most part the larger themes of the book have been ducked" by critics. "I thought that what was interesting about this book was that it was making some sort of tremendous, bizarre claims about New World masculinity," claims that unfold, paradoxically, not in the obviously historical and political portions of the book, but in its references to genre literature. "People want to feel that the historical footnotes are actually real," but "the history" is a "sleight of hand. I feel like the book's real arguments unfold in the parts that get ignored by everyone, which is the arguments that the book is making in its genre claims, which most people just dismiss as bells and whistles...as ornamentation."

The claims about genre are twofold. At one level they involve legitimating Oscar's interest in genre literature, linking it in positive ways to Oscar's masculinity and positioning it over against Yunior's machismo, which is directly connected to the form of "New World masculinity" Díaz associates with Trujillo. The other claim is to actually link the machismo of Oscar's superheroes to Trujillo's outsize sexuality, drawing a link between Trujillo's masculinity and that of some of his henchman Belicia becomes involved with in the Dominican Republic, and even the narrator, Yunior, whose machismo mirrors theirs. Indeed, according to Díaz, "one of the things that's really happening in this book is that Yunior is attempting to unlearn" that masculinity, but "unfortunately he's doing it in exactly the same way that the masculinity he's trying to undermine has always perpetuated itself, by being the only voice speaking," for if the book maps out how dominated Yunior is by the power of this model of masculinity, "the very map is a product of that power."

Yunior's Dominican machismo is a kind of curse, or fukú, and is linked to Trujillo's both directly in chapter 5 and indirectly in chapter 3. Both of these chapters take place in the Dominican Republic of Belicia's youth, and they present the brutality of the Trujillo regime through the lens of sexual violence. In chapter 5 this violence is associated directly with Trujillo, but in chapter 3 it surfaces in a character generically referred to as "the Gangster," a man Belicia falls in love with and who ends up being responsible for her having to flee the island for the United States. It is in this chapter that Díaz begins to link the worlds of Oscar and Lola with their mother's. Oscar's plight, it turns out, is a kind of reverse mirror of his young mother's in Santo Domingo. Where in chapters 1 and 2 Oscar emerges as a grossly overweight nerd, isolated from his peers at school and longing for the kind of sexual life Yunior has; in chapter 3, Belicia, as a dark-skinned girl living in Baní, is ostracized at school as an "ultra-dalit" (an Indian term for untouchables) but becomes empowered by a hypersexuality calculated to contrast with Oscar's nerdiness. The otherness of both these characters is figured in their bodies; Oscar's weight problem has its corollary in Belicia's blackness. Baní, where she lives, is, according to Yunior, "a city famed for its resistance to blackness," and Belicia is "the darkest character in our story" (78). For this reason she finds herself "exiled" in school:

> Her fellow ultra-dalits included: the Boy in the Iron Lung whose servants would wheel him into the corner of the class every morning and who always seemed to be smiling, the idiot, and the Chinese girl whose father owned the largest pulperia in the country and was known, dubiously, as Trujillo's Chino.... This was who Beli sat next to her first two years of high school. But even Wei had some choice words for Beli.
>   You black, she said, fingering Beli's thin forearm. *Black*-black. (84)

This scene is the mirror image of an earlier one in chapter 1 describing Oscar's life in high school. Don Basco Tech "was, for a fat sci-fi-reading nerd like Oscar, a source of endless anguish":

> For Oscar high school was the equivalent of a medieval spectacle, like being put in the stocks and forced to endure the peltings and outrages of a mob of deranged half-wits, an experience from which he supposed he should have emerged a better person, but that's not really what happened—and if there were any lessons to be gleaned from the ordeal of those years he never quite figured out what they were. (19)

The nerdiness that helps to marginalize Oscar is linked to his body, and through his body to his masculinity, for "he had none of the Higher Powers of your typical Dominican male, couldn't have pulled a girl if his life depended on it.... And most damning of all: no looks. He wore his semi-kink hair in a Puerto Rican afro" and "rocked enormous Section 8 glasses" (19–20). The reference to his kinked hair here links him to his dark mother (Yunior continually refers to him in the book as a ghetto "nigger"), and the use of "Higher Powers" to characterize Dominican masculinity is a subtle but unmistakably calculated link to the superheroes in Oscar's genre literature, who, later in the book, will be connected clearly to Trujillo's sexuality.

It is this sexuality that plagues both Oscar and his young mother. In contemporary Paterson Oscar's nerdiness isolates him from girls, yet he longs for romance: "Oscar was a social introvert.... His adolescent nerdliness vaporizing any iota of a chance he had for young love.... He cried often for his love of some girl or another" (22–24). Much of the book centers on Oscar's struggle to find love, or just to have sex with women, and along the way Yunior works to mentor Oscar in the ways of Dominican male sexuality (see, in particular, chapter 4). In Santo Domingo in the late 1950s, Belicia's similar longing for romance is also circumscribed by her "ultra-dalit" status, for in school she falls for a young light-skinned boy, Jack Pujols. He pays little attention to Belicia and her black body until she "hits the biochemical jackpot" (91) in the summer of her sophomore year:

> Where before Beli had been a gangly ibis of a girl, pretty in a typical sort of way, by summer's end she'd become un mujerón total, acquiring that body of hers, that body that made her famous in Baní...and if Trujillo had not been on his last erections he probably would have gunned for her. (91)

From this point forward, Belicia wields the sexual power Oscar will lack, but she does so in a way that brings her into disastrous conflict with the very form of Dominican masculinity we have seen Oscar yearn for, a sexuality Yunior traffics in and which, in the passage I have just quoted, is linked explicitly to Trujillo's. The connection between the contemporary Dominican model of masculinity Yunior embodies, and Oscar aspires to, and Trujillo's is made explicit late in chapter 3 when Belicia becomes involved with a figure Díaz calls "the Gangster." To underscore the paradigmatic nature of the Gangster's violent sexuality and how it stands for the kind of masculinity that preoccupies all men in the book from Trujillo to Yunior to Oscar, Díaz calls this section of the book "The Gangster We're All Looking For" (119).

Belicia meets the Gangster at a dance club in Baní called El Hollywood. He was "dressed in a ratpack ensemble of black smoking jacket and white pants and not a dot of sweat on him, like he'd been keeping himself in refrigeration. Handsome in that louche potbellied mid-forties Hollywood producer sort of way" (115). The Gangster, unbeknownst to Belicia, is a henchman for Trujillo, a hit man, money launderer, and brothel owner who "traveled the entire length of the Americas, from Rosario to Nueva York, in pimpdaddy style, staying at the best hotels, banging the hottest broads" (121), working for Trujillo in Batista's Cuba until Castro's revolution. As he "romanced the girl like only middle-aged niggers know how...treated her to plays, movies, dances, brought her wardrobes of clothes and pirate chests of jewelry, introduced her to famous celebrities, and once even to Ramfis Trujillo himself" (124), the link Díaz draws between the Gangster's masculinity and his political association with Trujillo's dictatorial rule becomes explicit. (Ramfis was Trujillo's son.) Díaz is not interested in exploring the clichéd world of Latin machismo for its own sake but to connect it to a colonizing and political model of masculinity first invoked in the novel's opening section on the New World curse he calls fukú and later traced through Trujillo and the Gangster to Yunior and Oscar. For this reason it is important that Belicia's disastrous affair be with a henchman of Trujillo, and that the narrator, Yunior, tries to get the reader to sympathize with him:

> He was a complicated (some would say comical), affable (some would say laughable) man who treated Beli very tenderly and with great consideration....He was un hombre bien social, enjoyed being out and about seeing and being seen, and that dovetailed nicely with Beli's own dreams. But also an hombre conflicted about his past deeds. On the one hand, he was proud of what he'd accomplished....On the other hand, he was tormented by his crimes...and it was he who taught her all about her body, her orgasms, her rhythms, who said, You have to be bold, and for that he must be honored, no matter what happened in the end. (125–27)

Yunior buys into the idea that the Gangster is both a "bien hombre" and a man "tormented by his crimes" because the kind of gangster sexuality he models is central to the form of masculinity Yunior has embraced and Oscar obsesses over, and so he can ask the reader to honor the Gangster's sexual power even though, by the end of the chapter, his henchman have beaten Belicia nearly to death (his wife turns out to be Trujillo's sister and is partly responsible for the beating) and her aunt, La Inca (who has taken her in) has to send her away to New York to begin the diasporic life her children will inherit.[7]

As the "Queen of Diaspora" (261), Belicia and her story create a web of connections between political and sexual violence in the historical Dominican Republic and the kind of masculinity Oscar and Yunior obsess over and, more generally, to the New World curse of colonization, slavery, and brutality evoked at the outset of the book. Even before the beatings that she is subjected to at the hands of Trujillo's henchman Belicia has "the inchoate longings of nearly every adolescent escapist, of an entire generation...she was suffering the same suffocation that was asphyxiating a whole generation of young Dominicans" after "twenty-odd years of the Trujillato" (80–81). The link in Belicia's story between masculinity, sexual violence, and political domination is key, and Díaz has spoken explicitly about his purpose in making this link. In the September 2007 interview with Christopher Lydon, Díaz stated that he wanted to make the violence of the Trujillo regime concrete in the book and so decided to represent that violence through the brutality of Belicia's treatment by the Gangster because it allowed him to make that violence "immediate."[8] This device serves to connect the book's preoccupation with brutal forms of masculinity and sexuality to colonizing forms of domination and the exercise of what is ultimately political power. Read as they are meant to be—in sync with the contemporary chapters on Oscar, Lola, and Yunior—the historical chapters set in the Dominican Republic have the effect not only of historicizing but also of politicizing the struggle of this younger generation with contemporary models of masculinity, femininity, and sexuality that have a hemispheric dimension. The forms of power Yunior loves to exercise in his sexual promiscuity and cavalier mistreatment of Lola (his on-again-off-again girlfriend, a women he would never let himself love), a sexual power Oscar is tormented by because he can never get it, is inextricably connected through these historical chapters to models of masculinity linked to the exercise of political power.

The book's preoccupation with nerd culture in contemporary Paterson might seem a world away from this subject, but it is in fact inextricably linked to it, albeit in complicated ways, for both the outsize model of masculinity and sexuality Yunior and Oscar aspire to and the theatrical nature of its performance are linked to modes of storytelling Díaz connects to genre literature, an aesthetic form he goes out of his way to root in the older Dominican world that brutalizes Belicia and that is explicitly connected to Trujillo's exercise of power.

These connections do not become clear until chapter 5. Here Díaz looks back past the years Belicia spent in Baní to tell the earlier story of her family, the Cabrals, who led a privileged, even aristocratic life during the Trujillato until Belicia's father, Abelard, was jailed, tortured, and killed for having thwarted Trujillo in his desire for one of his other daughters. Here Díaz not only focuses on Trujillo's brutally sexual masculinity as a symbol of the larger brutality of his dictatorship, but he links that brutality to some of the darker figures from the world of Oscar's genre literature. This link is immediately apparent in the epigraph used to open part 2 of the novel, a few pages before the beginning of chapter 5:

> Men are not indispensable. But Trujillo is irreplaceable. For Trujillo is not a man. He is…a cosmic force….Those who try to compare him to his ordinary contemporaries are mistaken. He belongs to…the category of those born to a special destiny. (204)

This quote (which Díaz attributes to *La Nación,* one of the main newspapers in the Dominican Republic), with its references to Trujillo as a "cosmic force" and a man born to a "special destiny" lends itself uncannily to the link Díaz draws in this chapter between the dictator's masculinity and some key antagonists from Oscar's genre literature. For example, at one point Trujillo's Dominican Republic is likened to Mordor, the land ruled by the evil Sauron in Tolkien's *The Lord of The Rings.*[9] At another point Díaz links Trujillo to the Jack the Ripper character, Dr. Gull, in Alan Moore's graphic novel, *From Hell.* (Trujillo became "like Dr. Gull in *From Hell;* adopting the creed of the Dionyesian Architects he aspired to become an architect of history" [224n27].)[10] Another key example connects Trujillo's rule to an episode from Rod Serling's *The Twilight Zone.* "In some ways," Díaz writes, "living in Santo Domingo during the Trujillato was a lot like being in that famous *Twilight Zone* episode that Oscar loved so much, the one where the monstrous white kid with the godlike powers rules over a town that is completely isolated form the rest of the world, a town called Peaksville....Santo Domingo was the Caribbean's very own Peaksville, with Trujillo playing the part of Anthony and the rest of us reprising the role of the Man Who Got Turned into Jack-in-the-Box" (224). All of these references take us back to the epigraph that opens the novel: "Of what import are brief, nameless lives...to *Galactus??*" This quote, taken from the "The Galactus Trilogy" in Marvel Comics' *Fantastic Four,* by Stan Lee and Jack Kirby, is from one of the comic books Oscar is so absorbed in. More important, it draws a link between the antagonist of the trilogy and Trujillo. Galactus is the evil villain of the trilogy, and as such his dismissal of the "brief, nameless lives" of those he oppresses is meant to invoke the nature of Trujillo's rule. Lee's characterization of the kind of villain Galactus is intended to represent models the link Díaz makes in the novel. Said Lee, "I created Galactus after we had done so many villains and wanted something different. I wondered, 'How could we get something bigger than a villain? Let's do a guy who's like a demigod.'"[11] Galactus's "demigod" status resonates with the quote about Trujillo from *La Nación* and the web of other allusions to superhero villains in the novel.

In chapter 5 this link is explicitly contextualized in relationship to Trujillo's outsize sexuality, for he emerges here as "the Number-One Bellaco in the Country" (217).[12] This chapter turns specifically on Trujillo's interest in Belicia's older sisters and her father Abelard's refusal to let them become subject to Trujillo's advances, but it paints a more general picture of how the brutality of his rule was characterized by systematized sexual terror. Writes Díaz:

> It's a well documented fact [that] in Trujillo's DR if you were of a certain class and you put your cute daughter anywhere near El Jeffe, within the week she'd be mamando his ripio.... Hiding your doe-eyed, large-breasted daughter from Trujillo,

however, was anything but easy.... In this climate, hoarding your women was tan-
tamount to treason; offenders who didn't cough up the muchachas could easily
find themselves enjoying the invigorating charm on an eight-shark bath. (217–18)

Abelard makes the mistake of keeping his daughters away from Trujillo and
is eventually arrested and tortured; he dies in prison just before Belicia is born.
The sexual brutality she experiences, as we have seen, is connected to Trujillo's,
which in Díaz's novel is meant to stand both for the general brutality of his regime and, more important to the book's overall aims, the dark side of the masculinity Yunior and Oscar are obsessed with. Díaz has made explicit in a number
of interviews the link in his book between writing, storytelling, and a dictatorial model of masculinity. When I interviewed him in March 2008, Díaz spoke
of being "obsessed with this idea that all these folks were dealing with this grand
narrative of this Trujillo masculinity." "I thought," he continued, "that what was
interesting about this book was that it was making some sort of tremendous, bizarre claims about new world masculinity." As I have stressed throughout this
chapter, "all these folks" includes Trujillo; his various henchman who torment
first Belicia, and then Oscar; and, of course, Belicia, Oscar, and Lola themselves.[13]
The idea that the New World suffers under a fukú or curse, raised as we saw
at the outset of the novel, is embodied in this web of brutality linked to Díaz's
"grand narrative of this Trujillo masculinity," a "New World masculinity" that
is meant to embody a transnationalized form of political domination.

Díaz makes clear the link in the novel between masculinity, dictatorial power,
and writing in an interview with Matthew Rothschild, editor of the *Progressive*
magazine. Here he first connects what he calls the "masculine economy" that
Oscar, Yunior, Belicia, and Lola have to deal with to the power of dictators like
Trujillo to tell stories, and then to the eerie power "Yunior" and he wield in telling the story in his novel. Dictators, he insists, are not "just about power" but
about "how good a story you tell...and dictators are superb storytellers.... The
stories they tell are very much directed at the blind spots in the culture who is
hearing it.... The best storytellers know how to play to that blind spot." The particular "blind spot" Díaz has in mind is that "we have a great dream of simplicity,
that there are simple answers." We do not, he insists, want "thirteen voices" but
one voice, the "straight talk." Díaz links this to a "dream of purity," embodied
both in the idea there is some kind of "pure America" and in our longing for
pure, "simple" stories. Simple stories, Díaz insists, play to our desire for simple
answers to complex questions. They depend on forgetting, or what he calls "strategic amnesia," the kind of historical forgetting that led to the Iraq war. Simple
stories are pitched to "myths about ourselves," and in the New World you "can't
have stories about yourself without forgetting the other stories, the ones that are

much more disturbing, much more real." The story Yunior tells is meant to contravene such simple stories, yet there is a paradox, for Yunior keeps verging to using the same dictatorial power and singular authority in a narrative that is meant to *critique* dictatorial power and singular authority. "One of the dangers of this novel," Díaz insists, "is that the very dictator everyone in this family is trying to flee, the very evil history that" his story is trying to expose, are exorcised by Oscar, Yunior, and Lola using the same storytelling power Trujillo wielded, and "to fight it the characters Oscar, Yunior, [and] Lola have to use the same tools, storytelling."

Díaz elaborated on the centrality of this paradox in his interview with me:

I always thought that there's this very interesting relationship with the paterfamilias, the sort of dominating father or the dominating masculinity, the dictator masculinity, and the role that one plays when one is an author of a book. I think that one of the things that's really happening in this book is that Yunior is attempting to unlearn and expiate himself, repent in some way, a penance. But unfortunately he's doing it in exactly the same way that the masculinity he's trying to undermine has always perpetuated itself, by being the only voice speaking. And I think that one of the most troubling things that's going through this book, and Yunior keeps giving very clear messages, that in some ways, look, guys, I'm trying to lay out a map of how fucked up I am and how fucked up this is but the very map is a product of that power, but also the desire that the reader has for that authoritative narrative.

Here we see Díaz foregrounding the issues that I have been arguing are key to understanding the novel, the relationship between masculinity, sexuality, power, and writing (including Diaz's interest in genre literature, his foregrounding of both Oscar's and Yunior's writing, *and* his self-reflexive interest in his own writing). The novel's self-reflexivity has partly to do with the author's attempt to *trouble* the kind of narrative it keeps trying to become as Yunior writes it. In his interview with Rothschild, Díaz contrasts simple stories with troubled ones. A troubled story applies the "brakes" to simplicity and "in itself questions its own authority." *The Brief Wondrous Life of Oscar Wao* is clearly calibrated by Díaz to model this kind of troubled narrative, though I would argue this is articulated more clearly in interviews than it is in the novel itself. Yunior's attempt to trouble his narrative comes most dramatically at the end and is connected to the surprising lesson he learns from Oscar's last letter from the Dominican Republic. Here, a novel that seems all about remembering history, political power, masculinity and sexuality becomes troubled by a new discourse about *intimacy*.

While the book Oscar wrote in his last months in the Dominican Republic never arrives as promised, Yunior does receive a letter from the now dead Oscar with "some amazing news" that he had succeeded in sneaking away with Ybon for a weekend of lovemaking. Here is what Yunior finds so amazing in Oscar's letter:

> What really got him was not the bam-bam-bam of sex—it was the little intimacies that he'd never in his whole life anticipated, like combing her hair or getting her underwear off a line or watching her walk naked to the bathroom or the way she would suddenly sit on his lap and put her face into his neck.... So this is what everybody's always talking about! Diablo! If only I'd known. The beauty! The beauty! (334–35)

In a surprising way that risks banality, Oscar discovers something he did not know he was seeking, intimacy. The important thing here is that the capacity for intimacy connects both Oscar and Yunior to a model of masculinity that *troubles* the brutal, dominating masculinity that has dominated the book. When I interviewed Díaz and told him I found this concluding scene surprising he responded that he felt this kind of surprise was "true about every quest narrative," that "what you discover is that the object of the quest is just a MacGuffin, and that what you learn in the journey is actually what was valuable. But you didn't know it because you were so focused on getting the ring, getting the spear, killing this creature, that you don't realize that there was something else." When intimacy trumps sex at the end of the novel the brakes are put on Yunior's narrative about Dominican masculinity. It becomes troubled not just thematically but in a political way, because the capacity for intimacy requires a capacity for vulnerability that is repressed in the exercise of power in which sexual brutality becomes the dominant metaphor.

Here is how Díaz explained this dynamic when we discussed it:

> The first rule of intimacy is that you have to drop your performances, that the "masks" have to drop. This is a book filled with characters wearing masks, and that's what's so disturbing, that we're narrative animals. We love to wear masks; that's the way we live. We perform. But yet, I really believe it's very difficult to connect at a human level without the dropping of masks. For me that's the art of stories. Stories are there so you can get to the point where you can finally take off that last mask. And I think that that's what growing up is. When you take your last mask off you are utterly vulnerable, you are utterly in another person's power. And what contemporary masculinity, what contemporary power structure ever puts itself utterly in someone else's power? Isn't storytelling the desire to put everything about the world in your power?

When Oscar discovers the capacity for intimacy at the end of his life (when he thought what he was after was sex) it becomes a lesson for Yunior, who has squandered his relationship with Lola by performing just the kind of swaggering sexualized masculinity Oscar was after and that ultimately gets them both nowhere. Yunior drops the mask and, by the end of the book, has married and settled down to his job teaching creative writing. In this way the novel ends by reiterating the complex link I have been arguing it establishes between the kind of destructive, sexualized masculinity Trujillo and his henchman represent, the wielding of political power, and storytelling as a kind of narrative performance that both enables brutality and masks vulnerability. What is most paradoxical about storytelling, Díaz seems to be insisting, is that it is about putting "everything about the world in your power" in the interests of critiquing the attempt to put everything about the world in your power.

This self-reflexivity distinguishes Díaz's novel from the others we have discussed. *The Brief Wondrous Life of Oscar Wao* shares with those novels an interest in tracing the transnational roots/routes of subjectivity across intersecting locations and shared political histories, linking the personal with the political and foregrounding the mobility of its characters under the accelerating forces of globalization. However, in linking a detailed analysis of masculinity, sexuality, and agency to the kind of political power exercised by the construction of narratives Díaz breaks new and important ground, for in doing so he calls attention to the power of storytelling to both critique and reverse dominant narratives, to, in effect, begin to undo the curse of colonizing power he links at the outset of his novel to the fúku. In this way his novel strikes a more hopeful tone than many of the others discussed here. Although Oscar's life is brief and ends violently, it is crafted to be wondrous. Compared to the bleak conclusions of *The God of Small Things, Moth Smoke,* and *The Inheritance of Loss,* the ending of Díaz's novel offers the tentative hope that in writing about systematic forms of injustice and brutality one might begin to undo them by weaving a counterspell that resists dominant narratives and brutalizing voices.

Conclusion

In the last chapter I argued that the curse or fukú in Díaz's novel could be linked to Zadie Smith's exploration of design and chance in *White Teeth* as well as to how the experiences of her younger characters are shaped by the colonial histories of their families. However, I also argued that Díaz's fúku, as a metaphor of the persistent historical effects of material and cultural colonization, stood in broader terms for the constellation of transnational historical forces at work in all of the novels discussed here. We saw that Díaz sets up Yunior's book as a kind of "counterspell" to a New World curse, invoking the idea that in the process of writing his book he might begin to undo a set of forces that have haunted the hemisphere since the arrival of Columbus. The nature of this effort calls our attention to something fundamental about both the fiction and the criticism I have been discussing, because, collectively, it deploys theoretical, critical, and imaginative thinking in order to both lay bare debilitating histories and imagine new, contemporary relationships and structures of power in an age in which the magnitude of change seems nearly overwhelming. At the center is the whole question of agency, explored by the critics in part 1 in terms of whether the forces of globalization flatten out (or homogenize) cultural differences and restrict rather than expand economic and cultural power, and by the novelists in part 2 in their linked explorations of how colonization, decolonization, and globalization have simultaneously disabled and enabled personal, cultural, and political agency.

The very idea of a curse raises the question of agency in the most explicit of terms, because to believe, as Yunior seems to at key points in *The Brief Wondrous Life of Oscar Wao,* that not only Oscar's family but the entire New World suffers under a curse brought from Spain by Columbus and from Africa by slavery suggests there is really little to be done, that no amount of struggle can counteract these historical forces as they continue to play themselves out in our own time. Believing in a curse like the fúku Díaz invokes runs the risk of giving up on the whole idea of agency, and thus of the possibility of real fundamental structural change in the dramatically uneven forms of power explored in all of the novels and each of the critics analyzed here. However, when I asked Díaz about this in the interview cited in chapter 9, he insisted this was wrong:

> I don't think even if the fukú is true, that it's a cop-out. Look, curses don't rob you, in literature, in the classic tradition, of making choices. I mean, that's agency, that you're supposed to make choices.... Everyone who is cursed in the classical tradition made a choice.... And so, it's not about robbing someone of agency.... [The] reason a curse is interesting narratively is because it makes the choices we make far more fraught.... [My] book can only be finished by its reader, and depending upon what decision the reader makes around the curse, around the fukú, around why Yunior is telling the story, around the historical and the nerdy.... It's only when the reader makes these decisions that the book finally assembles itself.

Díaz sees the curse as a literary device that foregrounds our need to make *choices* in the first place and underscores rather than contradicts the importance of agency. While this logic would extend to each of the novels discussed here, it also holds for the criticism discussed in part 1. The debates reviewed there about the historical nature of globalization and its relationship to colonial and postcolonial histories, about the vexing relationship between economic and cultural globalization, and about the whole complicated question of whether or not globalization homogenizes and contaminates cultural identities and what that means become more fraught when we think about them in terms of the conflict between the curse of domination (which surfaces in each of the novels in their stress on the *systematic* nature of oppression) and the liberating possibilities of agency. Novels like *White Teeth* and *The Brief Wondrous Life of Oscar Wao* mean to call our attention to how the roots/routes of colonial history become determinative to the point they seem like a curse, and how "root canals" like the one Irie Jones takes on in Smith's novel (researching and reconstructing for herself a kind of imaginary but liberating homeland in Jamaica) or the exhaustively researched and footnoted "counterspell" Yunior weaves in Díaz's novel dramatize the choice of agency over domination, a topic we have also seen at the center of critical debate.

Díaz has been treated in the popular press as both a new kind of "American" novelist and as a Latino writer whose work stretches the geographical and thematic range of literature written in the United States. While both of these characterizations are accurate, they miss the larger importance of his work, the fact that it transcends narrow national categories and instead embodies the transnational turn in English I have been discussing throughout this book. Díaz's novel is not just an American novel, it is an *Americas* novel, and the hemispheric and historical range of its reference suggests its affinity less with the tradition of the "American novel" than with the kind of transnational writer working in English discussed in this book. When I interviewed Díaz I asked him about his relationship to such writers, suggesting a kinship between his work and that of Smith, Desai, Roy, Chandra, and others such as Jhumpa Lahiri and Hari Kunzru. Here is part of his response:

> I was a Dominican kid who immigrated to the U.S. in the '70s, young, and settled in New Jersey and was trying to write to that experience. I could never have imagined a Zadie Smith growing up—that wasn't the sort of thing I was connecting to. I was sort of imagining, could I possibly contain New Jersey and the Dominican Republic? . . . . I was just a kid who was thinking of this very limited thing, dealing with Santo Domingo and New Jersey. But in the end I *am* part of a larger movement, and there is a lot of art trying to deal with this new condition, whether we call it transnationalism or something else. I'm from a family of illegal immigrants; my parents were illegal immigrants. It's very different from people whose parents were middle class or upper middle class, South Asian or Caribbean, who came to the metropole. But it doesn't change the fact that in our own ways and with our own class differences we're attempting to deal with similar issues.

Thinking of Díaz's novel within the older, narrow framework of "American" fiction obscures its connection to a "larger movement" that is trying to come to terms with a "new condition." This larger movement is embodied in the transnational turn in English. Díaz's insistence that beneath the class and geographical differences that separate his fictional world from Smith's, they are "attempting to deal with similar issues" underscores the fact of their struggling from different continents with a "new condition" put in motion by the long history of colonialism and postcolonialism and accelerating under the forces of globalization. This condition, as we have seen, is related in turn to the urgency of recognizing the transnational characters of our personal, cultural, and political experiences; confronting the challenge of how to make sense of the vexing category of identity; and trying to grasp the complex relationship between psychological, cultural, and economic forces that have shaped and continue to shape experience across what seem like increasingly arbitrary and historically contingent borders.

One of the other things that links *White Teeth* and *The Brief Wondrous Life of Oscar Wao* is that they both put the brakes on fantasies of purity and so trouble the dominant narrative of national belonging central to definitions of "Englishness" and what it means to be an "American." In this sense they take us back to the kind of world we saw Doris Sommer describe at the outset of this book, one in which cultures and literatures and the forms we use to study them have awakened from a romantic enchantment with singular languages and nations and in which "home means not a here but a there, somewhere else," a world in which "strangeness is the norm" (3). Both Smith and Díaz write this strangeness into the very structure of their novels. They trouble received national narratives, not by erasing them, but by resituating them within a broader, more complicated geographical and historical context dominated by a back-and-forth model of migration. From this perspective we can see how the relationship Díaz draws between the power of storytelling and the story Yunior struggles to write gets at something central in all of the fiction we have looked at here, and even in the critical writing. Each of the novels I have discussed engages the question of national belonging by focusing on larger transnational flows of people, commodities, and cultural forms that complicate simple versions of the stories we have told ourselves about the nation. Roy, Chandra, Hamid, and Desai, as well as Smith and Díaz, all develop troubled narratives that challenge fantasies of purity, and they do so in ways that parallel the focus on roots and routes in Gilroy, the relationship between culture and contamination in Appiah, the syncretizing work of the imagination in Appadurai, and by attending to Susan Stanford Friedman's insistence on the importance of resisting "simplistically universalist and binarist narratives" so as to focus on "multidirectional flows of power in [a] global context" that pays attention to "western forms of domination" (6).

This troubling of received and simple stories—about culture, identity, the nation and national belonging, the relationship between materiality and culture, the homogenizing threat of globalization, the origins and history of globalization and its relationship to colonialism and postcolonialism—animates both the body of criticism and the novels analyzed here. We do not end up after such an enterprise with simple answers to the questions I have been exploring. My aim has been less to provide singular and authoritative answers than to delve deeply and in a sustained way into the *questions,* posing some possible answers but playing them off one another in order to foreground the need for choice and agency in the critical and scholarly work we do. Few, if any, of the critical positions I have discussed here can be construed as axiomatic, empirically correct, or universally true. Some, however, come close.

First of all, it seems to me nearly axiomatic that the transnational turn in both literary production in English and in the approaches we take to teaching and writing about literature and culture is here to stay and will only accelerate. What Sommer calls our "romantic enchantment" with the nation and with commonality has given way for good to an interest in difference, so that "somewhere else" and "strangeness" will remain our focus for some time to come. This means that our approaches both to literatures historically linked to the nation and newer, emergent fiction like the novels examined here require theoretical frameworks and methodologies adequate to tracing the transnational character of their construction and dissemination, as well as to the subject matters they explore. Economic forces and cultural ones must be understood and studied as intersecting and mutually informing phenomena. We should not spend our time advocating for *either* materialist or culturalist approaches to the study of the literary and the cultural, since both forces intersect in their production and dissemination and so require a syncretic approach that pays attention to both. When it comes to the topic of culture, discourses of purity have become obsolete, for Appiah and a host of other critics have called our attention to the inevitable fact that what we call "culture" is a fluid and changing thing that thrives on forms of contact, exchange, and appropriation that belie insular notions of purity. This does not mean, as Appiah himself argues, that cultural objects and forms do not have traditions and a kind of integrity that ought to be supported when people want to protect them. However, preservation of tradition itself ought not to trump the aspirations of peoples to improve their economic situation or experiment with their cultural practices. And when it comes to the geographical frameworks in which we do our work, our whole approach to location must continue to evolve with the understanding that we largely create the areas we study. The relationship between the so-called core and the periphery has to continue to be rethought. Older one-way models of production and dominance (or the local and global) cannot account for the forms of appropriation and recirculation that characterize economic and especially cultural flows.

As we continue to refine our theoretical, methodological, and pedagogical approaches to the transnational turn in English and other literatures it is imperative that our work not reproduce new but uncomplicated narratives about history, identity, and belonging, narratives that simply reverse more traditional ones. One danger of the kind of focus on *difference* I have been discussing throughout this book is that it can lead to a hardening of identity categories that can divide groups off from one another, so that the older structures of division connected to the study of literature under a nationalist paradigm get replicated in the very context of its critique. This is the kind of danger we saw Paul Gilroy warning about in *The Black Atlantic* when he pointed out how critiques of traditional narratives of national belonging run the risk of creating absolutist categories of difference based on narrow notions of ethnic belonging. Virtually all of the novels I discussed in this book seek to find a way to work past such reductive categories. They do not provide simple answers to complex questions about identity, culture, and belonging, but rather they productively trouble the way we think about those questions. In so doing, they present a model for the critical work we do, for the very act of reading and understanding them.

NOTES

Introduction

1. See Appiah (2006), chap. 7.

2. Such a project is closer to the one taken up by David Damrosch, who looks at how modes of reading, translation, and circulation produce "world literature" written in and translated into many different languages.

3. These developments coincide with critiques of what Gerald Graff has called the field-coverage model in literary studies (see his *Professing Literature: An Institutional History*). While Graff's book, published in 1987, does not deal with the effects of globalization on the curriculum, his cogent criticisms of the historical-period paradigm in literary studies helped pave the way for rethinking the curriculum in literary studies in an age in which the effects of globalization on the production of literature have become much clearer. Bill Readings extends Graff's discussion in a way that connects it to late twentieth-century globalization.

4. For a discussion of some of the challenges of treating English globally, see Michael Bérubé's 2002 introduction to the special edition of *Modern Fiction Studies* on postmodernism and the globalization of English.

5. I borrow the concept of a "default narrative" for historical explanations from the historian Thomas Bender (see his *A Nation among Nations: America's Place in World History* and "No Borders: Beyond the Nation-State").

Chapter 1. Difference, Multiculturalism, and the Globalizing of Literary Studies

1. This observation is a recurrent one. See, for example, Susan Friedman (2007), who asks, "Why now—the naming of migrations, diasporas, and borders as a field? In a word, *globalization*, a term with

shifting meanings that spawn debate about its politics, its utopian possibilities and its dystopic realities" (261). "The rapid emergence of transnationalism and globalization as pervasive categories in literary studies," she continues, "helps explain the new significance of migration, diaspora, and borders as a cross-departmental and cross-specialty field of inquiry in the study of modern languages" (263).

2. For an earlier indication of the growing impact of globalization on the study of literature, see the January 2000 special issue of *PMLA* entitled "Globalizing Literary Studies."

3. Each of these chapters documents specific ways in which the field under consideration has developed a transnational emphasis over the last two decades.

4. See, in particular, Eagleton (1983) and Graff (1987).

5. See Culler's *Literary Theory: A Very Short Introduction,* 6–8.

6. For a discussion of its impact, see Daniels (2008).

7. See P. Jay (1998), G. Jay (1991), Porter (1994), and Saldívar (1991).

8. Near the beginning of the published version of her remarks, "Crossroads of Culture," Fishkin writes: "In many of its earliest incarnations American studies aspired to overarching generalities about the United States. The field had little room for the dissenting voices of minorities and women, and a fixation on American innocence blinded many scholars to the country's ambitious quest for empire" (20). Today, however, "another generative question in the spirit of those others is becoming increasingly salient: What would the field of American studies look like if the transnational rather than the national were at its center—as it is already for many scholars in this room?" (5). The rest of her essay is an exhaustive survey of such work.

9. The distinction between roots and routes was popularized by Paul Gilroy in his book, *The Black Atlantic* (1993), but it was first used in the late 1990s by the cultural anthropologist James Clifford.

10. On the transnational turn in American studies, see Fishkin's address to the American Studies Association published as "Crossroads of Culture" (2005). On the similar shift in modern studies, see Mao and Walkowitz in *PMLA* (2008).

11. A few important examples from the disparate fields of sociology, anthropology, cultural studies, American studies, and literary studies would include Roland Robertson's *Globalization* (1992); *Mapping the Futures: Local Cultures, Global Change,* edited by Jon Bird et al. (1993); Frederick Buell's *National Culture and the New Global System* (1994); Malcolm Waters's *Globalization* (1995); Bill Readings's *The University in Ruins* (1996); *Culture, Globalization, and the World-System: Contemporary Conditions for the Representation of Identity,* edited by Anthony King (1997); *Articulating the Global and the Local: Globalization and Cultural Studies,* edited by Ann Cvetkovich and Douglas Kellner (1987); Arjun Appadurai's *Modernity at Large: Cultural Dimensions of Globalization* (1998); Bruce Robbins's *Feeling Global* (1999); *The Cultures of Globalization,* edited by Frederic Jameson and Masao Miyoshi (1998); *PMLA's* January 2000 special issue, "Globalizing Literary Studies"; Tyler Cowen's, *Creative Destruction: How Globalization is Changing the World's Cultures* (2004); and *Globalization and the Humanities,* edited by David Li (2004).

12. For critical discussions of the role of nationalism in American literary studies see Buell (1994), Carafiol (1991), G. Jay (1991), P. Jay (1998), and Porter (1994).

13. While this is still technically true, authors of important books have begun to argue we are moving into an age in which global domination by the United States is on the wane, an effect both of the success of globalization and the failures of U.S. foreign policy under the George W. Bush administration. See, in particular, Parag Khanna's *The Second World* and Fareed Zakaria's *The Post-American World,* both published in 2008.

14. For an extended discussion of this concern, see Sabine Milz's "Global Literary Study, Postcolonial Study, and Their (Missing) Interrelations: A Materialist Critique," in which she reviews a number of complaints about the essays contained in *PMLA's* special issue on globalizing literary studies.

15. It is interesting to compare Miyoshi's rejection of the term *globalization* to Appiah's. While Appiah rejects it because he finds it banal and overused, Miyoshi bases his rejection of it on a substantive critique of the economic effects of globalization.

16. See "Ivory Tower in Escrow" (2002), 39–50.

17. Although their critical and political positions regarding globalization and its effects could hardly be more different, Miyoshi's concern with the stress on difference and relativism and the need for a totalizing perspective to counteract it is not all that far removed from Appiah's insistence that cosmopolitanism could go a long way toward creating an ethical framework with a totalizing perspective.

18. Such a pattern is quite clear in Gerald Graff's *Professing Literature: An Institutional History*.

19. I say "however awkwardly" because, as I have indicated, we do need to acknowledge that there are significant problems with both these discourses. I return to this topic in the chapters that follow.

20. Miyoshi's insistence that we ought to avoid critical discourses connected to multiculturalism and globalization because they have been co-opted, or are even directed by, the forces of global capitalism exhibits what I am tempted to call an anxiety about complicity that I think ends up being debilitating. I argued in 1992 in an essay on deconstruction and politics that Derrida was overly concerned with policing the political uses of deconstruction to avoid its being used by the wrong politics to the extent that he contributed to the misleading idea that deconstruction was not political (P. Jay 1992). Miyoshi, I believe, shares this kind of anxiety about complicity, a desire to keep one's theoretical and methodological positions free from the appearance of complicity with a bad politics. It seems to me this kind of anxiety about complicity is at times more debilitating than it is productive, based at it often is on a false idea that our work can be underwritten by some kind of pure or untroubled politics. I thank Nasrin Qader for a lively conversation in which this idea got worked out.

Chapter 2. What Is Globalization?

1. The acceleration of economic globalization in the late twentieth century (discussed at greater length in chapter 3) has been elegantly traced by Joseph Stiglitz. For Stiglitz, globalization in its contemporary form is reflected in attempts to manage institutionally a series of transnational crises including the Great Depression, the need to rebuild a devastated Europe at the end of World War II, the demise of colonialism in the 1950s and 1960s, and the collapse of Communism in the late 1980s. The need to manage these successive crises was accompanied by an "enormous reduction of costs of transportation and communication, and the breaking down of artificial barriers to the flows of goods, services, capital, knowledge, and (to a lesser extent) people across borders" (9), developments that accelerated the pace of long-standing economic and cultural exchanges across borders.

2. See, in particular, Jenkins's discussion of "corporate convergence" in his introduction and chapter 3, especially 109–12; and his discussion of the relationship between economics, politics, and media convergence, in chapter 6.

3. Sen deploys this historical analysis in the interests of his larger argument against two positions about globalization, one that sees globalization in wholly beneficial terms and as a "gift from the West to the world," and another that sees globalization as a form of "Western dominance" and a "continuation of Western imperialism" (1). Having demonstrated that globalization has a long history in the East and is not a product of Western capitalism or imperialism (although it becomes linked to these two processes), Sen goes on to argue the problem is not globalization itself but the need for an ethical and just regulation of its forces. "The central issue of contention is not globalization itself," he concludes, "nor is it the use of the market as an institution, but the inequity in the overall balance of institutional arrangements which produces very unequal sharing of the benefits of globalization" (8).

4. It is worth noting that opportunities for agency (economic, cultural, and personal) vary greatly at different periods in the history of globalization. The kind of agency Appadurai and Jenkins associate with convergence culture was not, of course, available at periods when globalization was being driven by the slave trade and colonization. Domination and exploitation associated with colonialism and the slave trade produced forms of hybridity, but in a much more asymmetrical and oppressive way than in our own time.

5. Arif Dirlik's position in "Rethinking Colonialism: Globalization, Postcolonialism, and the Nation" seems to come close to the "reconciliatory postcolonialism" that During describes here, but the political position he takes on colonialism hardly accords with the one During ascribes to a reconciliatory position. Dirlik argues that in spite of the violence and devastation it has caused, colonialism has utterly transformed the identities of colonized people everywhere. Everything from claims about the configuration of precolonial identity to the idea that all identities are hybrid can be traced back, in Dirlik's view, to colonialism. All identity, that is, is a product of colonialism, and its hybridization is an ongoing historical process. Dirlik's interest in globalization reflects his desire to move postcolonial studies away from a fixation on colonialism and identity and refocus its attention on the workings of global capitalism. This position does seem to attempt to reconcile the histories of colonialism, postcolonialism, and globalization, but

it doesn't embrace the reactionary political position During links to reconciliatory postcolonialism. Indeed, one could argue it mixes a reconciliatory and critical approach to postcolonialism in a way that belies During's distinction.

6. Harootunian insists that because of "the relentless kinship area studies formed with strategic policy making [during the cold war] serving national interests and 'contract research,' it was never able to free itself from the pursuit of a knowledge bonded to the necessities that had given it shape" (157).

7. Gikandi is quoting from Mike Featherstone's introduction to *Global Culture,* 2.

8. Gikandi's position is echoed by both Revathi Krishnaswamy (2002) and Supriya Nair (2001). Krishnaswamy questions Appadurai's "celebratory view of consumption as active and agential" (116), which he sees pushing "globalization theory toward an optimistic position that merges into a postmodern celebration of difference and differentiation" (115). Likewise, Nair questions the priority given to the "cultural" among critics like Appadurai and Gilroy, who link "migrancy and transcendence of national boundaries" with forms of resistance that are not available to those who, she points out, remain in the home country (267).

9. See, in this regard, Gikandi's discussion of Gayatri Spivak's distinction between "migrant" and "national" postcolonial subjects (Gikandi, 639–40). Gikandi makes the point that "postcolonial theories of globalization have been influential in the mapping of global culture because they have appeared to be focused on tropes that speak powerfully to the experience of migration. The downside to this focus on migrancy and its images, however, is that the national has tended to be negated" (640).

10. For another argument that postcolonial studies ought to stay focused on the nation, even as it pursues in interest in transnational and diasporic spaces, see Nair.

11. On the complexity of this phenomenon, see Appadurai's discussion of the "work of the imagination" (5–11).

12. For an extended discussion of this kind of syncretism in the Caribbean, see Antonio Benítez-Rojo's *The Repeating Island* and Paul Gilroy's *The Black Atlantic.*

Chapter 3. Economies, Cultures, and the Politics of Globalization

1. Stiglitz is unsparing in his criticism of how regulatory institutions have mismanaged globalization. These institutions, dominated by policymakers and bureaucrats from Western nations, "have pushed poor countries to eliminate trade barriers, but kept their own barriers" in place (6). The "free market mantra" of the 1980s, widely referred to as "the Washington Consensus," led to the imposition of policies for economic stabilization and growth in developing countries that trampled on their national sovereignty (19) and turned out to be "ill suited" to their needs (16). While globalization has improved economic conditions in some areas, "for millions of people globalization has not worked," indeed, many "have been made worse off" (248). According to statistics Stiglitz cites, during the last decade of the twentieth century "the actual number of people living in poverty has actually increased by almost 100 million" (5).

2. All of these problems are reflected in a country like India, where, for example, a Western-imposed "green revolution" forced poor farmers to abandon the use of local seeds for hybrid ones, which required the use of expensive and destructive pesticides, a practice that proved to be an unmitigated disaster. Crop production was uneven, and pesticides were so expensive that many farmers went broke, with some committing suicide by drinking the pesticides. See Vandana Shiva for a thorough study of the failure of the green revolution in India. Globalization in India has also produced a deepening divide between a vast impoverished class and those who have benefited economically from globalization that Stiglitz finds characteristic of globalization's processes. It has produced rapid and disruptive urbanization that has fueled poverty and overwhelmed the infrastructure in Indian cities. In addition, the cultural and social values of both traditional rural societies and urban ones have been radically disrupted, making India a case study of the uneven effects of globalization.

3. Helpful as this formulation is, it is a little unsatisfying. For example, it is not hard to see how the demagogic cultural politics of the Third Reich used culturalism, as Appadurai defines it, to perpetuate what he calls "culture." It would make more sense, it seems to me, for Appadurai to stress the relation between culturalism and culture instead of drawing such a rigid distinction between them and to acknowledge that culturalism can serve a retrograde, even violently discriminatory, cultural politics as well as a progressive and liberatory one.

4. For a discussion of diasporas and globalization, see Robin Cohen's *Global Diasporas,* especially chap. 7.

5. For a sustained argument about the homogenizing effects of globalization, see Bauman.

6. Appiah cites studies of the reception of U.S. television by the media scholar, Larry Strelitz, in making this argument (109–10).

7. For an extended analysis of this process, see George Lipsitz's *Dangerous Crossroads.*

8. See Stephen Frears's film, *Dirty Pretty Things* (2005) for a dramatic treatment of the place of the undocumented migrant worker in the economy of globalized metropolitan Western cities.

9. Globalization theory was until recently dominated by male academics who paid scant attention to gender and the role of women in globalization. All the founding figures—Wallerstein, King, Robertson, Featherstone, Hannerz, Giddens, Harvey, Appadurai—are men. All the principal critics whose work is collected in *Culture, Globalization, and the World-System* (King) are male, while women are relegated to the role of respondents (Abu-Lughod, Abou-El-Haj, Turim, and Wolff). As Wolff pointedly notes, there is an "indifference" to gender in these papers (169). This problem unfortunately persists in Miyoshi and Jameson's *The Cultures of Globalization,* where only three of the eighteen contributors are women and where gender and women's issues are not part of the discussion. This lack is beginning to be rectified in the work of feminist critics such as Kaplan, Friedman, Grewal, and Tiffin, many of whom intervene in globalization studies from the fields of literary and cultural studies.

10. Freeman goes on in her essay to analyze the female higgler (a kind of trader) in the region of the Caribbean, an analysis that "challenges any notion that global spaces are traversed by men and gendered masculine" (1012) while women's experience (and power) under globalization is simply relegated to the local.

Chapter 4. Border Studies

1. While the places and borders are not constructed, the *idea* of the nation and the various configurations of its identities are constructed by the scholars and critics who study them.

2. Although the field of border studies developed in the United States along the lines I am sketching out, it is important to recognize that the concept has spread to border regions in disparate parts of the globe. One example would be the field of partition studies, which focuses on the history and effects of partition in West Bengal. Another would be the Centre for Cross Border Studies, located in Armagh and Dublin, which, according to its website, "researches and develops cooperation across the Irish border (between Northern Ireland and the Republic of Ireland) in education, training, health, planning, public administration, communications, agriculture and the economy, and acts as secretariat for a number of cross-border educational networks." See http://www.crossborder.ie/.

3. See P. Jay (1998) for an overview of rise of U.S. border studies theory and criticism in the late 1980s and 1990s.

4. Pratt borrows the term "contact" from linguistics. In linguistics, she explains, "the term contact language refers to improvised languages that develop among speakers of different native languages who need to communicate with each other" (6). She equates the Creole or pidgin languages resulting from this improvisational interaction with the Creole or hybrid *cultures* that also result from this kind of sustained contact.

5. The character of Pratt's contact zone fits nicely with Appiah's theory that culture is always already contaminated. Indeed, it provides an explanation before the fact of how this contamination takes place.

6. For a critical discussion of this problem, see Kaup (2001), Fox (1999), and Sadowski-Smith (2008). Sadowski-Smith warns that one of "the more troubling aspects of liberating the border from its spatial referent to denote Chicana/o concerns with homeland, migration, identity, and aesthetics is that the voices of other border communities become muted" (35).

7. See Hortense Spillers for an excellent discussion of Faulkner's *Absalom, Absalom* in the context of "the politics of the New World" (1–16). See also Zamora's discussion of Faulkner in *Writing the Apocalypse* (32–45).

8. Those concerns are linked to what Gregory Jay calls "problematics," distinguished from "themes" in that they indicate "an event in culture made up simultaneously of material conditions and conceptual norms that direct the possibilities of representation" (277). The "problematics" he lists include origins, power, civilization, tradition, assimilation, translation, bodies, literacy, and borders.

9. See Goudie's *Creole America* for a sustained engagement with "Caribbean regionalism."

10. For example, George Washington Cable's *The Grandissimes* could be read in this context in ways that emphasized the role of the Haitian Revolution in heightening and complicating anxieties in Louisiana about its new role as part of the nation in the beginning of the nineteenth century, a much-neglected topic in criticism on the novel.

11. Geyer insists that a "multicultural" education in American literature and culture "requires... intellectual innovation—a general shift from places, ages, peoples of imperial settlement to places, ages, and peoples of unsettlement, from the grand efforts of authentication to the struggles of putting together many different strands of experience in the weave of culture. We may discover in due course that this condition of unsettlement (as opposed to that of imperial civilization) is rather the norm than the exception" (532). I would suggest that Geyer's focus on "unsettlement" encourages the same kind of historical focus we get in Glissant, O'Gorman, and Gilroy. See Carolyn Porter's brief discussion of Geyer (471–72).

12. Foucault argues the "hypothesis" that Kant's essay, "Was ist Aufklarung?" *is* "located in a sense at the crossroads of critical reflection and reflection on history. It is a reflection by Kant on the contemporary status of his own enterprise," which "we may call the attitude of modernity" (38).

13. Chevigny and Laguardia title their book *Reinventing the Americas,* and they make much the same argument O'Gorman does, yet seem completely unaware of his book.

14. The historically narrow-minded and patriarchal notion that "man" does all of this is part of the whole mythic conception of modernity O'Gorman is referring to and which needs to be critiqued in any contemporary approach to its "irruption." The fact that O'Gorman invokes the traditionally masculinist language of explanation here is hardly surprising, but it does not undercut the historical and philosophical accuracy to his observation about the invention of America.

15. For Pippin, the challenge of individual, social, and artistic/creative "autonomy" is the central problem of modernity. See, in particular, 1–13, 56–64, and 116–21.

16. O'Gorman is particularly careful, near the close of his book, to stress the development of various strategies concocted by the West to contain native populations, such as, "Christianize" them, breed with them, restrict them, eradicate them, and so on (138–45).

17. Gilroy briefly discusses in this light the work of Raymond Williams, E. P. Thompson, and Eric Hobsbawm (1–19). "For all their enthusiasm for the work of C. L. R. James," these critics, in Gilroy's view, "reproduced" the "nationalism and ethnocentrism" of nineteenth-century intellectuals like Turner and Ruskin, "denying imaginary, invented Englishness any external referents whatsoever" (14).

18. Here it is important to draw attention to how the forces of globalization in our own time were in place in Gilroy's black Atlantic, how contemporary globalization has been fueled by a dramatic transformation of those technologies and the speeds at which they unfold, and, of course, the development of globalization as an institutional practice as outlined and critiqued by Stiglitz.

19. For a thorough history of Spanish influence in North America, see Daniel Weber's *The Spanish Frontier in North America.*

20. Eric Lott makes a related point in his review of Gilroy's book in *The Nation,* in which he criticizes its "curious fixation on black culture in the United States, which may partly undermine the book's diasporic ambitions" (603). Lott would have liked to have seen Gilroy "invoke the range of black cultures ringing the Atlantic—at the very least the insurgent rhythms coming back over the airwaves to colonize the West in its turn. I miss here and at other moments the disparate ports of call *The Black Atlantic* seeks to map" (603).

21. For Mignolo's extended discussion of the problem of Indian doubt, see pages 727–31.

22. In stressing the need to complicate this center-periphery formulation, I certainly do not mean to play down the fundamentally asymmetrical nature of economic and cultural change under the regimes of colonialism or contemporary globalization. The production of hybridity and the inevitability of cultural exchange under colonialism take place in a fundamentally oppressive context, even if those exchanges are, as Gilroy stresses in his discussion of the production of "Englishness," bidirectional. And we have seen in our discussion of Stiglitz and other critics of contemporary globalization that although the developing world generally has more agency under globalization than it did under colonialism, agency is still too often restricted, and the hybrid or syncretistic can be imposed through hierarchical structures dominated by the West.

Part Two. Globalization in Contemporary Literature

1. "Mohsin Hamid," *Chronicle* [Duke University], February 18, 2000.

2. While I have limited myself to a discussion of narrative fiction here, a rich literature is developing in the analysis of transnational poetry. See Jahan Ramazani's "A Transnational Poetics" in *American Literary History*.

Chapter 5. Post–Postcolonial Writing in the Age of Globalization

1. Interview with Alex Wilber in "Plus," *Sunday Times,* October 19, 1997.

2. This includes, of course, attention to class, caste, and gender. See Gqola (2004), Tirhankar (1997), and Bose (1998) for discussions of these aspects of Roy's novel.

3. For a discussion of the role of the "personal" in Roy's novel, see Balvannanadhan (2002). For related treatments of the novel's more general engagement with subjectivity, see Sharma (2004), Elwork (2004), and Oumhani (2000).

4. See Durix (2002) for a discussion of the novel's engagement with postcolonialism. See Tickell (2003) for an exploration of the relationship between postcolonialism and cosmopolitanism in the novel.

5. For more on the treatment of history in Roy's novel see Needham (2005).

6. In addition to the exploration of the relationship between public and private, the novel has a complex engagement with location and place. See Susan Stanford Friedman (2005).

7. For other extended treatments in the book of the debilitating effects of globalization, see Roy's discussion of the fate of the Kathakali dancers, the transformation of the History House into a tourist hotel (119–20), the relationship between the History House and colonialism (52–54), and her use of the film *The Sound of Music (90–107)*. See also Sankaran (2006) for another way into exploring the novel's engagement with globalization.

8. It might be tempting to see the portions of the novel dealing with Sophic Mol's visit in 1967 and the more contemporary portions organized around the return of Estha and Rahel to Ayemenem in 1992 as reflecting a kind of division between a postcolonial and a globalized India, but I would argue Roy is more interested in creating a seamless link between the two periods.

9. This should not be surprising given Roy's political activism in India.

10. For another view of the novel's treatment of hybridity, see Mijares (2006). On its exploration of cross-cultural experience, see Salvador (2002).

11. See, for example, the episode concerning the British printer Markline, who insists that Sanjay study Aristotle's *Poetics* to purge himself of all things Indian. "There is much in here," Markline says, jabbing Sanjay on the chest, "we need to get rid of, much stuff we need to scoop out and throw away.... If you want to progress, you must cut yourself off from your past!" (298–99).

12. Sanjay and Abhay are also the principle narrators of the novel, and Chandra uses their collective work to develop the novel's meditation on storytelling. For a more extended analysis, see Ganapathy-Dore (2002).

13. Kathakali is a dance drama that originated in Kerala in the seventeenth century, but its roots run deep into India's past. In the novel, Kathakali dancing has been transformed by the global tourist industry into a relatively brief and entertaining bit of exotica. In a key scene, the men, who dance for the tourists "to stave off starvation," have stopped afterward at a temple "to ask pardon of their gods," to "apologize for corrupting their stories. For encashing their identities. Misappropriating their lives" (218). This scene is linked in complex ways to Roy's own approach to storytelling, but the more obvious point is to underscore the effects of global tourism on this ancient dance form and the dancers who perform it. Of the Kathakali dancer Roy writes that "in despair, he turns to tourism. He enters the market. He hawks the only thing he owns. The stories that his body can tell. He becomes a Regional Flavor" (219).

14. It is important to note that Abhay's access to the economic and cultural benefits of globalization are a function of his class, and thus imply the asymmetry of these benefits. He comes from a solidly middle-class family able to absorb the cost of his schooling in Southern California.

15. "Mohsin Hamid," *Chronicle* [Duke University], February 18, 2000.

16. See in particular Chacko's lecture on the subject (50–54).

17. By utilizing two narrators, one to tell the historical events covered by the novel (from the late eighteenth century through the Sepoy Rebellion of 1857) and another to register the more contemporary

dislocations of diasporic experience in the 1990s, Chandra draws a clear link between colonialism and the forces of globalization.

18. See in particular Mukherjee (1999) and Lahiri (1999).

19. See *World Bank Literature* (2002) for a collection of critical essays that explore in depth the relationship between economic globalization, literature, and literary studies, including essays about contemporary fiction dealing with the intersection of these issues.

20. For an overview of the problem of corruption in Pakistan and efforts to curb it, see the website of Transparency International Pakistan, an organization dedicated to monitoring and uprooting national and international corruption in Pakistan, at http://www.transparency.org.pk/index.htm.

21. In choosing the name Zulfikar Manto, Hamid is clearly alluding to the important and controversial writer Saadat Hasan Manto, who was born in the Punjab in 1912 and died in 1955.

22. The novel is framed by the story of Daru's trial; the sense that we are reading "testimony" is underscored by Mumtaz, who implies at the end of the book that the novel we have read is her own "half story" of Daru's "innocence" (245). However, at the outset of the novel, Daru refers to the witnesses at his trial as "liars all" and includes Mumtaz in the list. According to *Newsweek International* (July 24, 2000), Hamid submitted a version of the story as his JD thesis at Harvard Law School. The philosophical and legal issues treated in the book deserve the kind of lengthy analysis that falls beyond my scope.

23. "Mohsin Hamid," *Chronicle* [Duke University], February 18, 2000.

24. Loomba also articulates this position (1–19).

25. For a variety of perspectives on Pakistan's experience with globalization, see Husain (2000), Hasan (2000), Shirazi (2001), and Ahmed (2000). Husain, a former senior economist and director at the World Bank and since 1999 governor of the Central Bank of Pakistan, argues that Pakistan has not benefited much from globalization because it has failed to shift from a reliance on foreign aid and international financial institutions to international trade, foreign direct investment, labor flows, and technology. Shirazi, more skeptical about the benefits of globalization than Husain, insists that "local ownership and involvement must be central to any structuring of the economy" in Pakistan. Hasan, on the other hand, sees globalization as a direct threat to the autonomy of Pakistan, a new economic and political order imposed by the United States and Japan, "a threat, in many ways akin to the one posed by the English 200 years ago."

26. The Grameen Bank in Bangladesh began in the late 1970s with the aim of designing a credit delivery system aimed at supporting the rural poor. The bank lists its main objectives as extending banking facilities to poor men and women; eliminating the exploitation of the poor by money lenders and creating opportunities for self-employment; and assisting disadvantaged women from poor villages to develop techniques for household management. For background information on the Grameen Bank Project, see http://www.grameen-info.org/.

27. Although his novel is critical of globalization, Hamid himself has benefited rather spectacularly from it and has written elsewhere favorably about its potential for positive change. Hamid was a high school student at Lahore's prestigious Lahore American School, and he drafted *Moth Smoke* while studying at Princeton with Toni Morrison. He developed another draft while in law school at Harvard, and finished the novel while working as a highly paid management consultant in Manhattan for McKinsey and Company, a transnational consulting firm, where he reportedly specialized in developing "strategies for media and financial-sector clients." (See his interview with Terry Gross for National Public Radio's *Fresh Air,* September 20, 2001.) In "Mistrust in the West," a magazine article written just after the 9/11 attacks, Hamid wrote that Pakistan needs more economic and cultural globalization, not less. According to Hamid, his country needs "jobs and access to the markets and knowledge and entertainment of the wider world.... We need access to purchasers for our goods, investors in our industries. With these things come greater growth and stability, which then become self-reinforcing" (*Dawn: The Internet Edition,* November 1, 2001 (http://www.lib.virginia.edu/area-studies/SouthAsia/SAserials/Dawn/2001/nov0301.html#mist).

28. As we have seen, no such thing happens in *Moth Smoke.* Appadurai sees globalization as resulting from a rupture related to migration and the media, and, while Hamid focuses on how his characters migrate from Pakistan to America and back (part of Appadurai's financescape, he pays no attention to the media and tends to see the cultural effects of globalization as homogenizing.

Chapter 6. Globalization and Nationalism in Kiran Desai's *The Inheritance of Loss*

1. In Latin America, in the early twenty-first century, elected governments in Bolivia, Venezuela, Brazil, Argentina, and elsewhere are exerting unprecedented efforts to resist U.S. hegemony and take control of their natural (and cultural) resources. Eastern Europe and the former Soviet Union have witnessed in the last decade a proliferation of new nation-states structured along the lines of old historical affiliations and allegiances tied to ethnicity and religion. Responses to the U.S. intervention in the Middle East, particularly the occupation of Iraq, have led to a strengthening of governments (especially in Iran and Palestine, and perhaps in Iraq itself) that resist the kind of cosmopolitanism endorsed by Appiah and others. And nationalist movements throughout Africa and South Asia (from Kashmir and Sri Lanka to Indonesia) continue to splinter populations along ethnic, religious, and cultural lines in ways that counterbalance the supposedly homogenizing forces of globalization.

2. In this first basement room in Harlem, Biju "joined a shifting population of men camping out near the fuse box, behind the boiler, in the cubby holes, and in odd-shaped corners that once were pantries, maids' rooms, laundry rooms, and storage rooms at the bottom of what had been a single-family home" (51).

3. It is important to note that Desai's depiction of Nepalese in Kalimpong and of the GNLF was subjected to withering criticism by Nepalese living in Kalimpong, who complained about the relentlessly unsympathetic portrait they claimed she created. See Randeep Ramesh, "Book-Burning Threat over Town's Portrayal in Booker-Winning Novel," *Guardian*, November 2, 2006, http://www.guardian.co.uk/world/2006/nov/02/books.india.

4. This passage underscores the historically contested nature of the region and the range of national identities competing for recognition and power. Darjeeling is a relatively independent district in the Indian state of West Bengal, situated in the lower range of the Himalayas and adjacent to what is now Nepal, Tibet, and Bhutan. Originally a part of Sikkim, Darjeeling developed as a separate district under British rule in the early nineteenth century after Nepal ceded a part of its territory to the British, who in turn ceded the land to the raj of Sikkim. In February 1835 the British negotiated a lease of the land from Sikkim, and it became a municipality under British control in 1850.

5. Jemubhai's divided identity, along with his Anglophilia, have their roots in his father's complicity with the British Raj. His father had, Desai writes, "helped the right side in a certain skirmish between the English and the Gaekwads, and he was repaid by the regimental quartermaster with a contract to the official supplier of horse feed to the British military encampment" in his area (89).

6. While living at the convent, Sai is forced to learn the "English" way of making tea (6) and to appreciate how English cake is superior to the Indian laddoo (30). Much is made of how the young Jemubhai, arriving in England, does not know how to eat with a fork (38). Eventually he learns to avoid "Indian" food in London and learned to "eat shepherd's pie instead" (119). And Lola and Noni regularly shop for English desserts and vegetables (66). This focus on food and ways of eating as cultural markers is underscored by the prominence of the cook in the novel and by Biju's experiences working in restaurants in New York.

7. Desai actually narrates this scene in a way that underscores a persistent skepticism on the part of the narrator about the political project of the GNLF. During the march the insurgents are described as "behaving as if they were being featured in a documentary of war, and Gyan couldn't help but look on the scene already from the angle of nostalgia" (157). There are a number of other passages like this in which the insurgents are compared in a cynical way to characters in films. See, for example, pages 4 and 5, where they are described as being dressed in "universal guerilla fashion," behaving "as if in a movie," or, later, where Desai writes that the insurgents were "just boys, taking their style from Rambo, heads full up with kung fu and karate chops...living the movies" (294). These criticisms of the GNLF form the backbone of the book's unrelenting critique of nationalism; and, as noted earlier, her generally negative depiction of ethnic Nepalese in the book led to much protest in Kalimpong, especially after the novel won the Man Booker Prize.

Chapter 7. The Cultural Politics of Development in Zakes Mda's *The Heart of Redness*

1. Mda's heavy reliance on Jeff Peires's historical work *The Dead Will Arise: Nongqawuse and the Great Xhosa Cattle-Killing Movement of 1856–7* (1989) led to a charge by Andrew Offenburger that Mda

had actually plagiarized from Peires. Mda offered a rebuttal, and Peires has written in support of Mda's position in a statement issued by his publisher, Oxford University Press. See http://tinyurl.com/l7uaur for an article about the dispute that contains the statement by the Oxford University Press. Offenburger's charges and Mda's response appeared in the Fall 2008 issue of *Research in African Literatures*.

2. The Xhosa are a prominent tribe residing primarily in the southern and southern-central parts of South Africa. Under the pre-1994 system of bantustans, people of the Xhosa tribe were denied South African citizenship and restricted under supposed self-government to their "homelands." Prominent Xhosa include Nelson Mandela, Desmond Tutu, and Miriam Makeba. The cattle-killing movement was instigated by the vision of the young teenage girl Nongqawuse, who claimed she was visited by ancestral spirits near a lagoon who promised her that if the Xhosa slaughtered all of their cattle this ritual cleansing would lead to a renewal of their people and would drive the British from their land.

3. As a postapartheid returnee who has been away from Africa for thirty years, Camagu's biography is loosely connected to Mda's. *The Heart of Redness,* according to Mda, began as a commissioned television script about the Xhosa and Nongqawuse that he began to write after returning to South Africa from thirty years living in the United States. At the time, like Camagu, he was working as a teacher. For a discussion of this and other of his works, see the interview with Mda conducted by Elly Williams in *The Missouri Review.*

4. The "freedom dance" alludes to the toyi-toyi dance, a South African dance used in political protests against apartheid. It is characterized by foot stomping and rhythmic movement, and includes chanting, shouts, and singing. The dance became a popular way for unarmed protesters to confront and challenge the white government's riot police.

5. Camagu originally heads to Qolorha-by-Sea in search of a woman he glimpses at a wake. While Mda's interest in the cultural politics of development in the village takes center stage, Camagu's romantic involvement with a series of women is of central interest to himself.

6. For example, the first four chapters alternate regularly between the past and the present. The first twelve pages are set in the present, then on page 13 the narrative reverts to the nineteenth-century story of the Xhosa, then shifts back to the present on page 25, back to the past on 47, the present on 55, the past again on 75, the present on 87, and so on. These shifts in narrative time are overlaid with alternating perspectives on the Believers and Nonbelievers, told in a straightforward, nonjudgmental way. For example, pages 106–13 are focalized through the Believers, 123–28 through the Nonbelievers, and the narrative alternates in this way through page 187.

7. Historians distinguish nine frontier wars of increasing severity. The first occurred in 1779–81, with successive wars breaking out in 1793, 1779–1802, 1811–2, 1818–9, 1834–5, 1846–7, 1850–53, and 1877–8.

8. The history of the cattle-killing movement is covered in detail in Peires's *The Dead Will Arise.*

9. "Believing brothers fought against Unbelieving brothers. Unbelieving spouses turned against Believing spouses. Unbelieving fathers kicked Believing sons out of their homesteads. Unbelieving sons plotted the demise of Believing fathers. Unbelieving fathers attempted to kill Believing sons. Siblings stared at each other with eyes full of blood. Many amaXhosa killed their cattle in order to facilitate the resurrection. Many others killed them unwillingly under the threat of their Believing relatives." (86)

10. This mirrors Camagu's earlier situation in Johannesburg, where his experiences outside South Africa make him appear complicit with the West.

11. Redness in the novel is consistently linked to tradition and the "primitive," and to the extent to which the novel is sympathetic with the Xhosa who are Believers, the novel's title works as an ironic reversal of Conrad's *Heart of Darkness.* Where the "primitive" in Conrad's novel is connected in a negative way with barbarity and darkness, in Mda' novel it is associated in a positive way with tradition and belief.

12. Dalton's version of cultural tourism is mostly a dramatic performance perpetrated by what one character calls "con artists" by the name of NoManage and NoVangeli (96). When tourists come to the area, for example, "NoManage pretends she is a traditional healer, what the tourists call a witch doctor, and performs magic rites of her own concoction.... shenanigans are performed by these women in the full isiXhosa traditional costume of the amahomba" (96).

13. See Vital's 2005 essay for an excellent discussion of how the novel takes a "stance...towards the indigenous as a category" that "simultaneously" asserts its value and opens it to question (307).

14. Camagu's position here contrasts with an embrace of the traditional roots of his identity elsewhere in the novel. For example, he explicitly identifies with "Majola," the "totem snake" of his clan (150),

reminding one character, "I am not from America. I am an African from the amaMpondomise clan. My totem is the brown mole snake, Majola. I believe in him" (150). This is another example of the kind of balance between tradition and modernity Mda has Camagu trying to work out. He resists the casino development *and* Dalton's cultural heritage park, but he does develop a cooperative business focused on the production and sale of traditional ixiXhosa clothing and accessories, which he markets in Johannesburg (161). Unbelievers in the village accuse him of participating in a "backward movement" that reinforces the primitiveness of the Xhosa: "It is part of our history of redness... all this nonsense about bringing back African traditions! We are civilized people. We have no time for beads and long pipes!" (160).

15. See Vital for an astute discussion of Mda's treatment of ecology in the novel, particularly pages 309–11.

Chapter 8. Multiculturalism and Identity in Zadie Smith's *White Teeth*

1. The multicultural makeup of the United States is rooted in the histories of European immigration, the conquest of Native Americans, the slave trade, and the migration of people from Mexico, Latin America, Asia, and elsewhere to North America, whereas multiculturalism in England is largely the result of the migration of people formerly colonized by the British to many of its major metropolitan centers. While both societies are now "multicultural," it seems to me these different histories are important to keep in mind.

2. For a through discussion of the treatment of British multiculturalism in *White Teeth,* see Head (2003). Drawing on Bhabha's work on hybridization, he argues that Smith's novel deals with multiculturalism as a "transitional" phase in the complex history of hybridization, a phase in which multiculturalism is part of "an interactive, conflictual process" connected to "redefining and rewriting the nation from within" (108). For other treatments of multiculturalism, cosmopolitanism, and hybridity in Smith's novel, see Thompson (2005), Sizemore (2005), and Childs (2006).

3. See Laura Moss's interesting discussion of the pros and cons of seeing Smith's novel as "post–postcolonial" (11). She argues with an unnamed reviewer of *White Teeth* in the *Economist* who insists that "the real spark of the book is not post-colonial, but post–postcolonial," and that as a post–postcolonial novel it does not care about "history" (11). Moss is right, up to a point, in rejecting this assessment of the novel, for *White Teeth* is thoroughly engaged with multiple histories. However, whereas Moss seems to believe that a post–postcolonial position must be ahistorical, I would argue that we can understand Smith's novel as post–postcolonial precisely because of the way in which it *is* historical.

4. Magic Carpet of Cultures in London," by Yasmin Alibhai-Brown, *New York Times,* June 25, 2000.

5. This symbolism pops up in miscellaneous places throughout the novel. It's title comes from a scene in a chapter entitled "Molars" where an old pensioner tells some students about how, when he was a British soldier in the Congo, Africans could be spotted by their white teeth: "See a flash of white and bang! as it were" (144).

6. In such scenes the novel's dental imagery merges with its interest in the relationship between identity and historical memory. See, for example, chapter 10, which is entitled "The Root Canals of Mangal Pande," and chapter 13, "The Root Canals of Hortense Bowden." Root canals in both these chapters, and elsewhere, are a invoked as a trope for historical inquiry and understanding.

7. Gilroy's emphasis on "routes" over "roots" is connected to the sustained argument he makes against the notion that black identity can be located either biologically or in some other fundamental form of blackness, an argument, as we have seen, more recently taken up by Appiah in *Cosmopolitanism.*

8. Samad invokes Pande (usually spelled Pandey) throughout the novel as a central character in his own personal mythology, a hero against whom he measures himself. The historical Mangal Pande was a central figure in the instigation of the Sepoy Rebellion against the British on March 29, 1857. He was hanged for attacking British soldiers a few days after the rebellion was crushed.

9. See Walters (2005) for a discussion of the problem of national identity in the novel.

10. This discourse about assimilation, which draws a direct link between tradition and purity and assimilation and corruption, is both colored and complicated by the affair Samad is having with his sons' teacher, Poppy Burt-Jones, a character Smith associates with a naive and banal propensity for celebrating diversity in the classroom. Samad's preoccupation with corruption and purity dates back to the early

years of his marriage, deepens in the context of his feelings for Poppy, and only later is projected in a guilty transference onto his sons (115–33).

11. As a friend puts it, there are only two choices for Samad. "He can send 'em back there [Bangladesh] and have 'em brought up proper, by their granddads and grandmums, have 'em learn about their fucking culture, have 'em grow up with some fucking principles. Or…*Accept* it. He'll have to *accept* it…We're all English now, mate. Like it or lump it, as the rhubarb said to the custard" (160).

12. Samad's taking recourse to chance, to flipping a coin, recalls both how he decides to attempt suicide and an episode on the Russian front when Archie, faced with executing a prisoner, flips a coin to decide whether to kill the man or let him go (446–47). Scenes like these contribute to Smith's exploration in the novel of arguments about design and chance. See Sell (2006) for another discussion of the role chance plays in the novel.

13. "Raggastani" is an actual term used to characterize the blending of black, Caribbean, and South Asian cultural styles in contemporary Britain. The hybrid term contains "ragga" (alluding to the Indian musical form) and "reggae," and echoes "ragamuffin," a type of dance hall music in Jamaica. "Rag" also suggests the Hindi words "raj" (reign or rule) and "stani" (place). In this sense the word also conjures up Rajasthan (the largest state in India). In the novel this cultural style connects Irie's Jamaica and Magid and Millat's South Asia to contemporary youth culture.

14. KEVIN, like the earlier Raggastani, has its roots in the Caribbean and South Asia, thus mirroring the link between the Jamaican Bowdens and the Bengali Iqbals. The founder of the fictional organization KEVIN, Brother Ibrahim ad-Din Shukrallah, Smith writes, was "born Monty Clyde Benjamin in Barbados in 1960, the son of two poverty-stricken barefoot Presbyterian dipsomaniacs, he converted to Islam after a 'vision' at the age of fourteen. Aged eighteen he fled the lush green of his homeland for the desert surrounding Riyadh," where be became "disillusioned with much of the Islamic clerical establishment," developing a "belief that many radical modern political movements were relevant to Islam and moreover were to be found in the Qur'an if one looked closely enough" (388–89).

15. This does not come without some scolding from a black woman in the beauty shop who tells Irie, "You people think you're all Mr. Bigstuff….Some of us are happy with our African hair, thank you very much. I don't want to buy some poor Indian girl's hair. And I wish to God I could buy black hair products form black people for once. How we going to make it in this country if we don't make our own business?" (234).

16. Smith produces a mock family tree for the Bowdens full of uncertain paternities, unknown names or issues, and dead ends, meant to contrast with the elegant genealogy of the Chalfens (271).

17. The chapter is entitled "Chalfenism versus Bowdenism."

18. Her grandmother's library includes such obscure texts as *An Account of a West Indian Sanatorium* (1886) and *Dominica: Hints and Notes to Intending Settlers* (1906).

19. See Rushdie (1991).

20. Millat is also at one point associated with this desire for inhabiting a neutral space. Smith writes that "Millat was neither one thing nor the other, this or that, Muslim or Christian, Englishman or Bengali; he lived for the in between, he lived up to his middle name, *Zulfikar,* the clashing of two swords" (291).

21. One example is her very calculated send-up of the role liberal multiculturalism plays in the curriculum at Magid and Millat's grade school. Samad objects to the students being required to attend a harvest festival celebration, but he is told that "the school already recognizes a great variety of religious and secular events: among them, Christmas, Ramadan, Chinese New Year, Diwali, Yom Kippur, Hanukkah, the birthday of Haile Selassie, and the death of Martin Luther King. The Harvest Festival is part of the school's ongoing commitment to religious diversity" (108–9). Samad insists the harvest festival is not a Christian but a pagan practice and should therefore be removed from the school calendar. Smith uses the scene to question the lengths to which the school goes to celebrate what it defines as "religious diversity." Later, when Samad visits his sons' music class, the teacher mistakenly invokes Freddie Mercury, lead singer of the rock band Queen, as a British singer to scold her students about not being open to musicians from other cultures, missing the fact that "Freddie Mercury" was actually Farrokh Bulsara, born in Zanzibar of Parsi parents. He went to high school in India.

22. See, for example, the story of Moe Hussein, who joins KEVIN after enduring numerous racist beatings from both his customers and the police (391–92).

23. KEVIN's cultural argument, which is much more familiar now than it was in 2000 when Smith's novel was published, is elaborated near the end of the novel by its leader, Ibrahim ad-Din Shukrallah: "Look around *you*! And what do you see? What is the result of this so-called *democracy,* this so-called *freedom,* this so-called *liberty?* Oppression, persecution, *slaughter.* Brothers, you can see it on national television every day, every evening, every *night*! Chaos, disorder, *confusion.* They are not ashamed or embarrassed or *self-conscious*! They don't try to hide, to conceal, to *disguise*! They know as we know: the entire world is in a turmoil! Everywhere men indulge in prurience, promiscuity, *profligacy,* vice, corruption, and *indulgence.* The entire world is affected by a disease known as *Kufr*—the state of rejection of the oneness of the Creator—refusing to acknowledge the infinite blessing of the Creator" (387).

Chapter 9. Transnational Masculinities in Junot Díaz's *The Brief Wondrous Life of Oscar Wao*

1. By calling attention to the deep structural links between the characters in these various novels, I do not mean to suggest that their experiences are all the same. There are important historical and class differences between the characters in each of these novels that both enable and circumscribe their agency, and each is subject to different pressures under varying colonial and postcolonial regimes. We can observe this in the range of characters Desai treats in *The Inheritance of Loss,* and by comparing characters like Biju and Baby Kochamma with Chandra's Abhay or the characters in *The Brief Wondrous Life of Oscar Wao.* They may all, to some degree, be defined by their hybridity, but the forces that shape their identities are often very different.

2. This quote is transcribed from part 3 of the interview, which can be read and heard online at Open Source. http://www.radioopensource.org/at-home-and-global-in-america-junot-diaz/.

3. Díaz's narrative technique recalls Desai's in its orientation around shifting locations. Where Desai's moves between Kalimpong and New York, Díaz's moves between the Dominican Republic and New Jersey.

4. For a general treatment of the relationship between masculinity and political power in an international framework, see Charlotte Hooper's *Manly States: Masculinities, International Relations, and Gender Politics.*

5. This is another way in which Díaz is working territory Smith engages in *White Teeth.* Smith's attention to Magid's struggle with models of masculinity and his voracious sexuality and Irie's relationship to her raced body, anticipate Díaz's focus on gender and sexuality in *The Brief Wondrous Life of Oscar Wao.*

6. See "Junot Díaz Redefines Macho" in the April 14, 2008, edition of *In These Times* for a condensed version of this interview. http://www.inthesetimes.com/article/3616/junot_diaz_redefines_macho/.

7. In this section of the book Díaz is doing a kind of riff on our contemporary cultural fascination with the sexualized figure of "the gangsta" in hip-hop music.

8. Díaz obviously has some qualms about having this part of the book visit such violence on a woman. Regarding his using Belicia's beatings as a kind of metaphor for the brutality of the Trujillo regime, he muses in part 3 that it may have been a "kind of screwed up way of doing it." On the one hand, Díaz insists the book "lives and dies" by its female characters and that Belicia's is a too-often-untold story of woman and survival under the Trujillo regime, but, on the other hand, he recognizes the book ends up dramatizing the very brutality he means to be condemning.

9. "Trujillo was certainly formidable, and the regime was like a Caribbean Mordor" (226).

10. Moore is the author of *Watchmen,* another comic book series woven into *The Brief Wondrous Life of Oscar Wao. From Hell* is based on the story of Jack the Ripper. Wikipedia's plot summary makes clear the link Díaz has in mind between Trujillo and Dr. Gull. See http://en.wikipedia.org/wiki/From_Hell.

11. Quoted in "Galactus." http://en.wikipedia.org/wiki/Galactus.

12. "Bellaco" literally means "sly" or "cunning" in Spanish but is also, according to the Web-based *Urban Dictionary,* slang for "horny male." http://www.urbandictionary.com/define.php?term=bellaco.

13. Near the end of the book, Oscar returns to the Dominican Republic because he has fallen in love with a woman named Ybon, whose boyfriend, "the Captain," belongs to the Trujillato. Eventually his men track down and kill Oscar in a scene that repeats Belicia's beating in a cane field. This is another way in which Díaz draws a clear link between Belicia's suffering under the sexualized brutality of the regime and Oscar's.

Works Cited

Abou-El-Haj, Barbara. "Languages and Models for Cultural Exchange." In King, *Culture, Globalization and the World-System,* 139–44.

Abu-Lughod, Janet. *Before European Hegemony: The World System A.D. 1250–1350.* Oxford: Oxford University Press, 1989.

———. "Going Beyond Global Babble." In King, *Culture, Globalization and the World-System,* 131–37.

Ahmed, Sultan. "The Ill-Effects of Globalization." *Dawn: The Internet Edition.* March 2, 2000. http://www.sbp.org.pk/about/speech/Impact_of_globalization_Mahboobul_Haq.pdf.

Alibhai-Brown, Yasmin. "A Magic Carpet of Cultures in London," *New York Times.* June 25, 2000.

Anderson, Amanda, and Joseph Valente, eds. *Disciplinarity at the Fin De Siècle.* Princeton: Princeton University Press, 2002.

Anzaldúa, Gloria. *Borderlands/La Frontera: The New Mestizo.* San Francisco: Aunt Lute Books, 1987.

Appadurai, Arjun. *Modernity at Large: Cultural Dimensions of Globalization.* Minneapolis: University of Minnesota Press, 1996.

Appiah, Kwame Anthony. *Cosmopolitanism: Ethics in a World of Strangers.* New York: W. W. Norton, 2006.

Aravamudan, Srinivas. *Tropicopolitans: Colonialism and Agency, 1688–1804.* Durham: Duke University Press, 1999.

Balvannanadhan, Aida. "Re-Membering Personal History in *The God of Small Things.*" *Commonwealth Essays and Studies* 25, no. 1 (2002): 97–106.

Baudrillard, Jean. *America.* London: Verso, 1989.

Bauman, Zygmunt. *Globalization: The Human Consequences.* New York: Columbia University Press, 2000.

Bender, Thomas. *A Nation among Nations: America's Place in World History.* New York: Hill and Wang, 2006.

——. "No Borders: Beyond the Nation-State." *History News Network.* April 17, 2006. http://hnn.us/articles/23913.html.

Benítez-Rojo, Antonio, *The Repeating Island: The Caribbean and the Postmodern.* Durham: Duke University Press, 1996.

Berman, Marshall. *All That Is Solid Melts into Air: The Experience of Modernity.* New York: Penguin Books, 1988.

Bertens, Hans. *Literary Theory: The Basics.* London: Routledge, 2001.

Bérubé, Michael. "Introduction: Worldly English." *Modern Fiction Studies* 48, no. 1 (2002): 1–17.

Bhabha, Homi. "Cultural Diversity and Cultural Differences." In *The Post-Colonial Studies Reader.* Ed. Bill Ashcroft, Gareth Griffiths, and Helen Tiffin, 206–9. London: Routledge, 1995.

——, ed. *Nation and Narration.* London: Routledge, 1990.

Bose, Brinda. "In Desire and in Death: Eroticism as Politics in Arundhati Roy's *The God of Small Things. Ariel: A Review of International English Literature* 29, no. 2 (1998): 59–72.

Breckenridge, Carol A., Sheldon Pollock, Homi K. Bhabha, and Dipesh Chakrabarty, eds. *Public Culture (special issue on cosmopolitanism)* 12, no. 3 (Fall 2000).

Brennan, Timothy. *At Home in the World: Cosmopolitanism Now.* Cambridge: Harvard University Press, 1997.

Buell, Frederick. *National Culture and the New Global System.* Baltimore: Johns Hopkins University Press, 1994.

——. "Nationalist Postnationalism: Globalist Discourse in Contemporary American Culture." *American Quarterly* 50, no. 3: 548–91.

Cable, George Washington. *The Grandissimes.* New York: Penguin Books, 1988.

Canclini, Nestor Garcia. *Hybrid Cultures: Strategies for Entering and Leaving Modernity.* Trans. Christopher L. Chiappari and Silvia L. Lopez. Minneapolis: University of Minnesota Press, 1995.

Carafiol, Peter. *The American Ideal: Literary History as a Worldly Activity.* Oxford: Oxford University Press, 1991.

Carpentier, Alejo. *The Harp and the Shadow.* Trans. Thomas Christensen and Carol Christensen. San Francisco: Mercury House, 1990.

Chandra, Vikram. *Red Earth and Pouring Rain.* New York: Little, Brown, 1995.

Chevigny, Bell Gale, and Gari Laguardia, eds. *Reinventing the Americas: Comparative Studies of Literature of the United States and Spanish America.* Cambridge: Cambridge University Press, 1986.

Childs, Elaine. "Insular Utopias and Religious Neuroses: Hybridity Anxiety in Zadie Smith's *White Teeth. Proteus: A Journal of Ideas* 23, no. 1 (2006): 7–12.

Chittenden, Maurice. "Zadie Didn't Tell the Real Race Story." *Times Online* (London). February 19, 2006. http://www.timesonline.co.uk/tol/news/uk/article732529.ece.

Clifford, James. "Traveling Cultures." In *Cultural Studies.* Ed. Lawrence Grossberg et al., 96–112. New York: Routledge, 1992.

Cohen, Robin. *Global Diasporas: An Introduction.* Seattle: University of Washington Press, 1997.

Cohen, Robin, and Simon Learmount, eds. *Conceiving Cosmopolitanism: Theory, Context, and Practice.* New York, Oxford University Press, 2003.

Coser, Stelamaris. *Bridging the Americas: The Literature of Toni Morrison, Paule Marshall, and Gayl Jones.* Philadelphia: Temple University Press, 1994.

Court, Franklin E. *Institutionalizing English Literature: The Culture and Politics of Literary Study, 1750–1900.* Stanford: Stanford University Press, 1992.

Cowen, Tyler. *Creative Destruction: How Globalization Is Changing the World's Cultures.* Princeton: Princeton University Press, 2004.

Culler, Jonathan. *Literary Theory: A Very Short Introduction.* Oxford: Oxford University Press, 1997.

Cvetkovich, Ann, and Douglas Kellner, eds. *Articulating the Global and the Local: Globalization and Cultural Studies.* Boulder, CO: Westview Press, 1997.

Damrosch, David. *What Is World Literature?* Princeton: Princeton University Press, 2003.

Daniels, Roger. "The Immigration Act of 1965: Intended and Unintended Consequences." 2008. http://www.america.gov/st/educ-english/2008/April/20080423214226eaifas0.9637982.html.

Deleuze, Gilles, and Felix Guatarri. *Anti-Oedipus. Capitalism and Schizophrenia.* New York: Penguin Classics, 2009.

Desai, Kiran. *The Inheritance of Loss.* New York: Atlantic Monthly Press, 2006.

Díaz, Junot. *The Brief Wondrous Life of Oscar Wao.* New York: Riverhead Books, 2007.

Dirlik, Arif. "Rethinking Colonialism: Globalization, Postcolonialism, and the Nation." *Interviews* 4, no. 3 (2002): 428–48.

Dirty Pretty Things. Written by Steven Knight. Directed by Stephen Frears. Miramax Films, 2002.

During, Simon. "Postcolonialism and Globalization: Towards a Historicization of Their Inter-Relation." *Cultural Studies* 14, no. 3–4 (2000): 385–404.

Durix, Jean-Pierre. "The Post-Coloniality of *The God of Small Things*." In *Reading Arundhati Roy's The God of Small Things.* Ed. Jean-Pierre and Carole Durix, 145–62. Dijon, France: Éditions Universitaires de Dijon, 2002.

Dussel, Enrique. "World-System and 'Trans'-Modernity." *Nepanthla* 3, no. 2 (2002): 221–44.

———. *The Invention of the Americas: Eclipse of "the Other" and the Myth of Modernity.* London: Continuum Publishing Group, 1995.

Eagleton, Terry. *Literary Theory: An Introduction.* Minneapolis: University of Minnesota Press, 1983.

Elwork, Paul. "The Loss of Sophie Mol: Debased Selfhood and the Colonial Shadow in Arundhati Roy's *The God of Small Things.*" *South Asian Review* 25, no. 2 (2004): 178–88.

Featherstone, Mike, ed. *Global Culture: Nationalism Globalization and Modernity.* Newbury Park, CA: Sage Publications, 1990.

———. "Global and Local Cultures." In *Mapping the Futures: Local Cultures, Global Change.* Ed. Jon Bird et al., 169–87. London: Routledge, 1993.

Fishkin, Shelley Fisher. "Crossroads of Cultures: The Transnational Turn in American Studies." *American Quarterly* 57, no. 1 (March 2005): 17–57.

Foucault, Michel. "What Is Enlightenment?" In *The Foucault Reader.* Ed. Paul Rabinow, 32–50. New York: Pantheon Books, 1984.

Fox, Claire F. *The Fence and the River: Culture and Politics at the U.S.-Mexican Border.* Minneapolis: University of Minnesota Press, 1999.

Freeman, Carla. "Is Local: Global as Feminine: Masculine? Rethinking the Gender of Globalization." *Signs* 26, no. 4 (Summer 2001): 1007–37.

Friedman, Susan Stanford. *Mappings: Feminism and the Cultural Geographies of Encounter.* Princeton: Princeton University Press, 1998.

———. "Migrations, Diasporas and Borders." In Nicholls, *Introduction to Scholarship in Modern Languages and Literatures,* 260–93.

———. "Spatial Poetics and Arundhati Roy's *The God of Small Things.*" In *The Blackwell Companion to Narrative Theory.* Ed. James Phelan and Peter Rabinowitz, 192–205. Oxford: Oxford University Press, 2005.

Friedman, Thomas L. *The Lexus and the Olive Tree: Understanding Globalization.* New York: Knopf, 2000.

Fukuyama, Francis. *The End of History and the Last Man.* New York: Avon Books, 1992.

Gallagher, Catherine. "Historical Scholarship." In Nicholls, *Introduction to Scholarship in Modern Languages and Literatures,* 171–93.

Ganapathy-Dore, Geetha. "The Story-Teller's Voice in Vikram Chandra's *Red Earth and Pouring Rain:* Much More Than a Novel." In *Ontological Boundaries.* Ed. Ramón Plo-Alastrué and María Jesús Martínez-Alfaro, 175–84. Heidelberg, Germany: Carl Winter Universitatsverlag, 2002.

Garcia, Cristina. *Dreaming in Cuban.* New York: Ballantine Books, 1992.

George, Rosemary Marangoly. *The Politics of Home: Postcolonial Relocations and Twentieth-Century Fiction.* Cambridge: Cambridge University Press, 1996.

Geyer, Michael. "Multiculturalism and the Politics of General Education." *Critical Inquiry* 19, no. 3 (1993): 499–533.

Giddens, Anthony. *The Consequences of Modernity.* Cambridge, UK: Polity Press, 1990.

Gikandi, Simon. *Maps of Englishness: Writing Identity in the Culture of Colonialism.* New York: Columbia University Press, 1996.

Gilroy, Paul. *The Black Atlantic: Modernity and Double Consciousness.* Cambridge: Harvard University Press, 1993.

Glissant, Edouard. *Caribbean Discourse: Selected Essays.* Ed. and trans. Michael Dash. Charlottesville: University Press of Virginia, 1989.

Goudie, Sean X. *Creole America: The West Indies and the Formation of Literature and Culture in the New Republic.* Philadelphia: University of Pennsylvania Press, 2006.

Gqola, Pumla. "'History Was Wrong-Footed, Caught Off Guard': Gendered Caste, Class and Manipulation in Arundhati Roy's *The God of Small Things. Commonwealth Essays and Studies* 26, no. 2 (2004): 1007–19.

Graff, Gerald. *Professing Literature: An Institutional History.* Chicago: University of Chicago Press, 1987.

Grameen Bank. http://www.grameen-info.org.

Greenblatt, Stephen. *Marvelous Possessions: The Wonder of the New World.* Chicago: University of Chicago Press, 1992.

Grewal, Inderpal, and Caren Kaplan, eds. *Scattered Hegemonies: Postmodernity and Transnational Feminist Practices.* Minneapolis: University of Minnesota Press, 1994.

Gross, Terry. "Pakistani Novelist and New Yorker Mohsin Hamid." *Fresh Air.* April 3, 2007. http://freshair.npr.org.

Gruzinski, Serge. *The Conquest of Mexico: The Incorporation of Indian Societies in the Western World, 16th–18th Centuries.* Trans. Eileen Corrigan. Cambridge, UK: Polity Press, 1993.

Gunn, Giles, ed. "Globalizing Literary Studies." Special issue, *PMLA* 116, no. 1 (January 2001).

Habermas, Jürgen. *The Philosophical Discourse of Modernity: Twelve Lectures.* Trans. Frederick Lawrence. Cambridge: MIT Press, 1987.

Hall, Kim. *Things of Darkness: Economies of Race and Gender in Early Modern England.* Ithaca: Cornell University Press, 1996.

Hamid, Mohsin. "A Call to Arms for Pakistan." *Newsweek International Online.* July 24, 2000. http://www.msnbc.com/news/nw-int_front.asp?cp1=1.

———. "Mistrust in the West." *Dawn: The Internet Edition.* November 1, 2001. http://www.dawn.com/2001/11/01/op.htm#4.

————. *Moth Smoke.* New York: Farrar, Straus and Giroux, 2000.

————. *The Reluctant Fundamentalist.* New York: Harcourt, 2007.

Hannerz, Ulf. "Scenarios for Peripheral Cultures." In King, *Culture, Globalization, and the World-System,* 107–28.

————. *Transnational Connections: Culture, People, Places.* London: Routledge, 1996.

Harasym, Sarah, ed. *The Post-Colonial Critic: Essays, Strategies, Dialogues.* New York: Routledge, 1990.

Hardt, Michael, and Antonio Negri. *Empire.* Cambridge: Harvard University Press, 2000.

Harootunian, H. D. "Postcolonality's Unconscious / Area Studies' Desire." In Miyoshi and Harootunian, *Learning Places,* 150–74.

Harvey, David. *The Condition of Postmodernity: An Enquiry into the Origins Of Cultural Change.* Cambridge, MA: Blackwell, 1990.

Hasan, Mubashir. "The Menace of Globalization." *Dawn: The Internet Edition.* February 5, 2000. http://www.dawn.com/2000/02/25/op.htm.

Head, Dominic. "Zadie Smith's *White Teeth:* Multiculturalism for the Millennium." In *Contemporary British Fiction.* Ed. Philip Tew. Cambridge, UK: Polity Press, 2003.

Hicks, Emily. *Border Writing: The Multidimensional Text.* Minneapolis: University of Minnesota Press, 1991.

Holquist, J. Michael. "Comparative Literature." In Nicholls, *Introduction to Scholarship in Modern Languages and Literatures,* 194–208.

Hooper, Charlotte. *Manly States: Masculinities, International Relations, and Gender Politics.* New York: Columbia University Press, 2001.

Horkheimer, Max, and Theodor Adorno. *Dialectic of Enlightenment.* Trans. John Camming. New York: Continuum, 1982.

Horowitz, David. "Academic Bill of Rights." Temple Association of University Professionals. http://www.taup.org/TAUPWEB2006/HR177/ABoRHorowitz.pdf; http://www.taup.org/TAUniversity.

Houpt, Simon. "Novelist by Night." *The Globe and Mail* (Toronto). http://www.globebooks.com/interviews/mohsinhamid.html.

Hulme, Peter. *Colonial Encounters: Europe and the Native Caribbean, 1492–1797.* London: Methuen, 1986.

Husain, Ishrat. "Impact of Globalization on Poverty in Pakistan." February 2000. http://www.sbp.org.pk/about/speech/2001/Impact_of_globalization_Mahboobul_Haq.pdf.

Huyssen, Andreas. *After the Great Divide: Modernism, Mass Culture, Postmodernism.* ACLS e-Book, 2008.

Jameson, Fredric, and Masao Miyoshi, eds. *The Cultures of Globalization.* Durham: Duke University Press, 1998.

————. "Notes on Globalization as a Philosophical Issue." In Jameson and Miyoshi, *Cultures of Globalization,* 54–77.

Jardine, Alice. *Gynesis: Configurations of Woman and Modernity.* Ithaca: Cornell University Press, 1986.

Jay, Gregory. "The End of 'American' Literature: Toward a Multicultural Practice." *College English* 53, no. 3 (1991): 264–81.

Jay, Paul. "Beyond Discipline? Globalization and the Future of English." In Gunn, "Globalizing Literary Studies," 32–47.

————. "Bridging the Gap: The Position of Politics in Deconstruction." *Cultural Critique* 22 (Fall 1992): 47–74.

————. "Globalization and the Postcolonial Condition." In Li, *Globalization and the Humanities,* 79–100.

———. "The Myth of 'America' and the Politics of Location: Modernity, Border Studies, and the Literature of the Americas." *Arizona Quarterly* 54, no. 2 (1998): 165–92.

———. "Junot Díaz Redefines Macho." *In These Times*. April 14, 2008. http://www.inthese times.com/article/3616/junot_diaz_redefines_macho.

Jenkins, Henry. *Convergence Culture: Where Old and New Media Collide*. New York: New York University Press, 2006.

Kaplan, Caren. *Questions of Travel: Postmodern Discourses of Displacement*. Durham: Duke University Press, 1996.

Kaup, Monica. *Rewriting North American Borders in Chicano and Chicana Narrative*. Frankfurt, Germany: Peter Lang, 2001.

Khanna, Parag. *The Second World: Empires and Influence in the New Global Order*. New York: Random House, 2008.

King, Anthony, ed. *Culture, Globalization, and the World-System: Contemporary Conditions for the Representation of Identity*. Minneapolis: University of Minnesota Press, 1997.

Kingston, Maxine Hong. *Woman Warrior: Memoir of a Girlhood Among Ghosts*. New York: Vintage Books, 1975.

Knight, Franklin W. *The Caribbean: The Genesis of a Fragmented Nationalism*. 2nd ed. New York: Oxford University Press, 1990.

Krishnaswamy, Revathi. "The Criticism of Culture and the Culture of Criticism: At the Intersection of Postcolonialism and Globalization Theory." *Diacritics* 32, no. 2 (Summer 2002): 106–26.

Krupat, Arnold. *Ethnocentrism: Ethnography, History, Literature*. Berkeley: University of California Press, 1992.

Kumar, Amitava. *World Bank Literature*. Minneapolis: University of Minnesota Press, 2002.

Kutzinski, Vera. *Sugar's Sweet: Race and the Erotics of Urban Nationalism*. Charlottesville: University of Virginia Press, 1993.

Lahiri, Jhumpa. *Interpreter of Maladies*. Boston: Houghton Mifflin, 1999.

Learmount, Simon, and Robin Cohen, eds. *Conceiving Cosmopolitanism: Theory, Context, and Practice*. New York: Oxford University Press, 2003.

Li, David, ed. *Globalization and the Humanities*. Hong Kong: Hong Kong University Press, 2004.

Lipsitz, George. *Dangerous Crossroads: Popular Music, Postmodernism and the Poetics of Place*. London: Verso, 1994.

Loomba, Ania. *Colonialism/Postcolonialism*. London: Routledge, 1998.

López, Iraida H. "'…And There Is Only My Imagination Where Our History Should Be': An Interview with Cristina Garcia." *Michigan Quarterly Review* 33, no. 3 (Summer 1994): 605–17.

Lott, Eric. "Routes" Review of *The Black Atlantic*, by Paul Gilroy. *The Nation* 17 (May 2, 1994): 602–4.

Lydon, Christopher. "At Home in Global America: Junot Díaz." *Open Source*. September 14, 2007. http://www.radioopensource.org/at-home-and-global-in-america-junot-diaz/.

Mao, Douglas, and Rebecca Walkowitz. "The New Modernist Studies." *PMLA* 123, no. 3 (2008): 737–48.

Marcus, Leah. "Textual Studies." In Nicholls, *Introduction to Scholarship in Modern Languages and Literatures,* 143–59.

Matthiessen, F. 0. *American Renaissance: Art and Expression in the Age of Emerson and Whitman*. New York: Oxford University Press, 1941.

Mda, Zakes. *The Heart of Redness*. New York: Farrar, Straus and Giroux, 2000.

———. "A Response to 'Duplicity and Plagiarism in Zakes Mda's *The Heart of Redness,*' by Andrew Offenburger." *Research in African Literatures* 39, no. 3 (Fall 2008): 200–203.

Mignolo, Walter. "The Many Faces of Cosmo-polis: Border Thinking and Critical Cosmopolitanism." *Public Culture* 12, no. 3 (Fall 2000): 721–45.

Mijares, Loretta. "Mapping Hybridity: Historicizing Cultural and Racial Hybrids in Vikram Chandra's *Red Earth and Pouring Rain." South Asian Review* 27, no. 1 (2006): 30–52.

Miller, J. Hillis. *Black Holes.* Stanford: Stanford University Press, 1999.

Milz, Sabine. "Global Literary Study, Postcolonial Study, and Their (Missing) Interrelations: A Materialist Critique." *Postcolonial Text* 2, no. 1 (2006), an open source journal. http://post colonial.org/index.php/pct/article/view/429/152.

Miyoshi, Masao. "'Globalization,' Culture, and the University." In Jameson and Miyoshi, *Cultures of Globalization,* 247–69.

Miyoshi, Masao, and H. D. Harootunian, eds. *Learning Places: The Afterlives of Area Studies.* Durham: Duke University Press, 2002.

——."Ivory Tower in Escrow," in *Learning Places,* 19–60.

Morley, David, and Kevin Robins. *Spaces of Identity: Global Media, Electronic Landscapes and Cultural Boundaries.* London: Routledge, 1995.

"Mohsin Hamid." *Chronicle* [Duke University]. February 18, 2000. http://www.chronicle. duke.edu/vnews/display.v/ART/2000/02/18/3d768e32061ef?in_archive=1.

Moss, Laura. "The Politics of Everyday Hybridity: Zadie Smith's *White Teeth." Wasafiri: The Transnational Journal of International Writing* 39 (2003): 11–17.

Mukherjee, Bharati. *The Middleman and Other Stories.* New York: Grove Press, 1999.

Murrin, John M. "Beneficiaries or Catastrophe: The English Colonies in America." In *The New American History.* Ed. Eric Foner, 3–24. Philadelphia: Temple University Press, 1990.

Nair, Supriya. "Diasporic Roots: Imagining a Nation in Earl Lovelace's *Salt." South Atlantic Quarterly* 100, no. 1 (2001): 259–85.

Needham, Anuradha. "'The Small Voice of History' in Arundhati Roy's *The God of Small Things." Interventions: International Journal of Postcolonial Studies* 7, no. 3 (2005): 369–91.

Nicholls, David G., ed. *Introduction to Scholarship in Modern Languages and Literatures.* New York: MLA, 2007.

Offenburger, Andrew. "Duplicity and Plagiarism in Zakes Mda's *The Heart of Redness." Research in African Literatures* 39, no. 3 (Fall 2008): 164–99.

O'Gorman, Edmundo. *The Invention of America: An Inquiry into the Historical Nature of the New World and the Meaning of Its History.* Bloomington: Indiana University Press, 1961.

Oumhani, Cécile. "Hybridity and Transgression in Arundhati Roy's *The God of Small Things." World Literature Written in English* 22, no. 2 (2000): 85–91.

Owens, Louis. "'The Song Is Very Short': Native American Literature and Literary Theory." *Weber Studies* 12, no. 3 (1995): 51–62.

Peires, Jeff. *The Dead Will Arise: Nongqawuse and the Great Xhosa Cattle-Killing Movement of 1856–57.* Indianapolis: University of Indiana Press, 1989.

Pérez-Firmat, Gustavo. *Do the Americas Have a Common Literature?* Durham: Duke University Press, 1990.

Pippin, Robert. *Modernism as a Philosophical Problem: On the Dissatisfactions of European High Culture.* Oxford: Basil Blackwell, 1991.

Porter, Carolyn. "What We Know That We Don't Know: Remapping American Literary Studies." *American Literary History* 6, no. 3 (1994): 467–526.

Pratt, Mary Louise. *Imperial Eyes: Travel Writing and Transculturation.* London: Routledge, 1992.

Raiskin, Judith L. *Snow on the Cane Fields: Women's Writing and Creole Subjectivity.* Minneapolis: University of Minnesota Press, 1996.

Ramazani, Jahan. "A Transnational Poetics." *American Literary History* 18, no. 2 (2006): 332–59.

Readings, Bill. *The University in Ruins.* Cambridge: Harvard University Press, 1996.

Reising, Russell. *The Unusable Past: Theory and the Study of American Literature.* New York: Methuen, 1986.

Reuter, E. B. *Race and Cultural Contacts.* New York: McGraw-Hill, 1934.

Rich, Adrienne. "Notes Toward a Politics of Location." In *Blood, Bread, and Poetry: Selected Prose, 1979–1985,* 210–31. New York: W. W. Norton, 1986.

Robbins, Bruce. *Feeling Global: Internationalism in Distress.* New York: New York University Press, 1999.

Robertson, Roland. *Globalization.* London: Sage, 1992.

Rosaldo, Renato. Foreword to *Hybrid Cultures: Strategies for Entering and Leaving Modernity,* by Néstor García Canclini. Trans. Christopher L. Chiappari and Silvia L. Lopez, xi–xvii. Minneapolis: University of Minnesota Press, 1993.

Roy, Arundhati. *The God of Small Things.* New York: Random House, 1997.

Rushdie, Salman. *The Ground Beneath Her Feet.* New York: Picador, 2000.

——. *Imaginary Homelands.* New York: Viking, 1991.

Sadowski-Smith, Claudia. *Border Fictions: Globalization, Empire, and Writing at the Boundaries of the United States.* Charlottesville: University of Virginia Press, 2008.

Said, Edward. *Culture and Imperialism.* New York: Vintage, 1994.

——. "Globalizing Literary Study." In Gunn, "Globalizing Literary Studies," 64–68.

Saldívar, José David. *The Dialectics of Our America: Genealogy, Cultural Critique, and Literary History.* Durham: Duke University Press, 1991.

Salvador, Dora Sales. "Vikram Chandra's Transcultural Narrative: *Red Earth and Pouring Rain,* Much More than a Novel." In *Beyond Borders: Re-defining Generic and Ontological Boundaries.* Ed. Ramón Pló-Alastrué and María Jesús Martínez-Alfaro, 175–84. Heildelberg, Germany: Universitätsverlag C. Winter, 2002.

Sankaran, Chitra. "Ethics, Aesthetics and the Globalized Other in Arundhati Roy's *The God of Small Things.*" In *Global Fissures: Postcolonial Fusions.* Ed. Clara Joseph and Janet Wilson, 103–19. Amsterdam/New York: Editions Rodopi B. V., 2006.

Scholes, Robert. *The Rise and Fall of English.* New Haven: Yale University Press, 1998.

Sell, Jonathan. "Chance and Gesture in Zadie Smith's *White Teeth* and *The Autograph Man.*" *Journal of Commonwealth Literature* 41, no. 3: 27–44.

Sen, Amartya. "How to Judge Globalism." *American Prospect,* January 1, 2002. http://www.prospect.org/cs/articles?article=how_to_judge_globalism.

Sharma, Maya. "Translating Subjects to Selves in Arundhati Roy's *The God of Small Things.*" *South Asian Review* 25, no. 2 (2004): 124–34.

Shirazi, Usuf. "'Glocalization'—Not Globalization." *Dawn: The Internet Edition.* December 31, 2001. http://www.dawn.com/2001/text/ebr6.htm.

Shiva, Vandana. *India Divided: Diversity and Democracy Under Attack.* New York: Seven Stories Press, 2005.

Simpson, David. *Situatedness, or, Why We Keep Saying Where We're Coming From.* Durham: Duke University Press, 2002.

Sizemore, Christine. "Willesden as a Site of 'Demotic' Cosmopolitanism in Zadie Smith's Postcolonial City Novel *White Teeth.*" *Journal of Commonwealth and Postcolonial Studies* 12, no. 2 (2005): 65–83.

Smith, Zadie. *On Beauty.* New York: Penguin, 2005.

——. *White Teeth.* New York: Random House, 2000.

Sommer, Doris. "Language, Culture, and Society." In Nicholls, *Introduction to Scholarship in Modern Languages and Literatures,* 3–19.

Spillers, Hortense. "Who Cuts the Border?: Some Readings on 'America.'" *Comparative American Identities: Race, Sex, and Nationality in the Modern Text.* Ed. Hortense Spillers, 1–25. London: Routledge, 1991.

Spivak, Gayatri. *In Other Worlds: Essays in Cultural Politics.* New York: Methuen, 1987.

Stiglitz, Joseph. *Globalization and Its Discontents.* New York: W. W. Norton, 2002.

Stokes, Carla E. "Representin' in Cyberspace: Sexual Scripts, Self-Definition, and Hip Hop Culture in Black American Adolescent Girls' Home Pages." *Culture, Health and Sexuality* 9, no. 2 (2007): 169–84.

Suri, Manil. *The Death of Vishnu.* New York: W. W. Norton, 2001.

Syal, Meera. *Anita and Me.* New York: New Press, 1977.

——. *Life Isn't All Ha Ha Hee Hee.* New York: New Press, 2000.

Thompson, Molly. "'Happy Multicultural Land'? The Implications of an 'Excess of Belonging' in Zadie Smith's *White Teeth.*" *Write Black, Write British.* Ed. Kadija Sesay, 122–40. Hertford, UK: Hansib, 2005.

Tickell, Alex. "*The God of Small Things:* Arundhati Roy's Postcolonial Cosmopolitanism." *Journal of Commonwealth Literature* 38, no. 1 (2003): 73–89.

Tirhankar, Chandra. "Sexual/Textual Strategies in *The God of Small Things.*" *Commonwealth Essays and Studies* 20, no. 1 (1997): 38–44.

Turim, Maureen. "Specificity and Culture." In King, *Culture, Globalization and the World-System,* 145–48.

Viswanathan, Gavri. *Masks of Conquest: Literary Study and British Rule in India.* London: Oxford University Press, 1998.

Vital, Anthony. "Situating Ecology in Recent South African Fiction: J. M. Coetzee *The Lives of Animals* and Zakes Mda's *The Heart of Redness.*" *Journal of Southern African Studies* 31, no. 2 (2005): 297–313.

Wallerstein, Immanuel. *The Modern World System.* New York: Academic Press, 1981.

——. "The National and the Universal: Can There Be Such a Thing as World Culture?" In King, *Culture, Globalization and the World-System,* 91–105.

Walters, Tracey. "'We're All English Now Mate Like It or Lump It': The Black/Britishness of Zadie Smith's *White Teeth.*" *Write Black, Write British.* Ed. Kadija Sesay, 314–22. Hertford, UK: Hansib, 2005.

Waters, Malcolm. *Globalization.* London: Routledge, 1995.

Weber, Daniel J. *The Spanish Frontier in North America.* New Haven: Yale University Press, 1992.

Williams, Elly. "An Interview with Zakes Mda." *Missouri Review* 28, no. 2 (Fall 2005): 62–79.

Wilson, Rob. "Imagining 'Asia Pacific' Today." In Miyoshi and Harootunian, *Learning Places,* 231–60.

Wolff, Janet. "The Global and the Specific: Reconciling Conflicting Theories of Culture." In King, *Culture, Globalization and the World-System,* 161–73.

Yelin, Louise. "Globalizing Subjects." *Signs: Journal of Women in Culture and Society* 29, no. 4 (2004): 439–64.

Young, Robert. *Colonial Desire: Hybridity in Theory, Culture, and Race.* London: Routledge, 1995.

Zakaria, Fareed. *The Post-American World.* New York: W. W. Norton, 2008.

Zamora, Lois Parkinson. *Writing the Apocalypse: Historical Vision in Contemporary U.S. and Latin American Fiction.* Cambridge: Cambridge University Press, 1989.

Index